THE OUTDOOR MUSEUM

(not your usual images of NEW YORK)

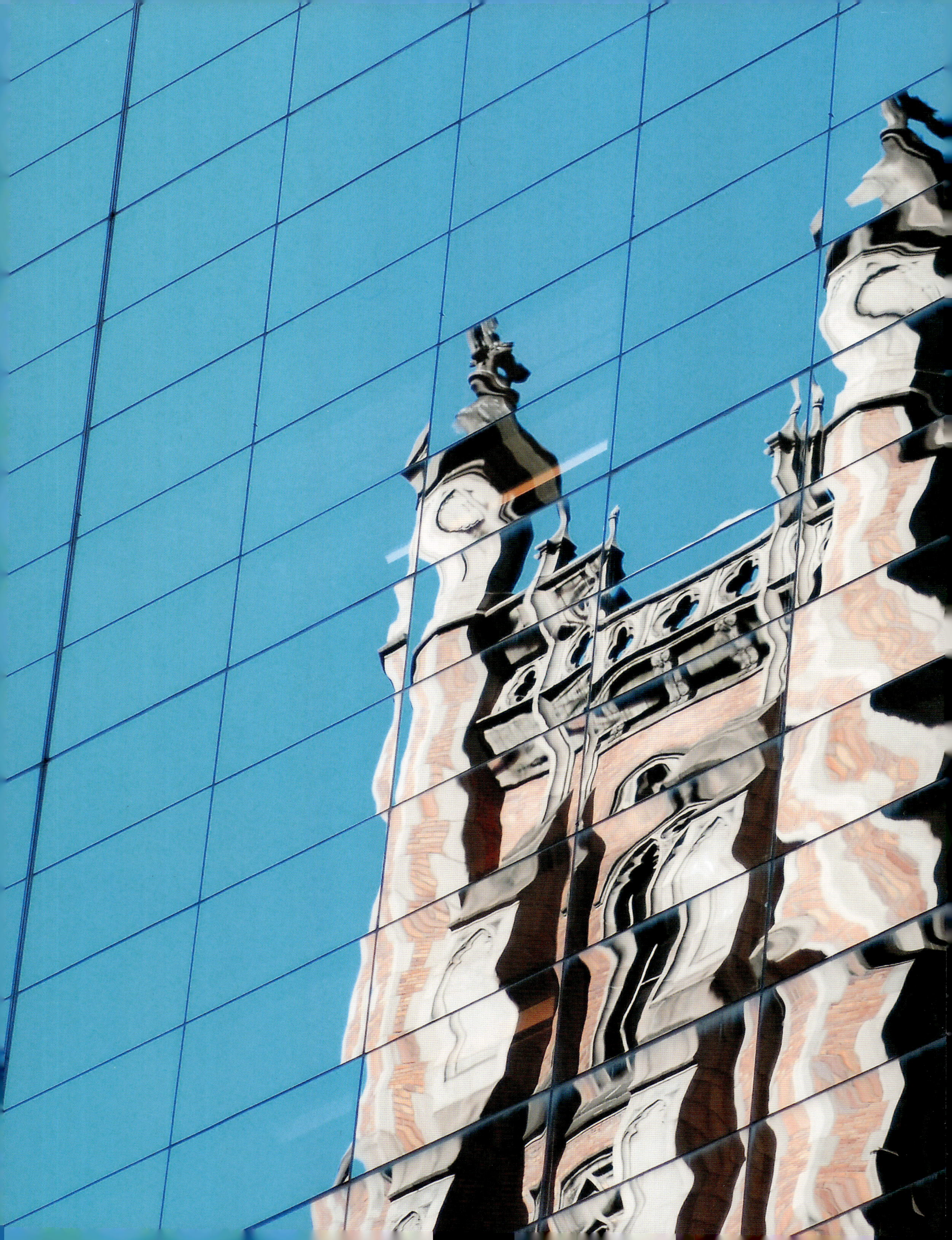

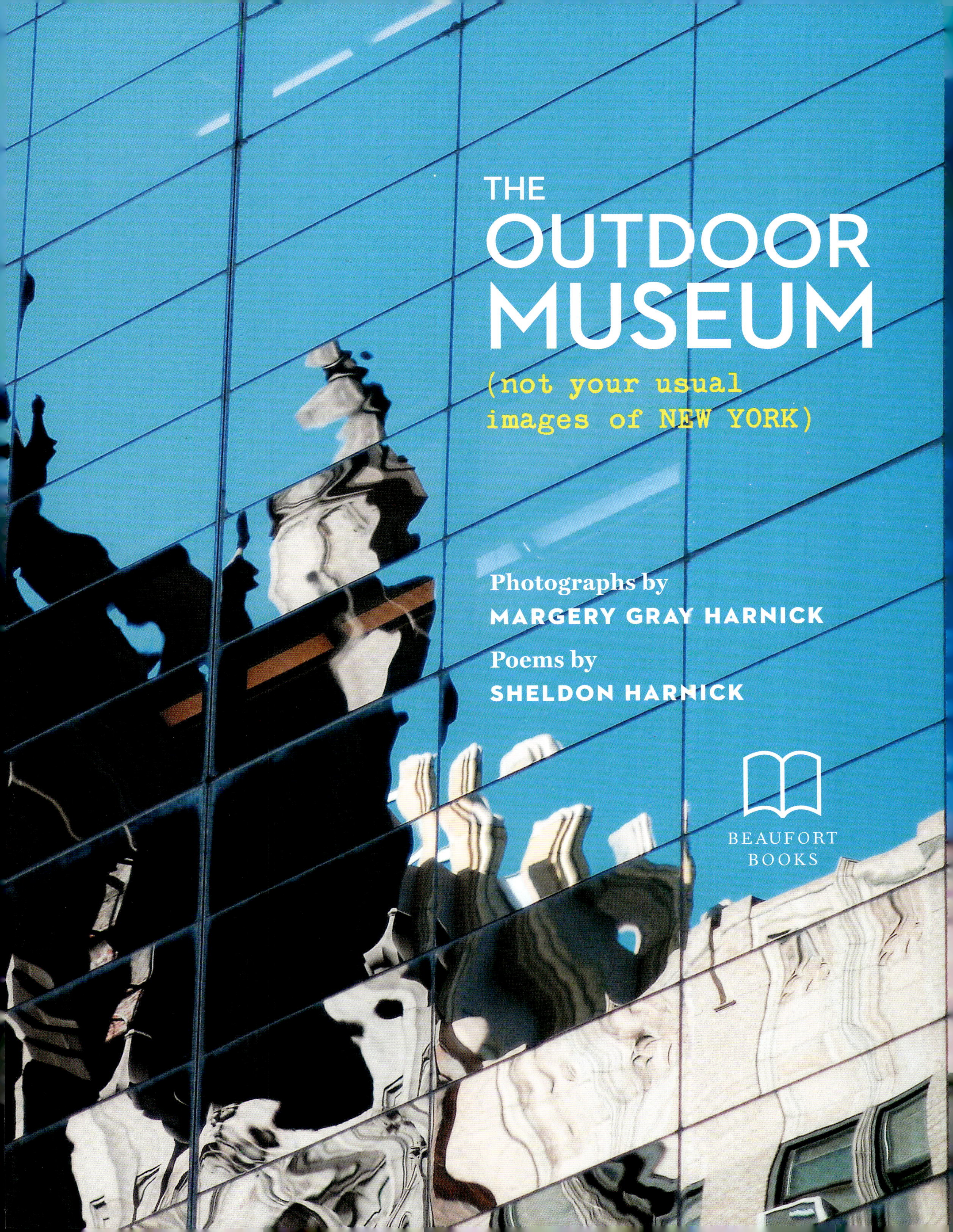

THE OUTDOOR MUSEUM

(not your usual images of NEW YORK)

Photographs by
MARGERY GRAY HARNICK

Poems by
SHELDON HARNICK

BEAUFORT BOOKS

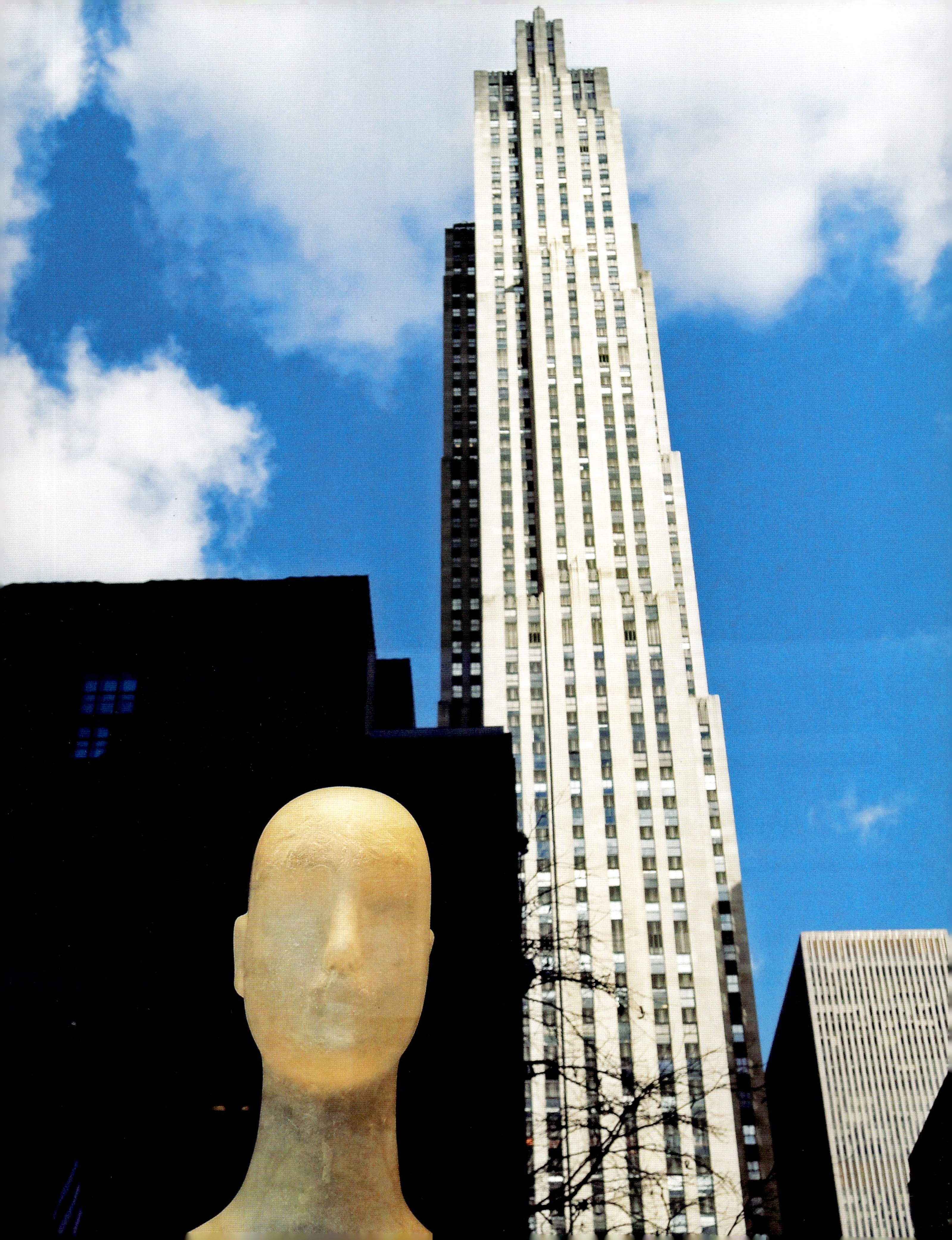

DEDICATION

To our beloved children: Beth Harnick Dorn, easily the wife and mother of the year (if not the century!), and Matthew Harnick, a passionate naturalist and a superb photographer in his own right.

•

ACKNOWLEDGMENTS

Our boundless thanks to Jane Lahr, without whose expertise, belief, and enthusiasm this book might never have become a reality, and to her extraordinary team: Lyn DelliQuadri, Celia Fuller, and Stephen Stinehour, for bringing this book to vibrant life. Our deep gratitude to Margot Atwell for responding to our work so quickly and so affirmatively and to Sarah Lucie for her invaluable editorial assistance. Our son Matt deserves a medal for the countless hours he devoted to this project. A special thank you to Henry Grossman for his kindness and his wonderfully helpful professional advice.

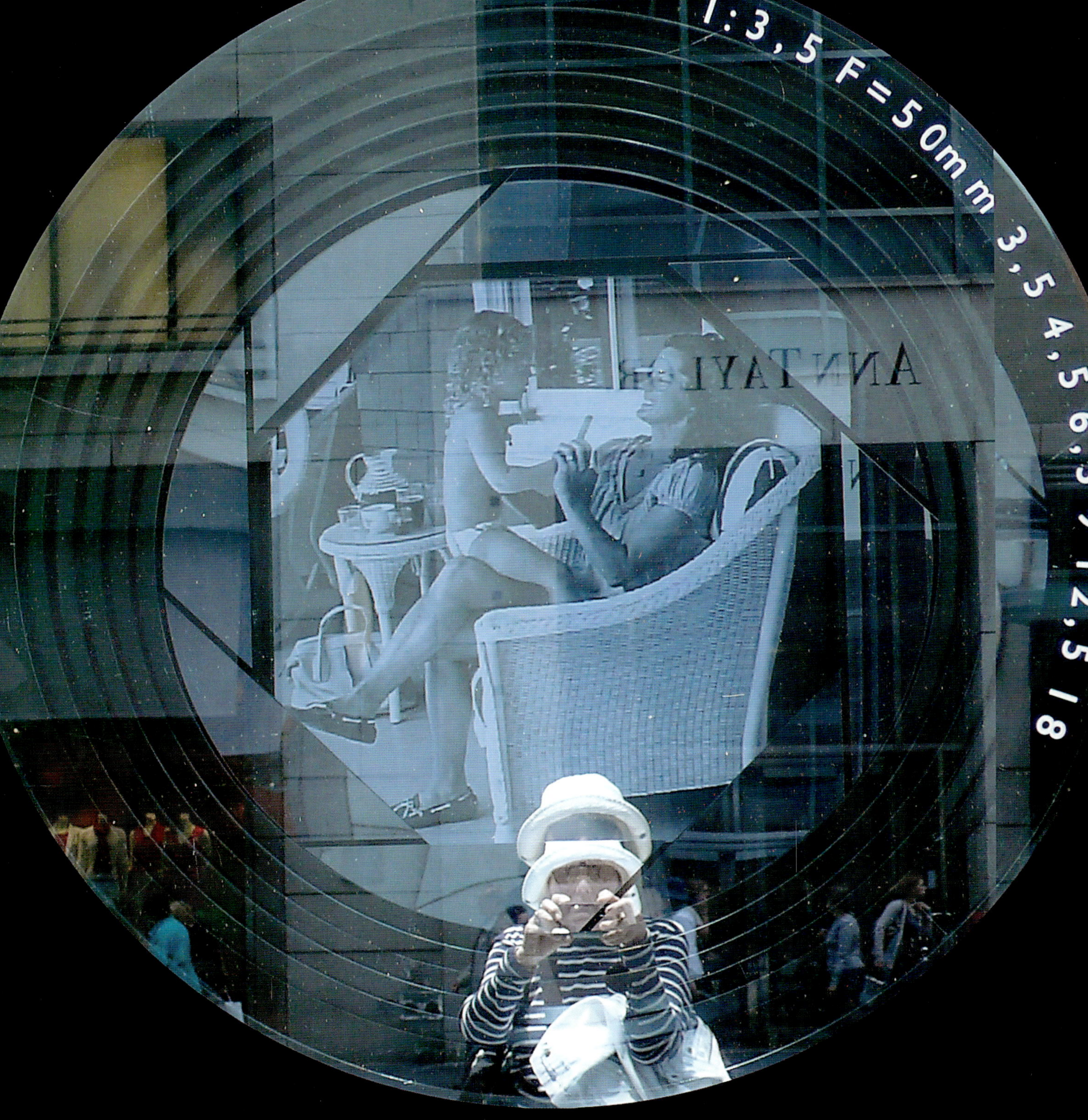
1:3,5 F=50mm 3,5 4,5 6,3 9 12,5 18

CONTENTS

FOREWORD

BY MIKE NICHOLS

New York is infinite. In analyzing its unlimited aspects, E. B. White wrote:

There are roughly three New Yorks. There is, first, the New York of the man or woman who was born there, who takes the city for granted and accepts its size, its turbulence as natural and inevitable. Second, there is the New York of the commuter—the city that is devoured by locusts each day and spat out each night. Third, there is the New York of the person who was born somewhere else and came to New York in quest of something. Of these trembling cities the greatest is the last—the city of final destination, the city that is a goal. It is this third city that accounts for New York's high strung disposition, its poetical achievements.

Margie and Sheldon Harnick see and record their own New York. Their astonishing book finds new things in every direction and sees the often-observed landmarks in a completely new way. It is as though two poets were taking a walk through the city side by side, looking at different things and sometimes the same things through their different eyes and souls, humming different tunes in the same key, sometimes joining in complex harmonies. They see beauty in things that, once seen, will never again be seen in the same way: a puddle reflecting a shiny new building and its own reflections until the puddle dries or a car blasts through it and all disappears. Landmarks change through their eyes into something never seen, stunning and with the shock of the new.

Look through their eyes at the familiar sights of Central Park and swans in the lakes, or mannequins in store windows, or the homeless, and they all take on new and startling aspects. Look at the art-by-accident of demolished buildings, graffiti, abandoned City of New York fixtures, and all the things that look different since Andy Warhol combined art and fashion, apparently forever.

Look at the Macy's Parade and some of the trademarked creatures made to sell to the little guys who have no opinions yet and love most fuzzy things they see on television. Look at the homeless woman, with all her possessions in plastic bags, peering in the Bulgari window. Here's a guy jubilantly kissing a girl just outside the backstage entrance of the theater where Jude Law is playing Hamlet. Is Jude the kisser? Looks just like him. We don't know for sure and, by the way, neither does Margie.

One of the many things this book is about is marriage. Sheldon may not have written a verse about it, but through the marriage of pictures and poems, the book itself expresses some of the complex wonders of two into one. A story, which Sheldon told me so long ago that both of them have forgotten it, illustrates for me the pleasures that this greatest adventure holds for those who fully invest in it. On a quiet evening at home in a cold month, Sheldon said to Margie. "It's so nice, the times we have together sharing silence and music and doing our work. It makes me happy." "For your information," said Margie, "for the past week, I have not been speaking to you."

And that's what a true marriage does. It turns conflict into laughter, time into memory, and two people into a searchlight, showing the rest of us the horizon in wonder and joy.

MIKE NICHOLS
New York, 2011

THE OUTDOOR MUSEUM

1.

There are masterpieces
hallowing the halls
and ennobling the walls
of the mighty Metropolitan,
the Whitney and the Guggenheim,
the Morgan and the Frick
and, of course, the Modern Art . . .
masterworks that offer us
banquets for the eye,
brandy for the brain,
candy for the soul
and manna for the heart.

2.

Our town is rich in shrines
where miracles of art
are known to appear,
prodigies of painting and sculpture
that all of us idolators
are prone to revere.

Whether Guggenheim or Whitney,
the Morgan or the Frick,
the Modern or the Met,
most of us, I think,
have a favorite shrine,

one we've come to love.
You probably have yours.
I certainly have mine
and it's none of the above.
Mine is not some gallery,
museum (or what have you),
that shelters all its treasures
in air-conditioned spaces.
No.
Mine displays its riches
in unprotected places
exposed to wind and weather.
For mine
is that cultural anomaly:
The Outdoor Museum,
the vast and varied pile
that is the City of New York itself.

3.

Admission free.
Open daily.
Never shuts its doors—
there are no doors to shut.
Come stroll with me
and let us see
what's on display
today.

4.

What have we here?
It seems to be
a crumbling wall,
no more, no less;
a crumbling wall,
that's all.

But study it more closely.
That wild, haphazard pattern,
that look of ordered chaos
could be by Jackson Pollock.
Yes, what we first ascribed
to erosion and decay
could be, if not by Pollock,
a capital example
of *art brut* by Dubuffet.

5.

Further down the block
there's a standpipe on display
that is either by Duchamp
or, quite possibly, Léger.

6.

And there, between opposing curbs,
behold: a most unlikely sight.
This cannot be! And yet
there they stand before us:
a flock of sheep
in the jungle of the city!
Delectable tableau.
It must be something by Rousseau.

7.

Greenwich Village, so I hear,
has acquired a new addition.
Come with me and we'll search
for that recent acquisition.
(Cue the music by Mussorgsky:
"Pictures at an Exhibition".)

Ah! There it is!
That explosion of graffiti
on the door across the way
was created, like as not,
in the mottled atelier
of the artist Basquiat.

8.

In The Outdoor Museum
there are sculptures by the thousand.
True, I've yet to see a piece
 by Michelangelo
or a work that I'd attribute
 to Rodin.
Still, with all the striking sculptures
by so many other artists
I feel it ill-behooves me
 to be choosy.
For example,
that sleek streamlined owl
might well be a Brancusi.

9.

We've had our stroll.
Now you're on your own.
When you go exploring,
stay alert, look around.
Hiding in plain sight
are remarkable creations
in improbable locations
waiting to be found.
Here a Turner,
a Constable, a Klimt,
there a Picasso,
a Magritte or Clyfford Still.
Be attentive and you'll find them,
these weathered works of art,
in that cultural anomaly,
that grand improbability:
The Outdoor Museum
of the City of New York.

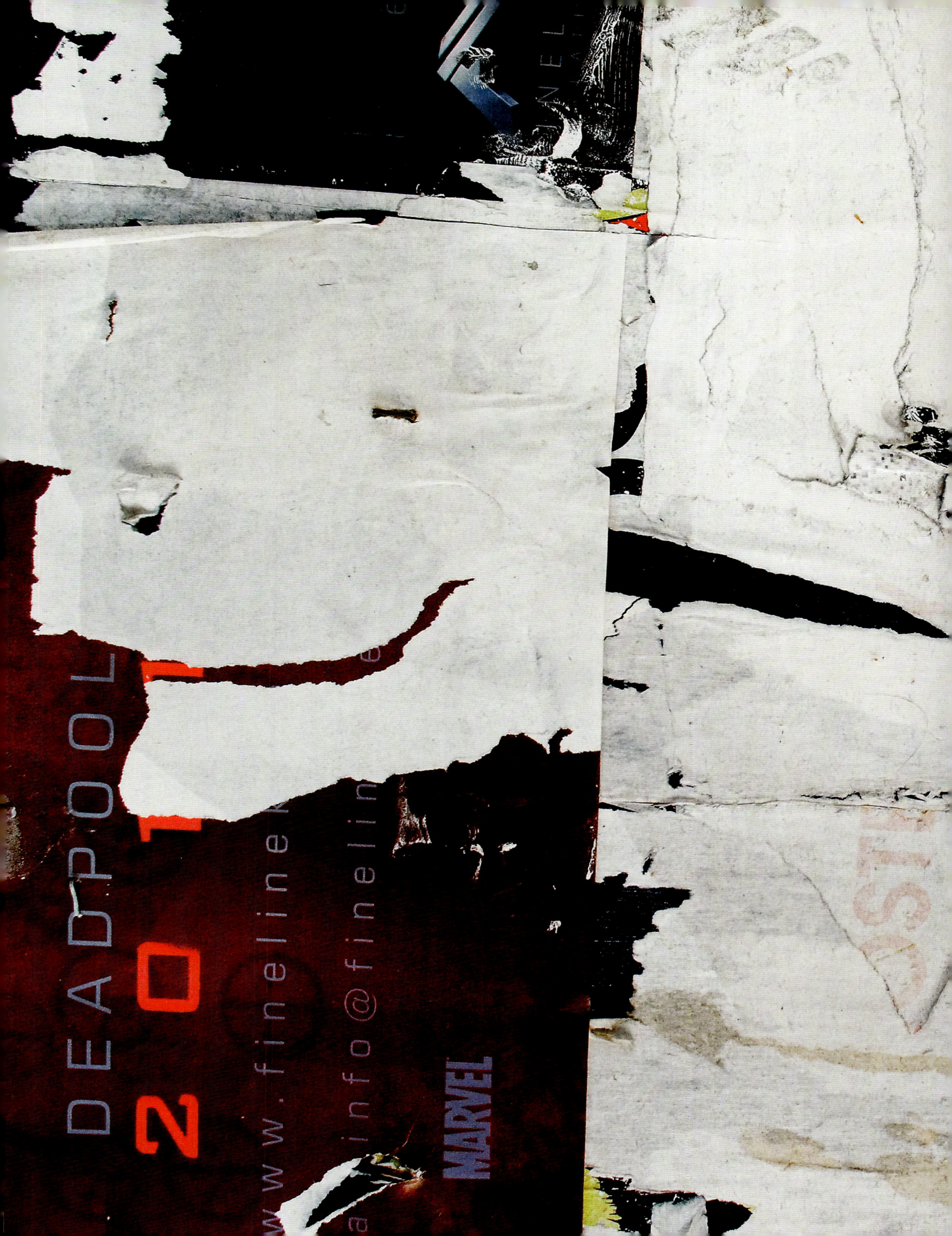
DEADPOOL
www.fineline
info@fineline
MARVEL

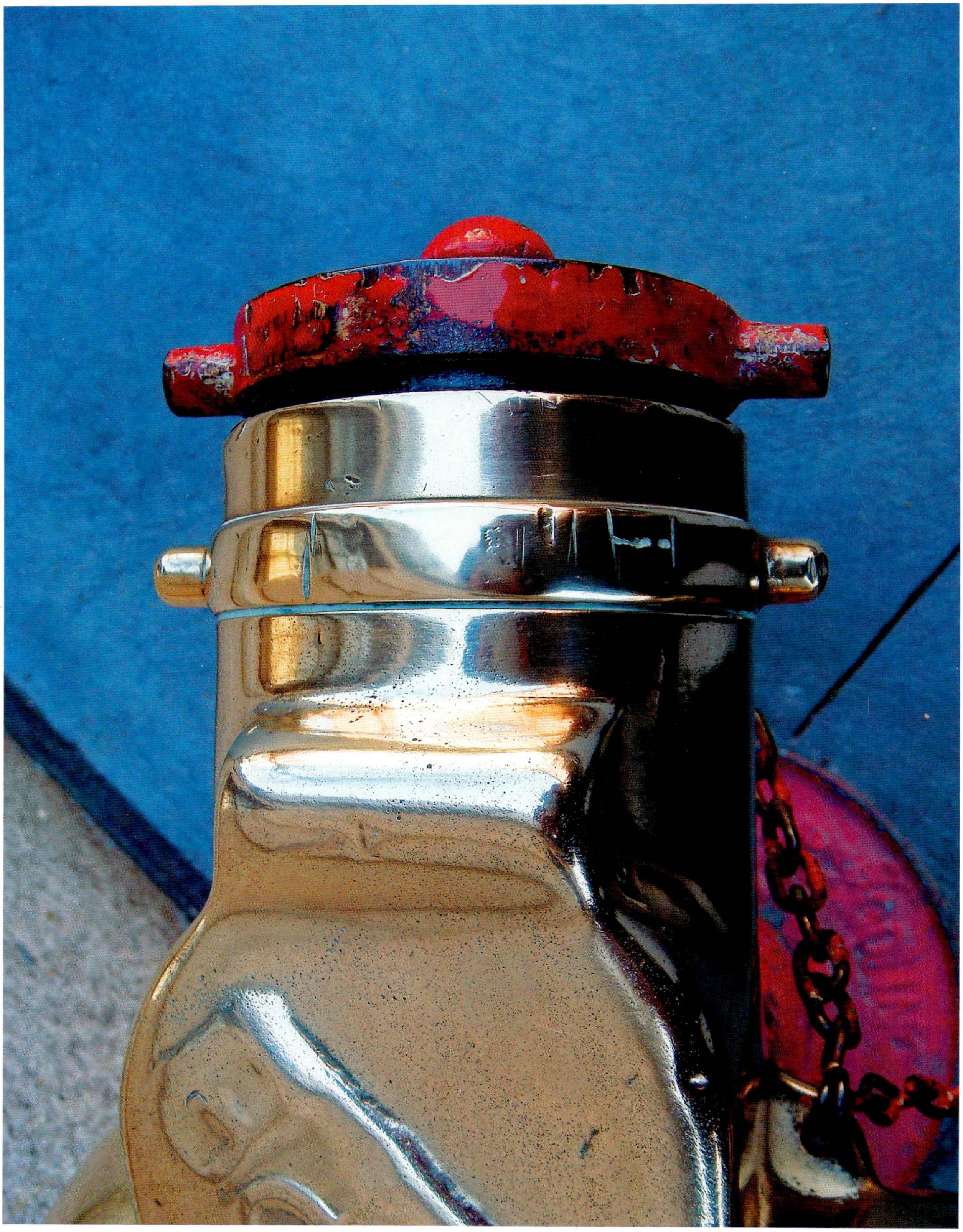

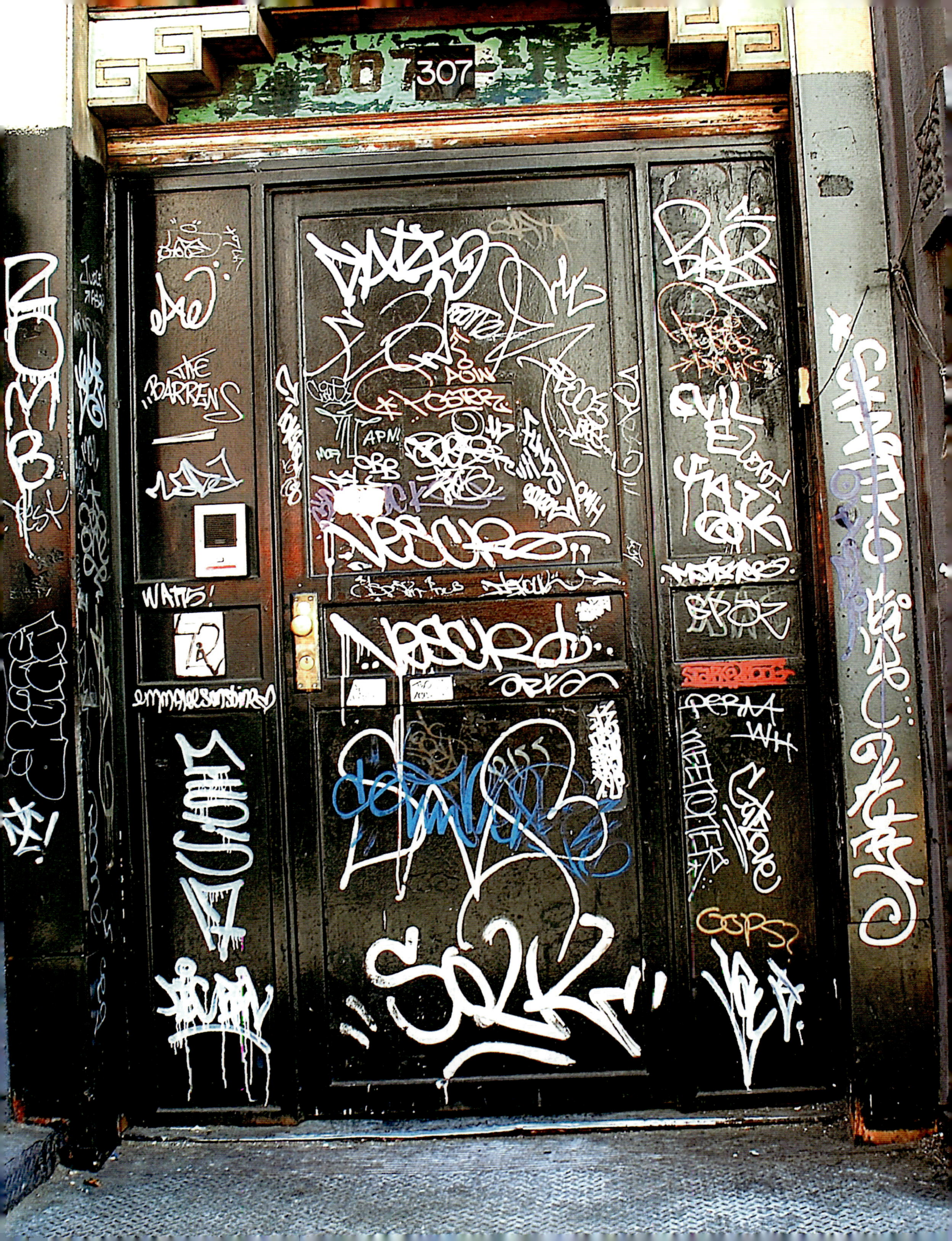
307
THE BARRENS
WATTS!

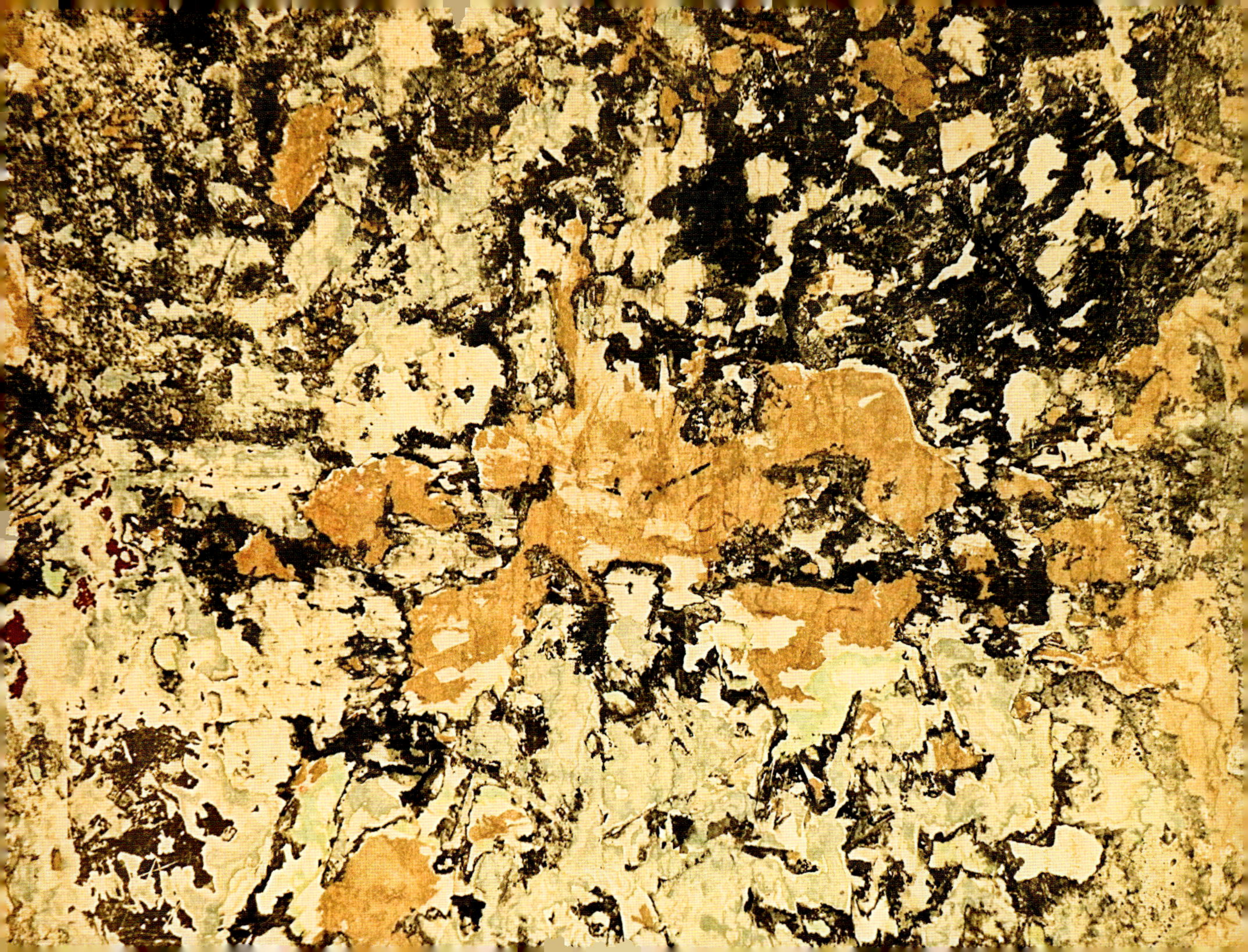

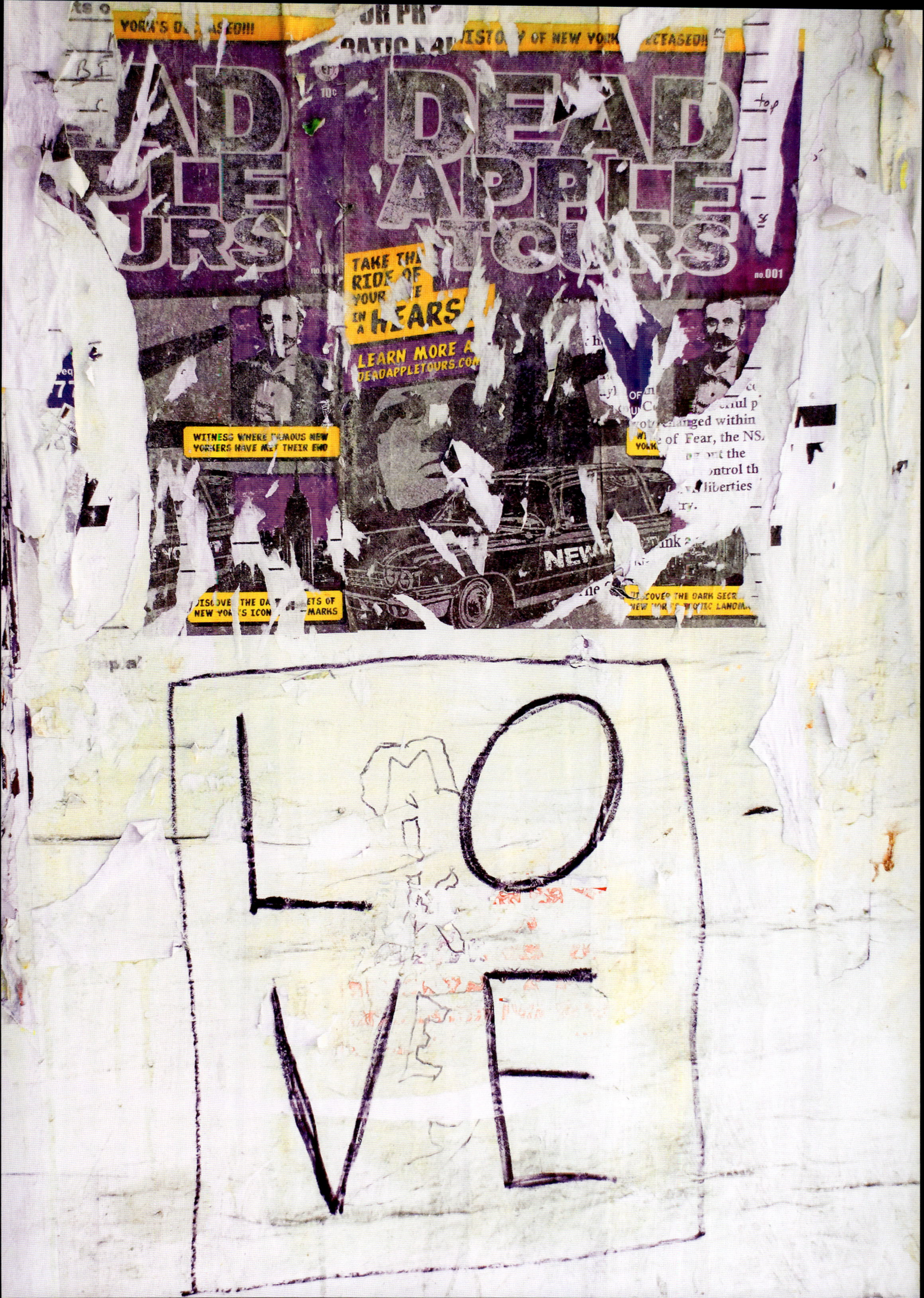
DEAD APPLE TOURS
no.001
LEARN MORE A
WITNESS WHERE FAMOUS NEW YORKERS HAVE MET THEIR END
LOVE

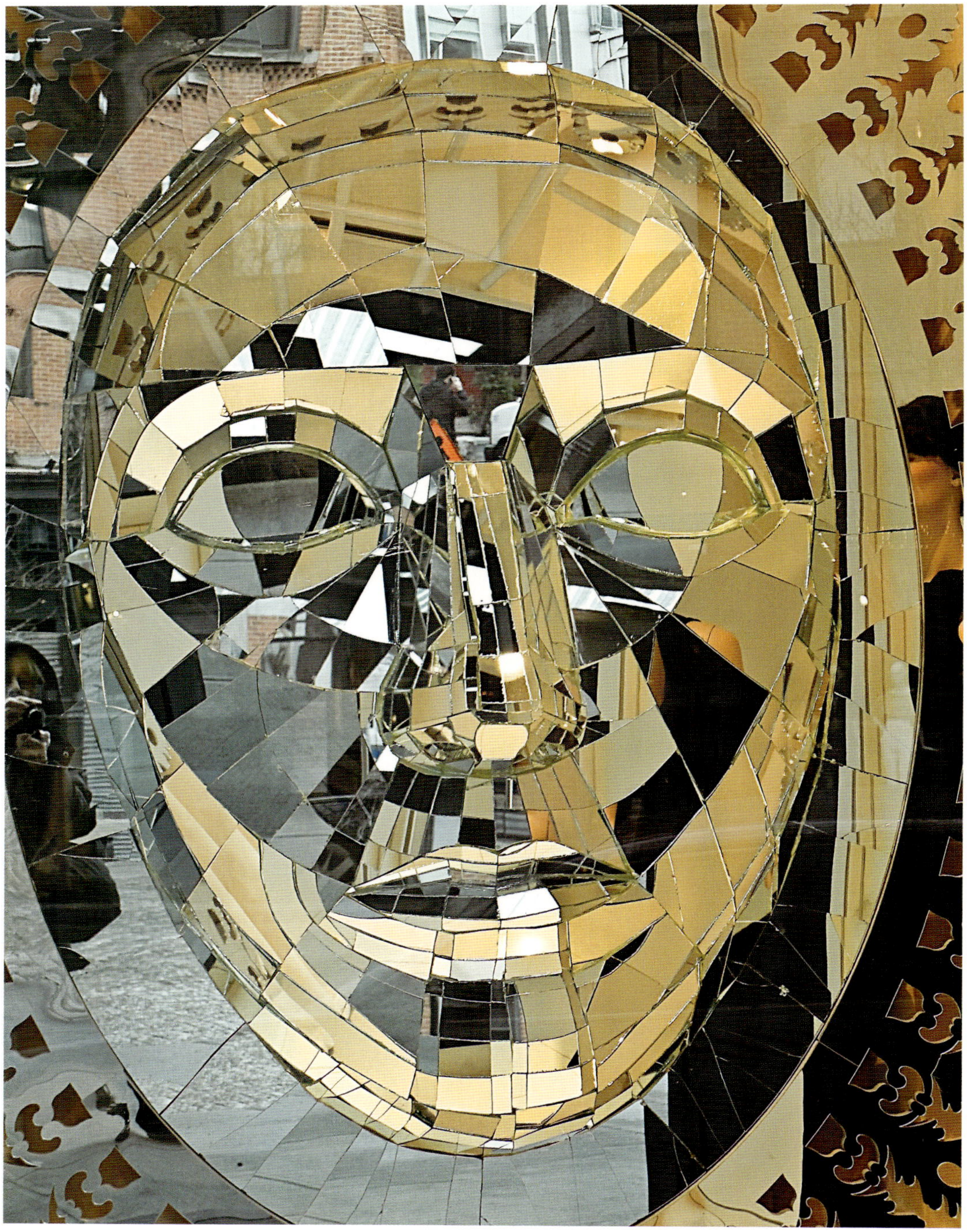

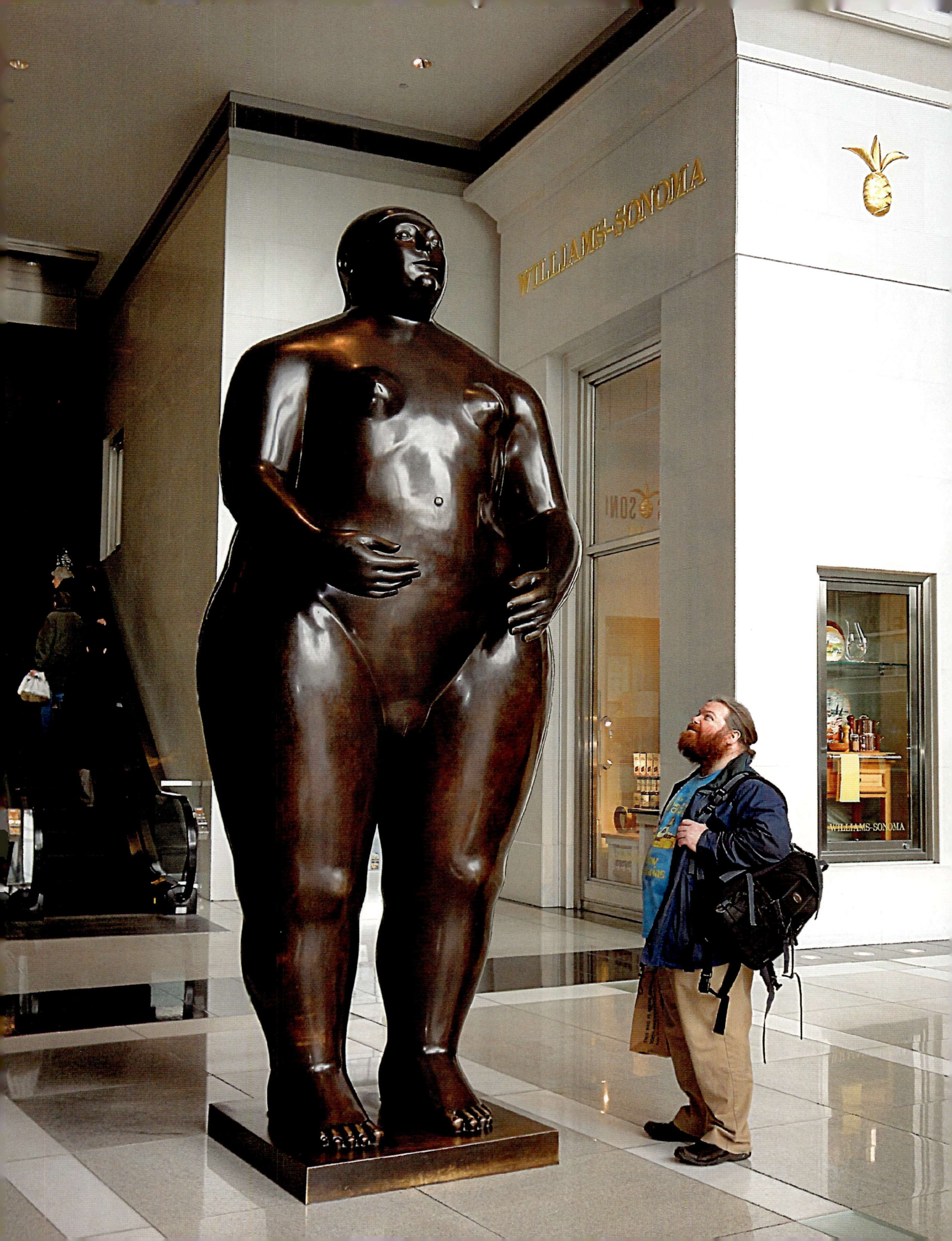
WILLIAMS-SONOMA
WILLIAMS-SONOMA

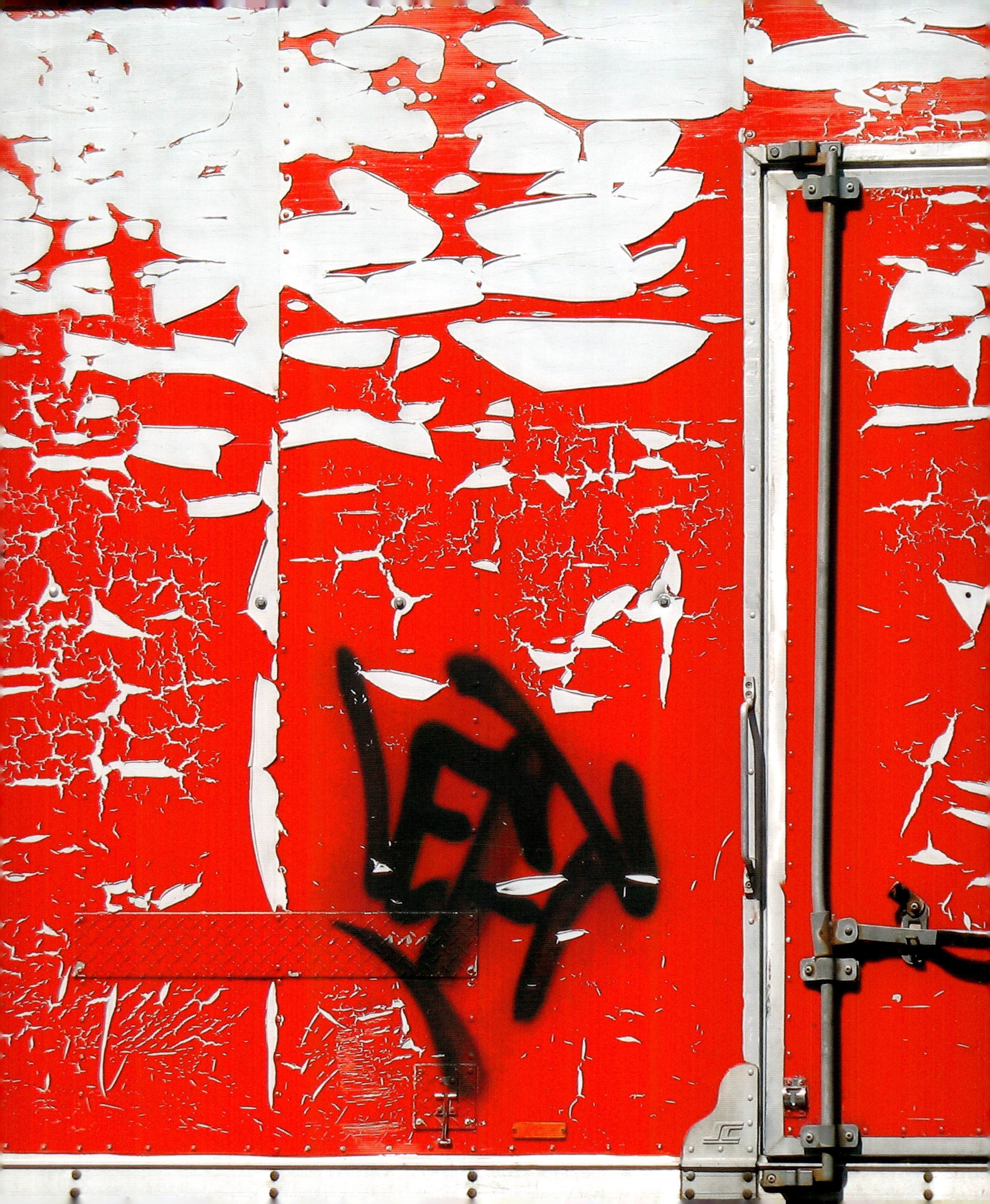

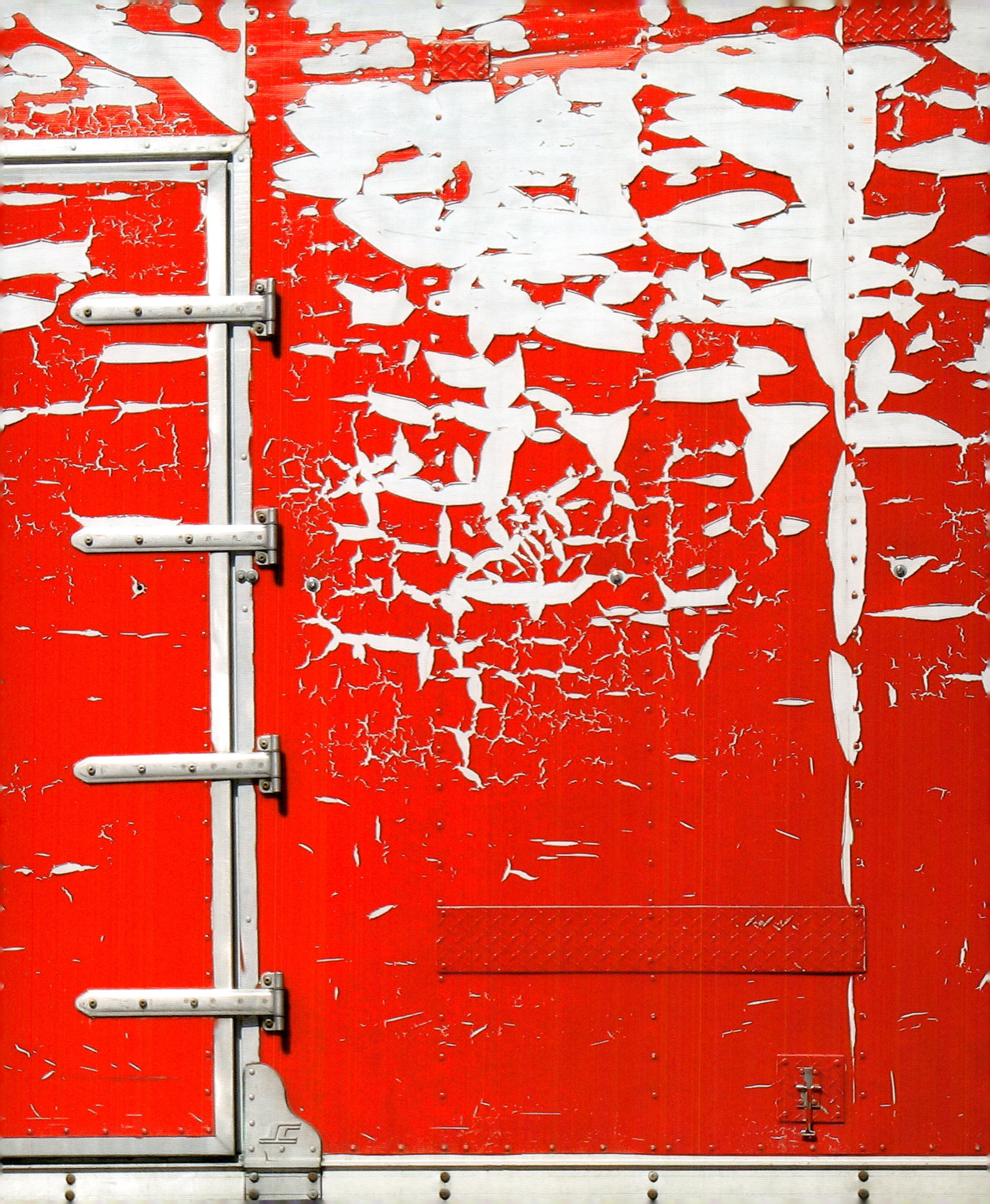

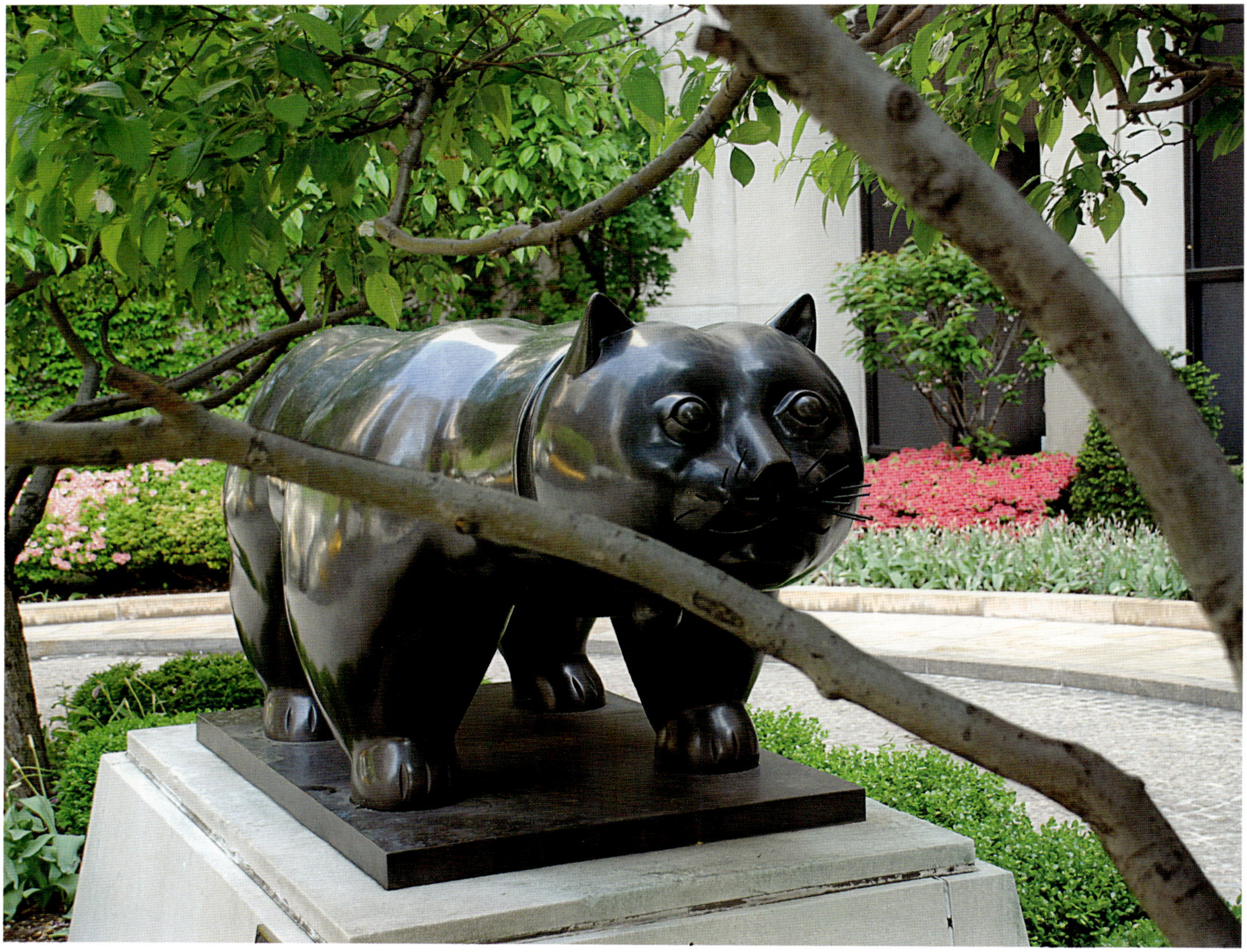

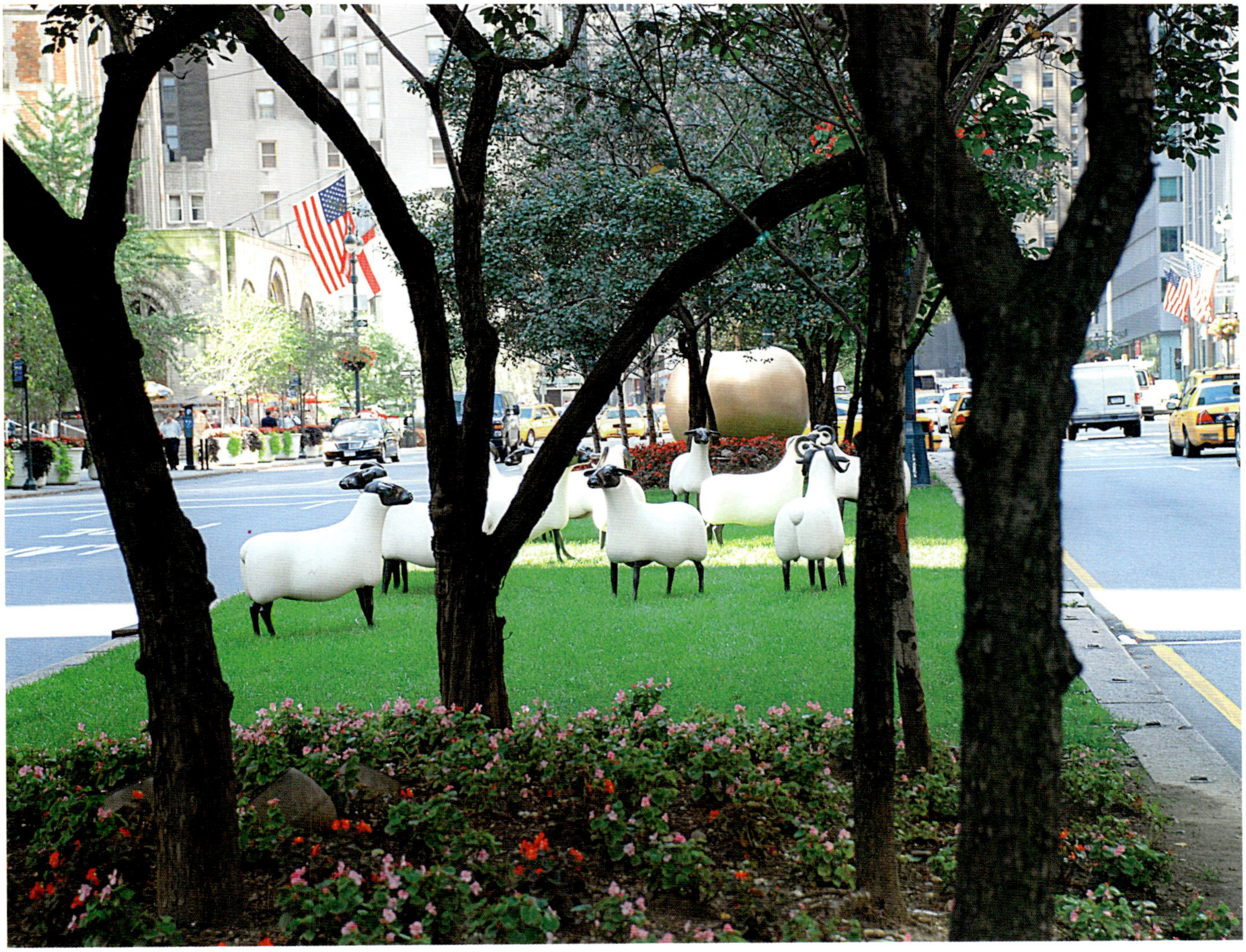

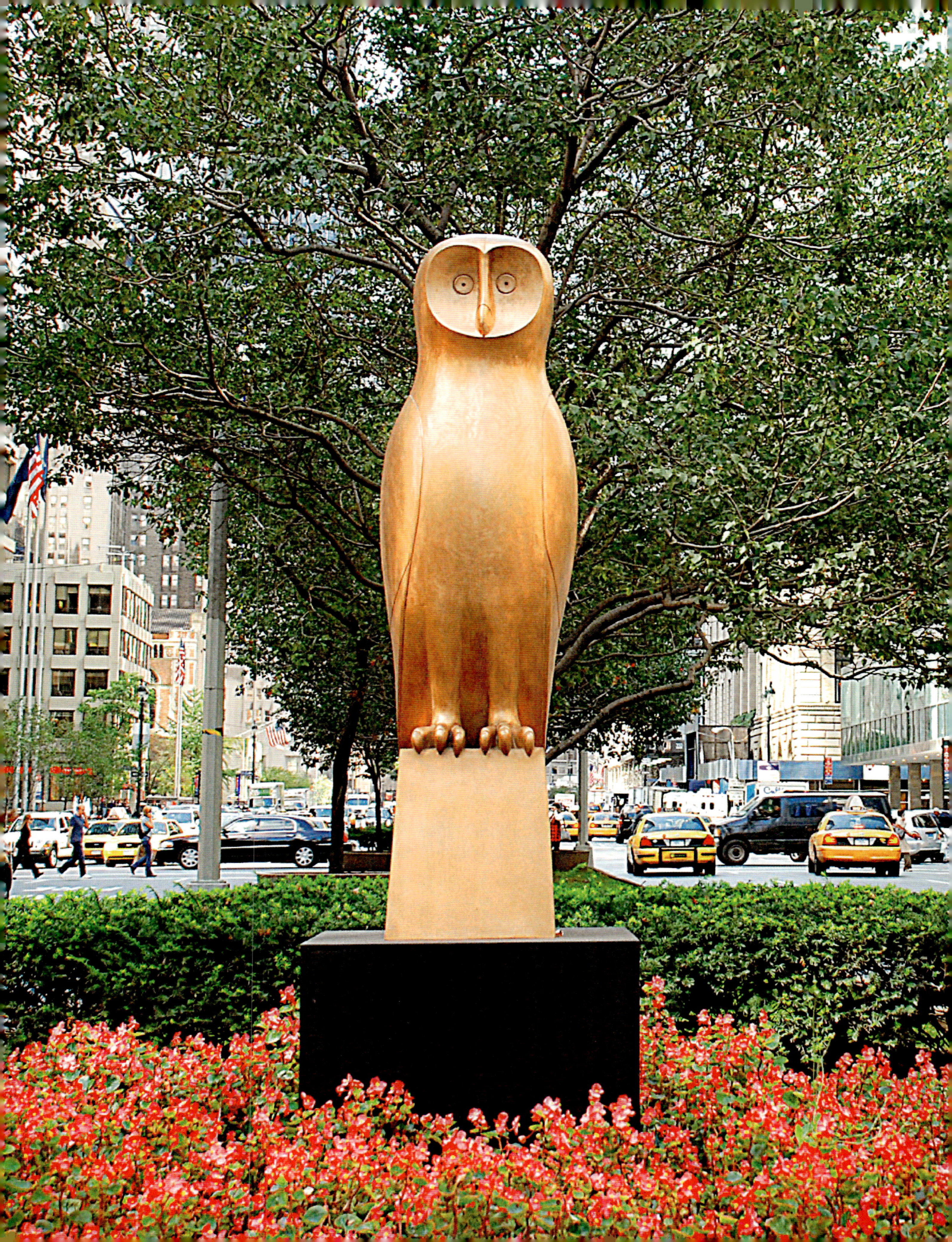

2

DEBUSSY IN NEW YORK

1.

When Debussy
advised Satie
to pay more heed to form,
I think he was revealing,
  in effect,
how much he longed to be
  an architect.

2.

If he had shed
  his music maker's coat,
he would have been
  an architect of note,
a member of
  that small inventive band
whose startling work
  is always in demand.

And as his new
  career began to hum,
from everywhere
  commissions would have come.

In no time, he'd
  have seen his buildings rise
to ornament Man-
  hattan's crowded skies.

With his innate
  impressionistic bent,
his structures would
  have caused astonishment
and had New Yorkers
  visually hooked.
One has to wonder
  how those buildings
would have looked!

3.

In my opin-
ion they'd have been
impressionistic,
light and airy,
liquid, lambent,
visionary,
even more than, say,
Frank Gehry.

That's how they'd have looked,
  I suspect,
if Debussy had been
  an architect.

4.

As for Ravel . . .
well . . .

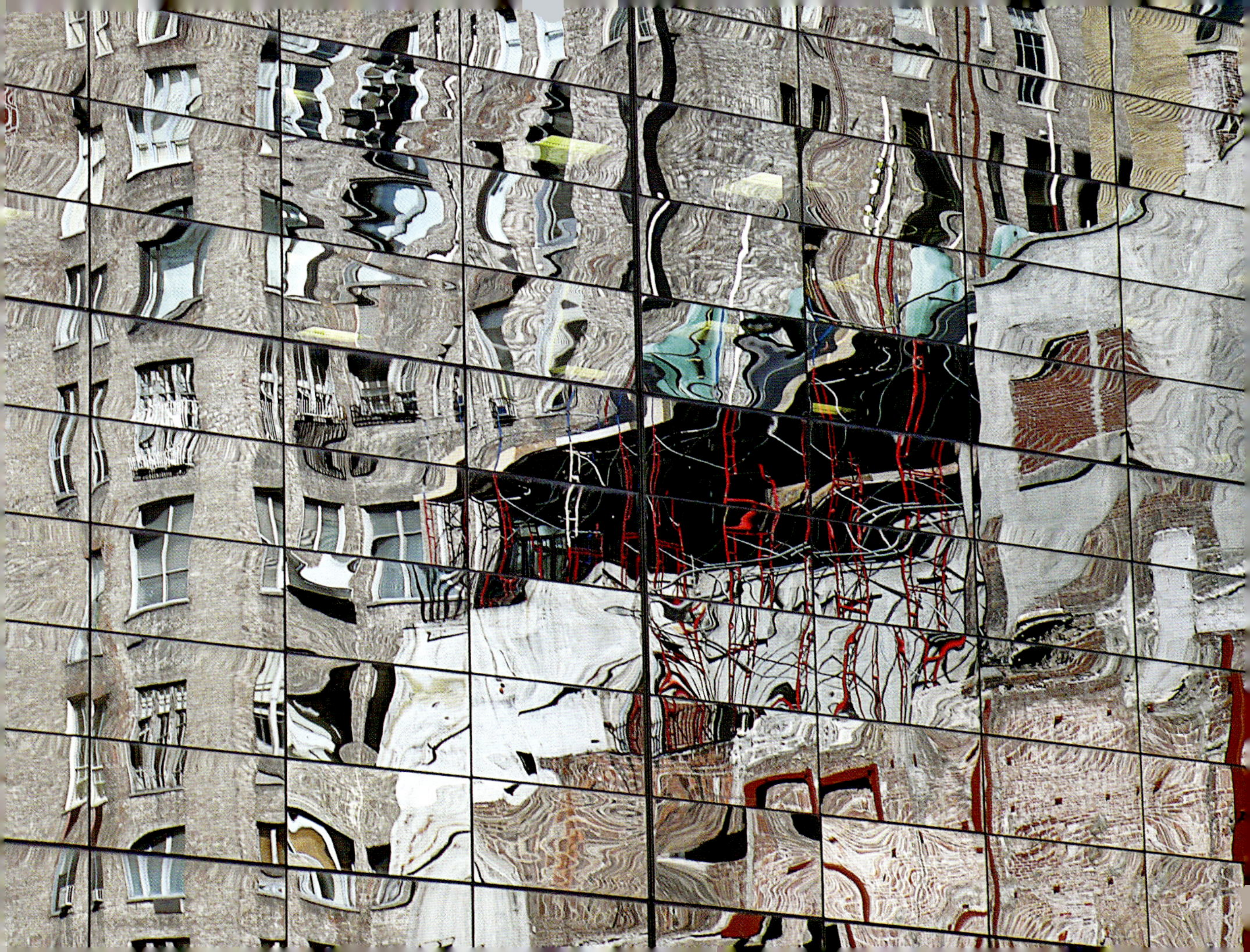

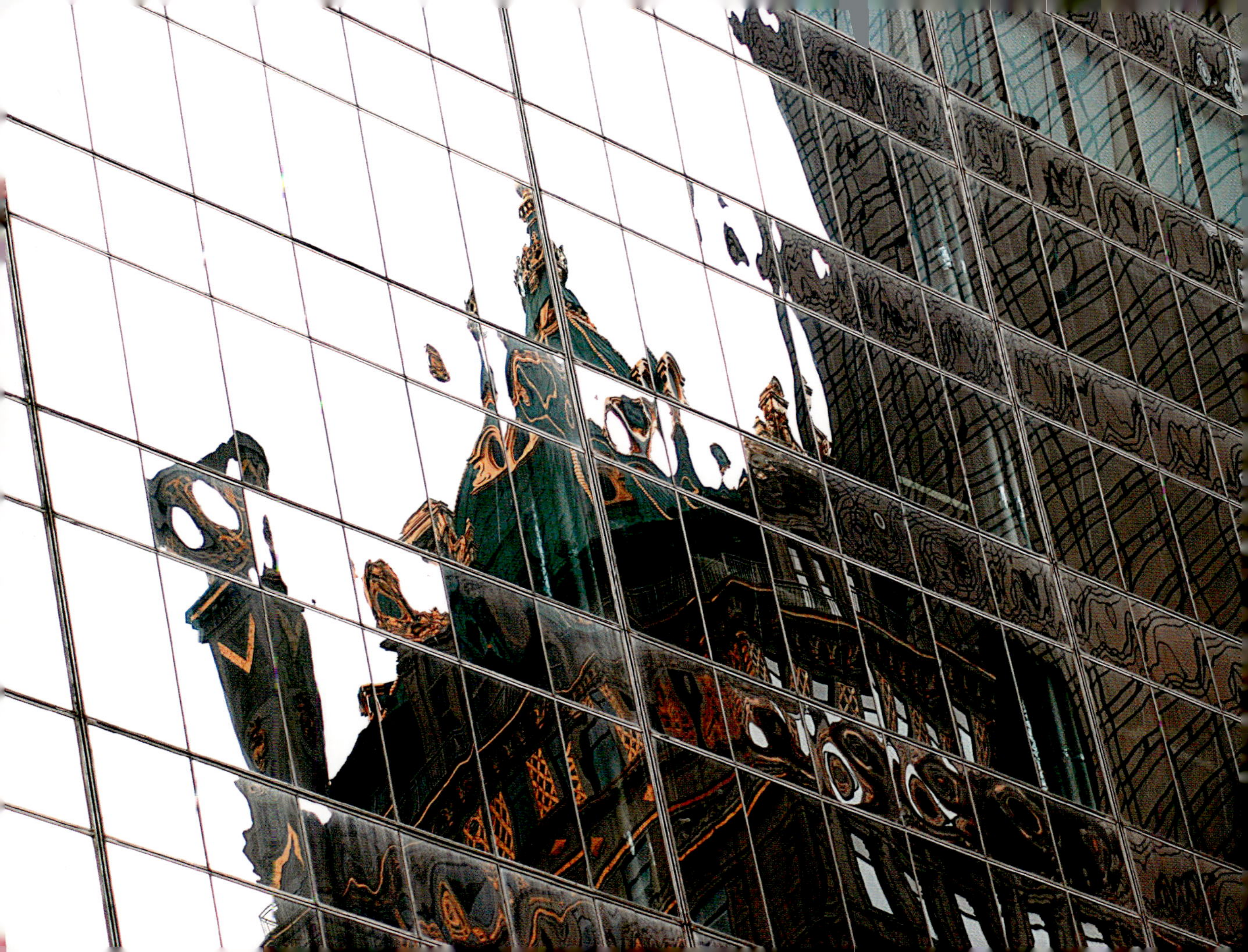

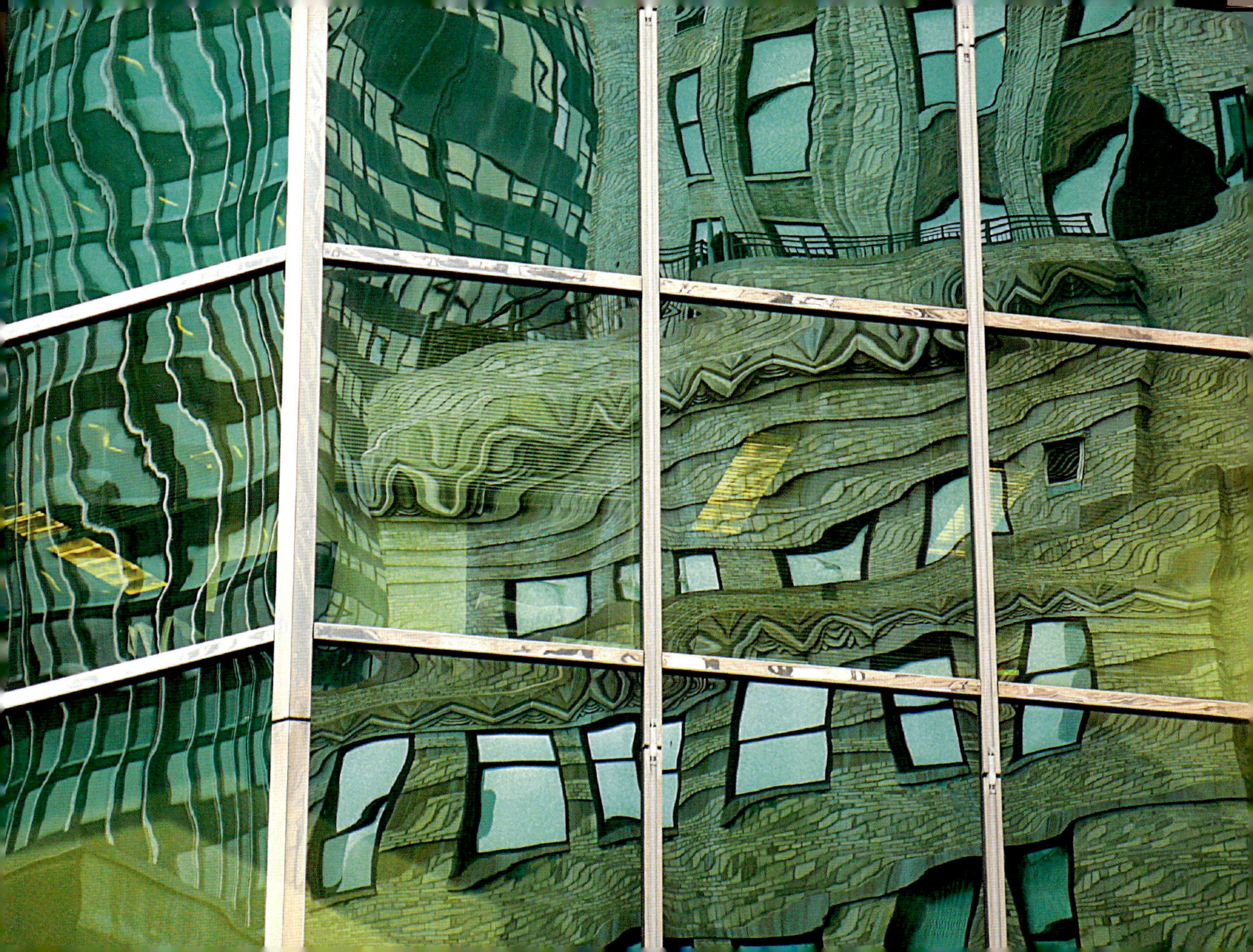

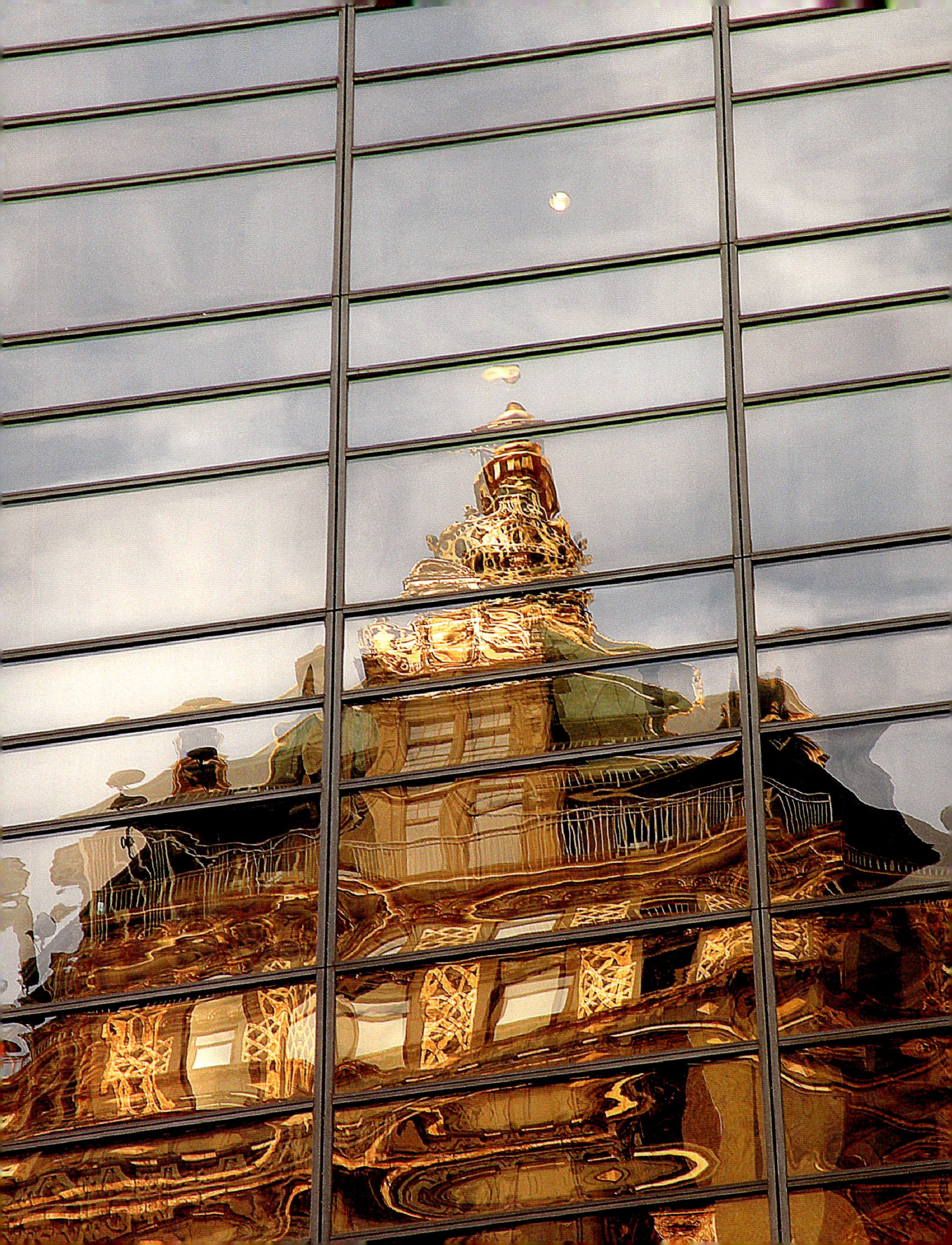

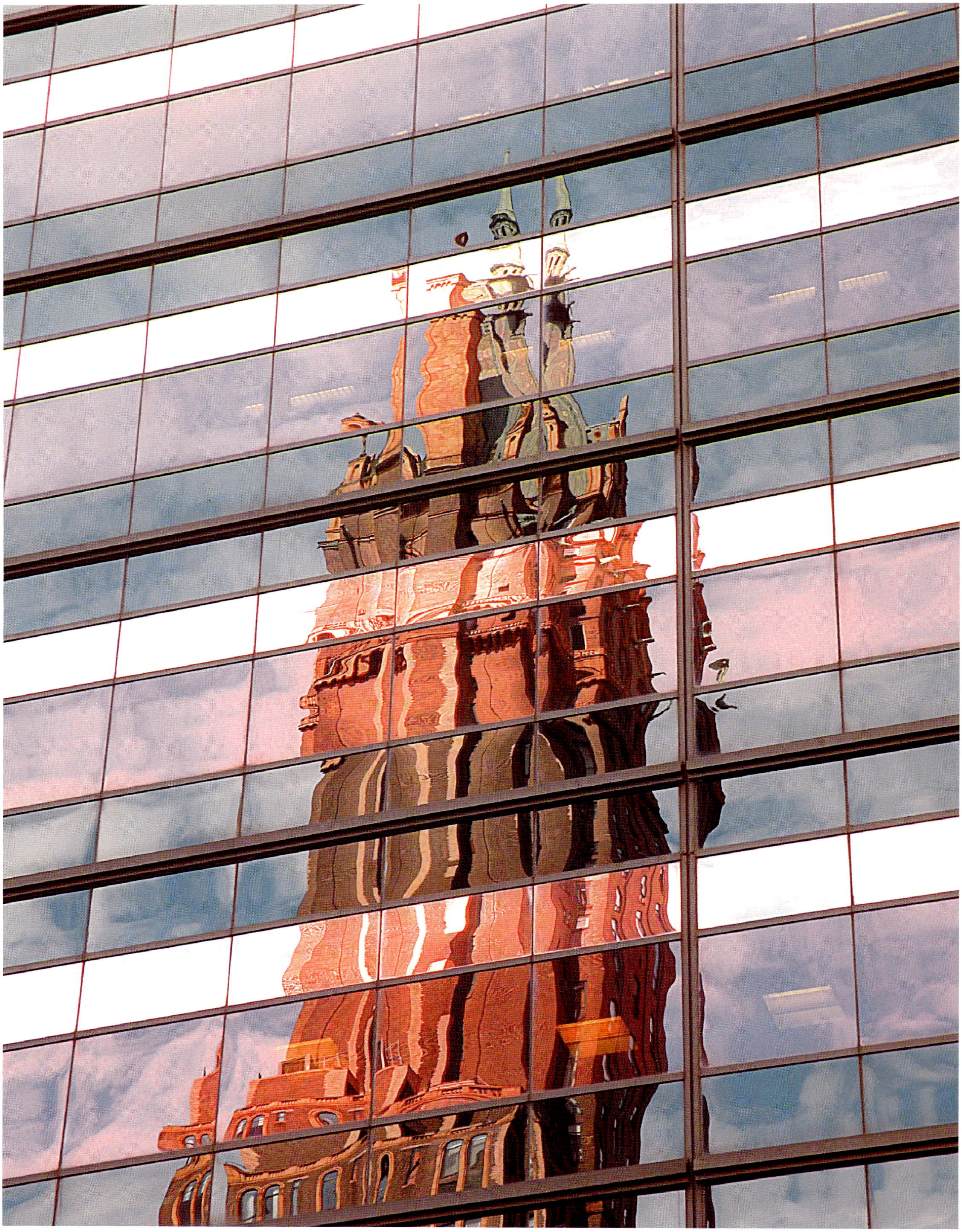

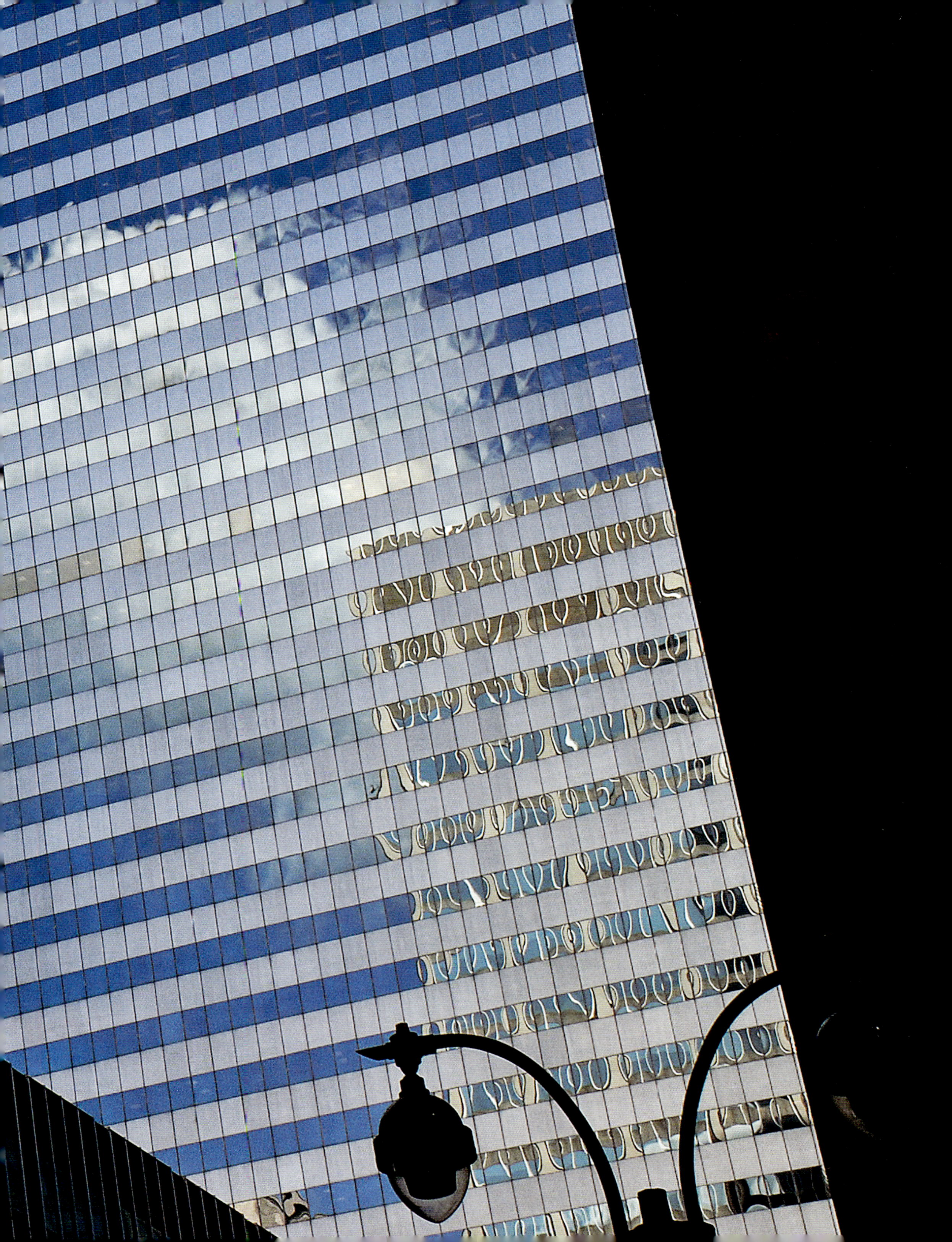

7 SUBWAY HAIKU

"... And the people ride
in a hole in the ground."

BETTY COMDEN
AND ADOLPH GREEN

I

Riding the D train
reading, all cares forgotten,
I went past my stop.

II

The Local goes where
the Express goes. It just takes
longer to get there.

III

Claustrophobia
tends to make most everyone
more considerate.

IV

If your train pulls in
just as you arrive, this does
not mean God loves you.

V

Subway musicians
all too often tend to make
low-level music.

VI

Those flamboyant scrawls
spray-painted on subway walls . . .
are these our Lascaux?

VII

We have all taken,
at one time or another,
the wrong train. That's life.

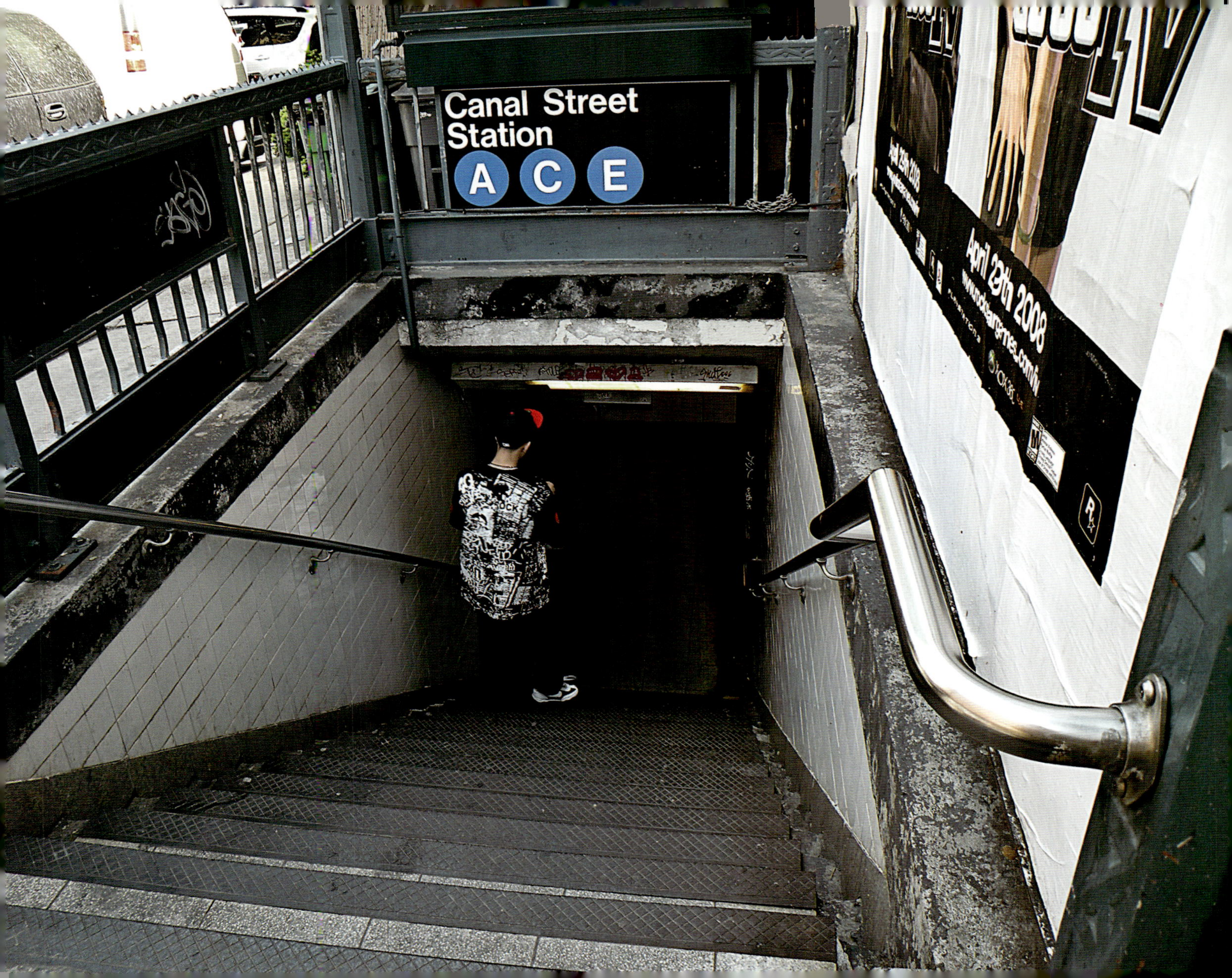
Canal Street
Station
A C E
April 29th 2008

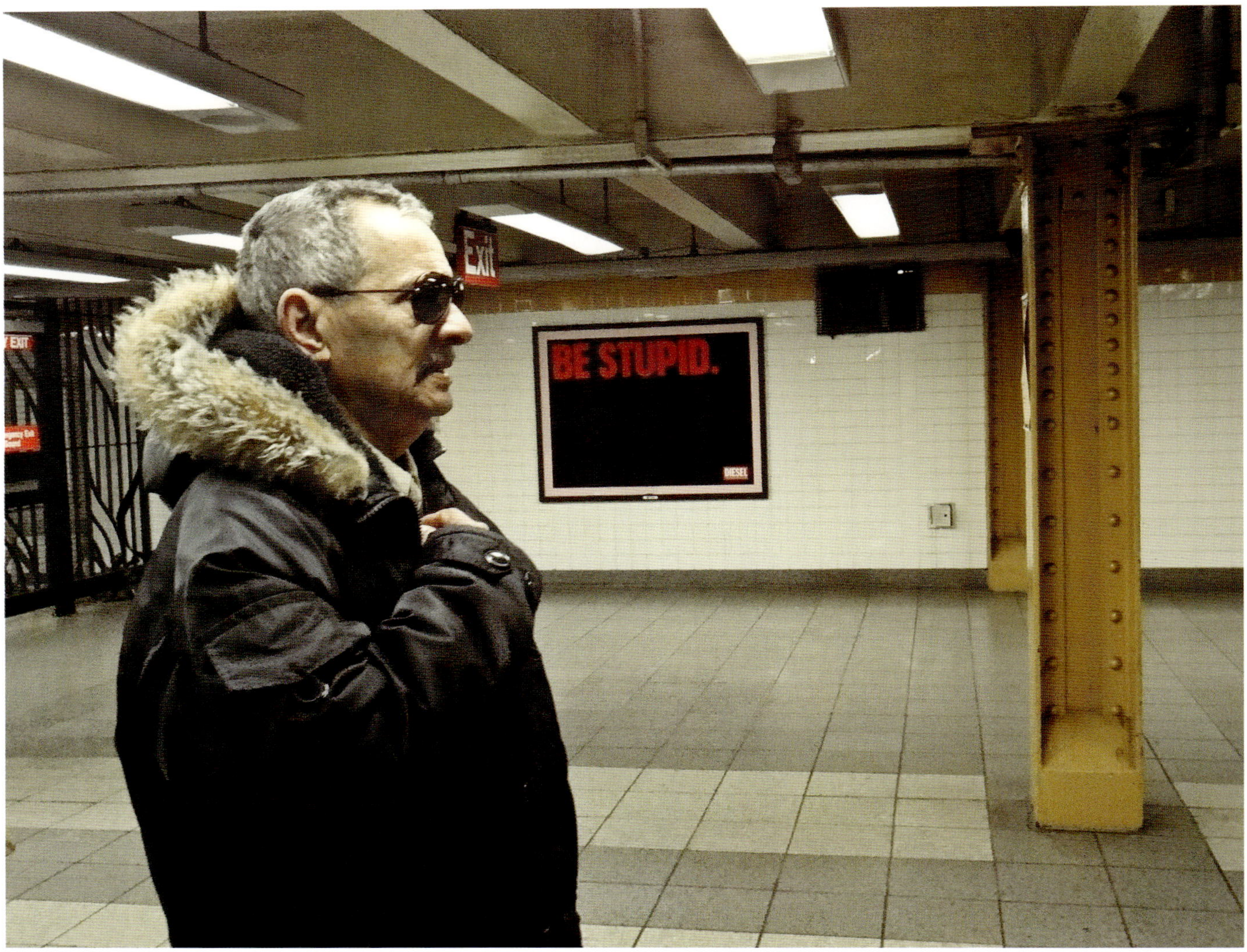
Exit
BE STUPID.
DIESEL

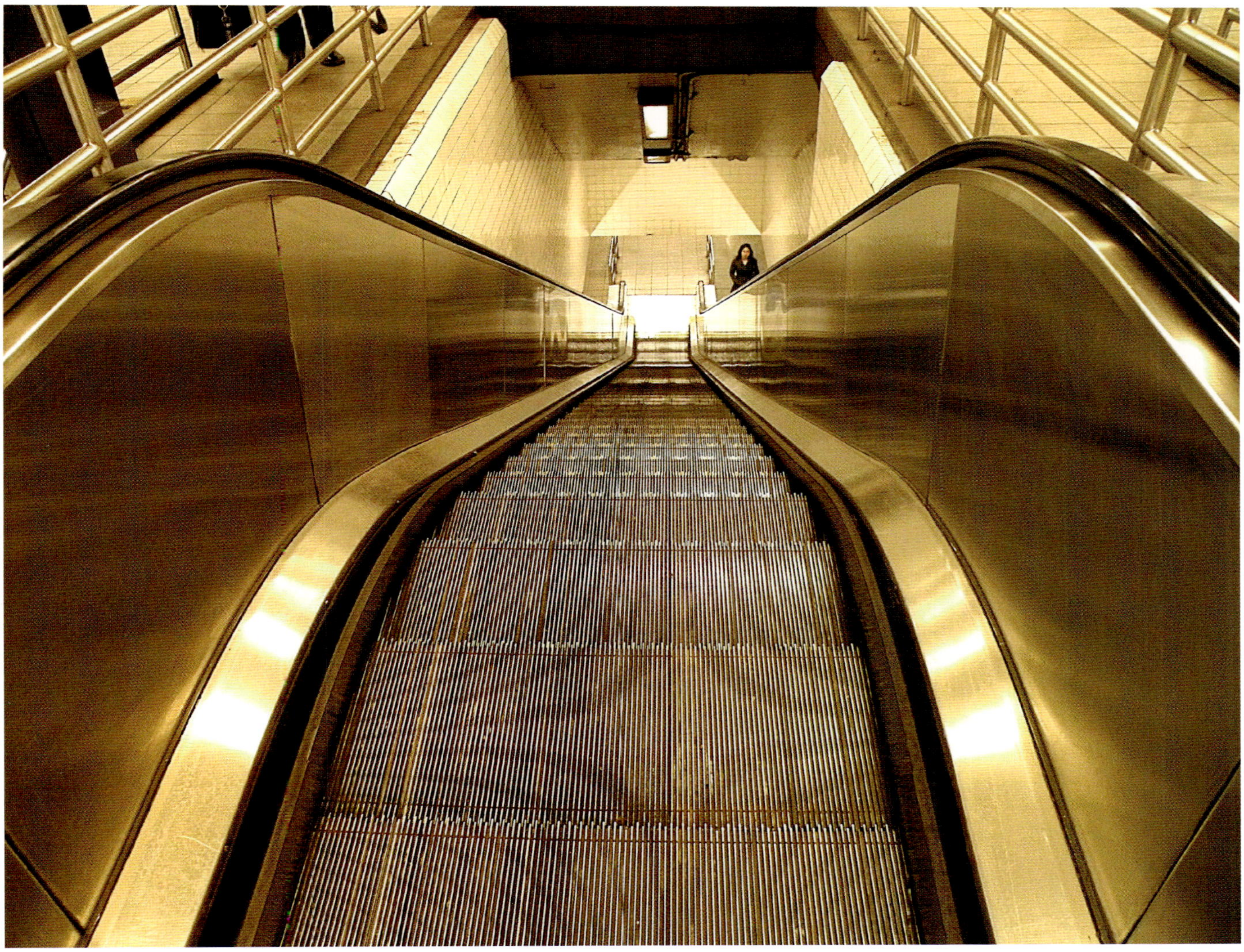

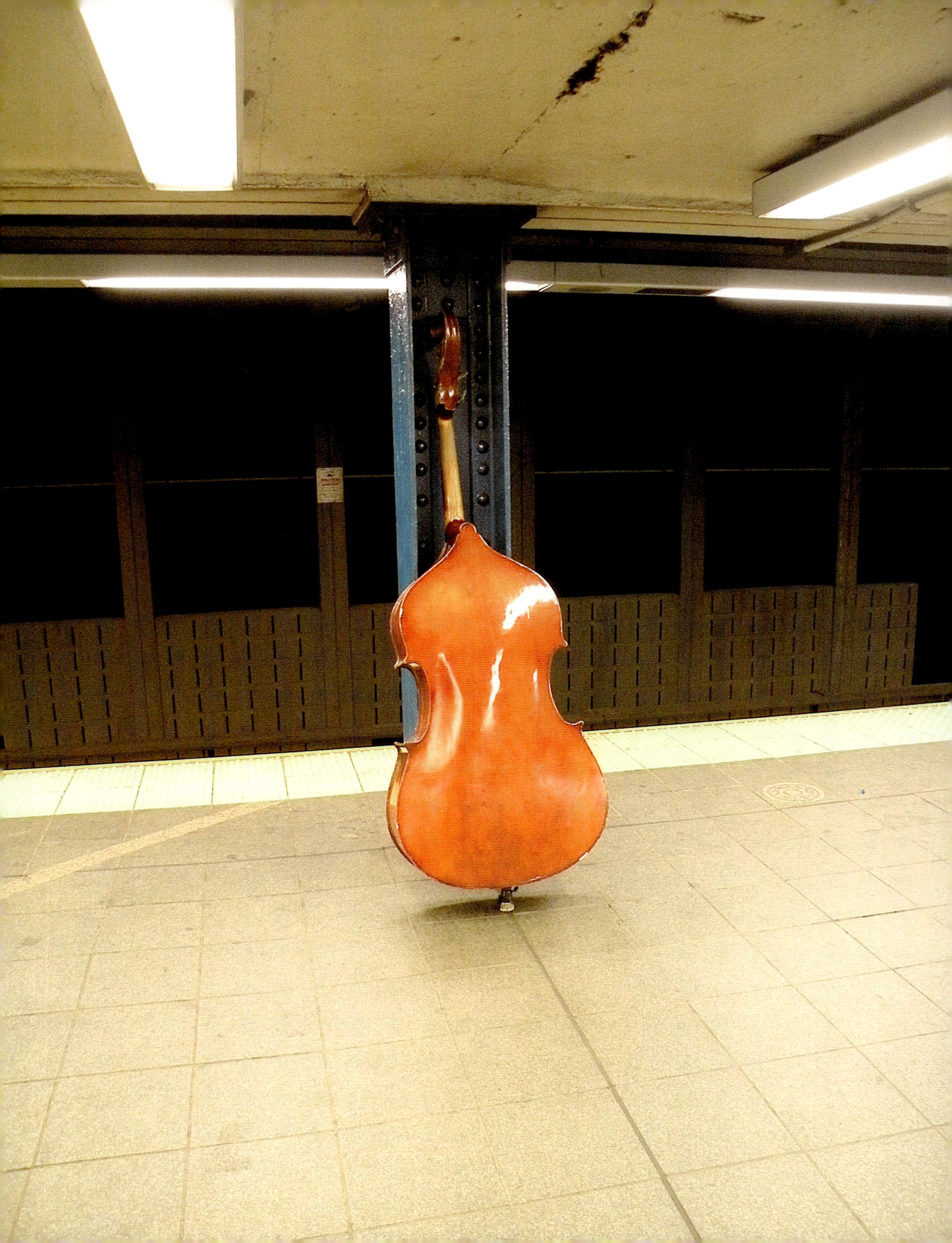

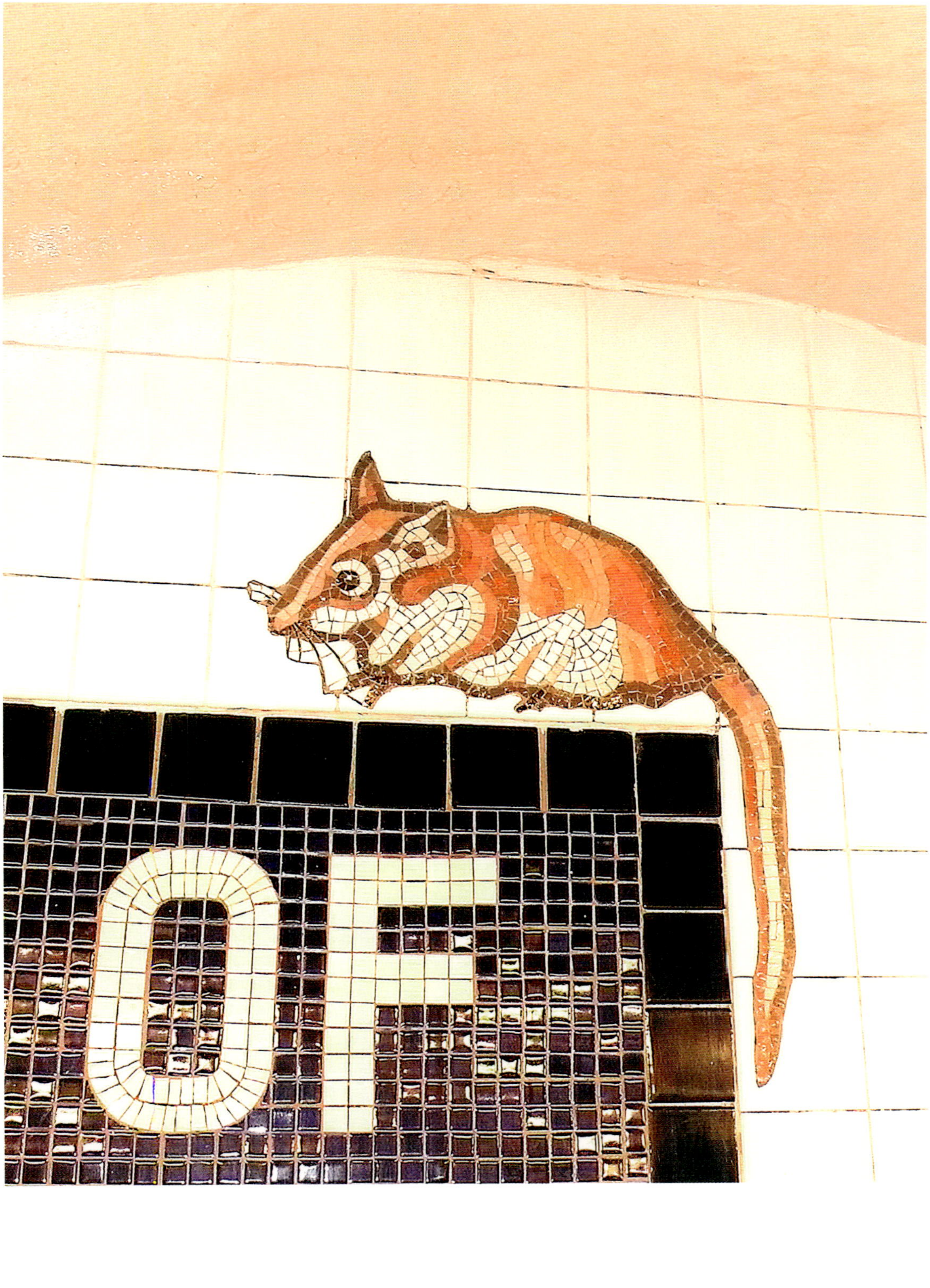
OF

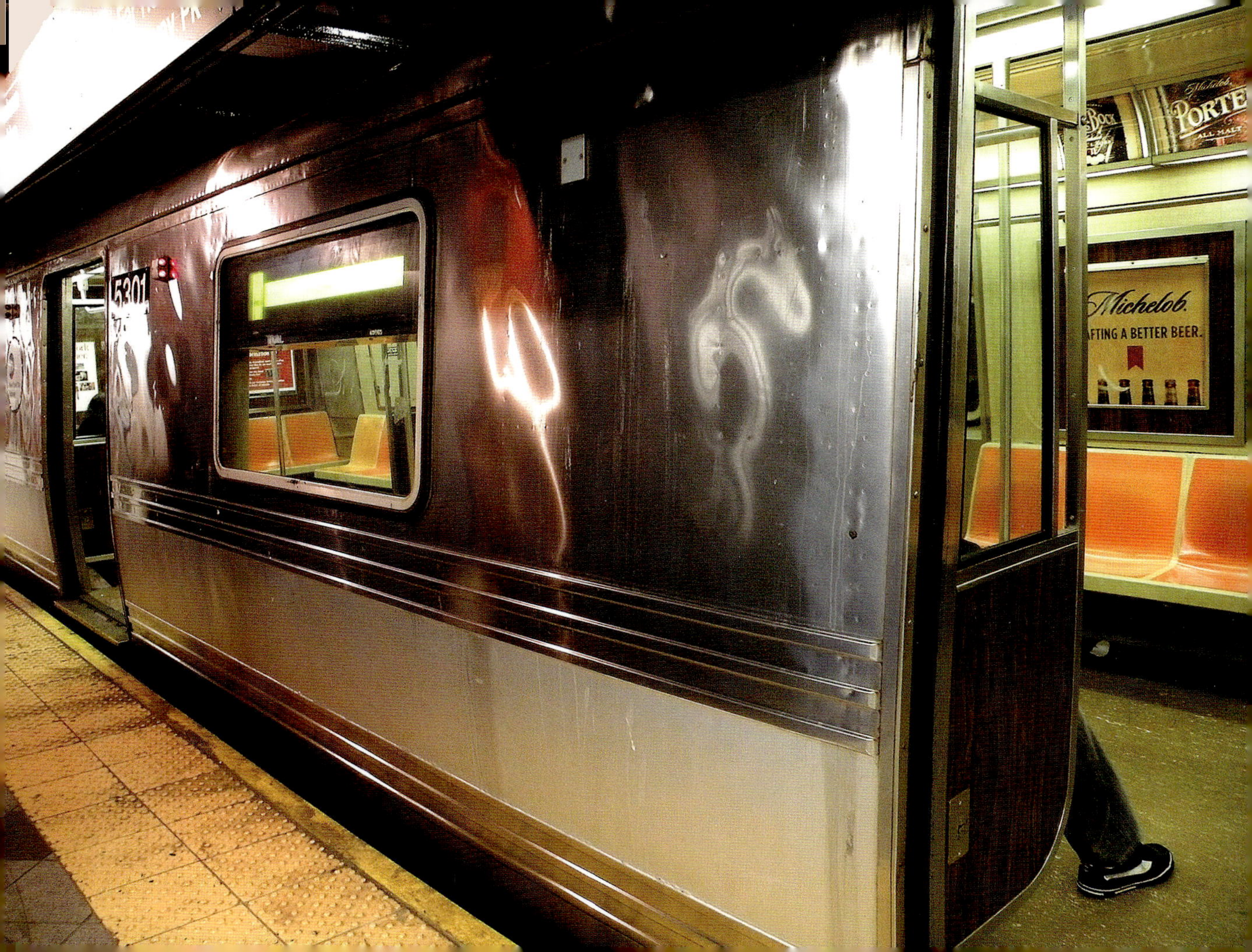
5301
Michelob.

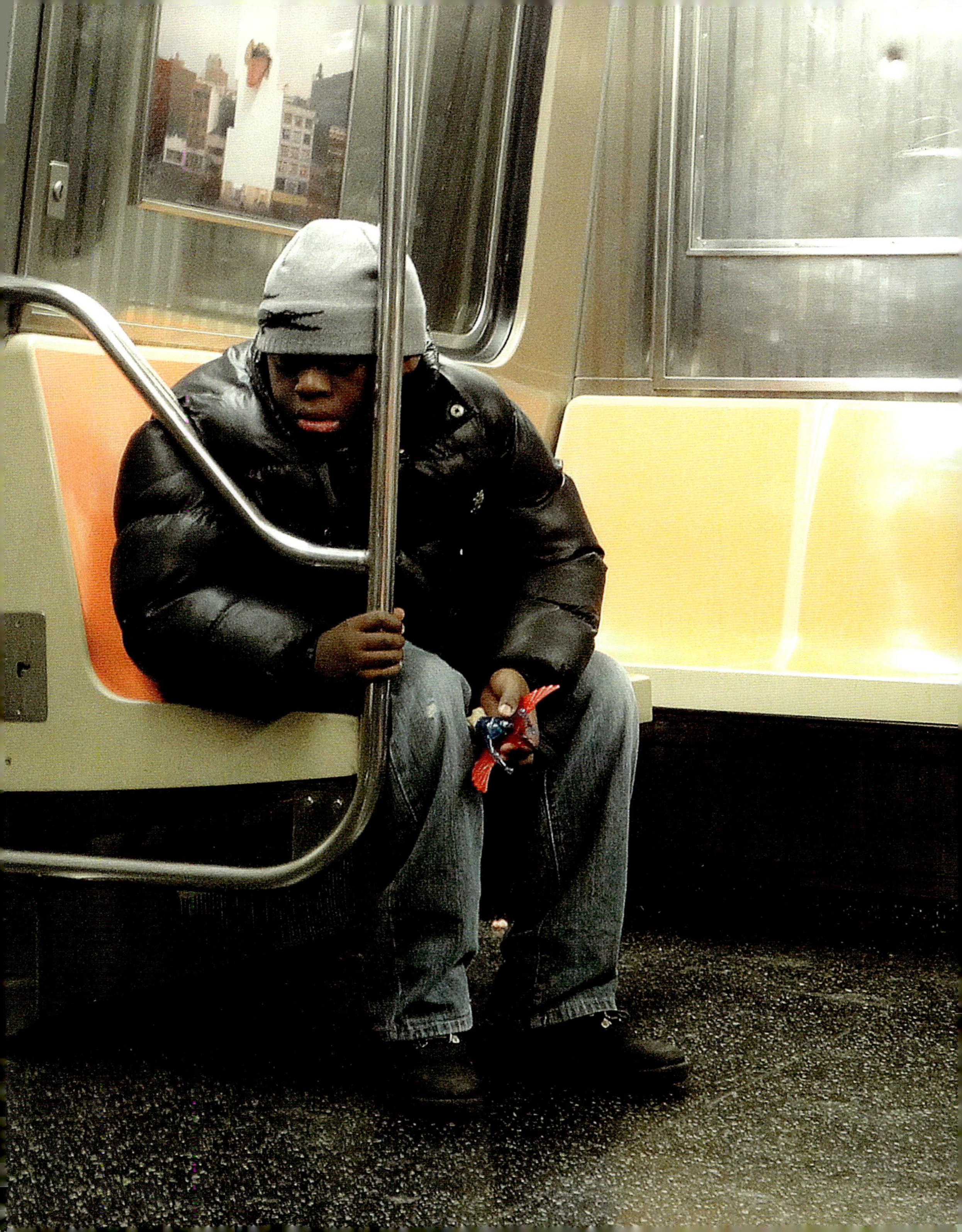

4

PUDDLES

Manhattan puddles, I suspect, are vain.
If so, then this must be the reason why:
Manhattan puddles know that they reflect
Manhattan buildings, trees and sky.

But other puddles, too, may be as proud,
Content to dwell in town and countryside.
Reflecting the locales that gave them birth,
They glow with chauvinistic pride.

I wonder if beneath their calm facades,
They tremble when they contemplate their fate.
They know reflected glory's a mirage
And will, in time, evaporate.

Aware that their existence may be brief,
They take the onward rush of time to heart
And choose to spend their dwindling span of days
Becoming works of art.

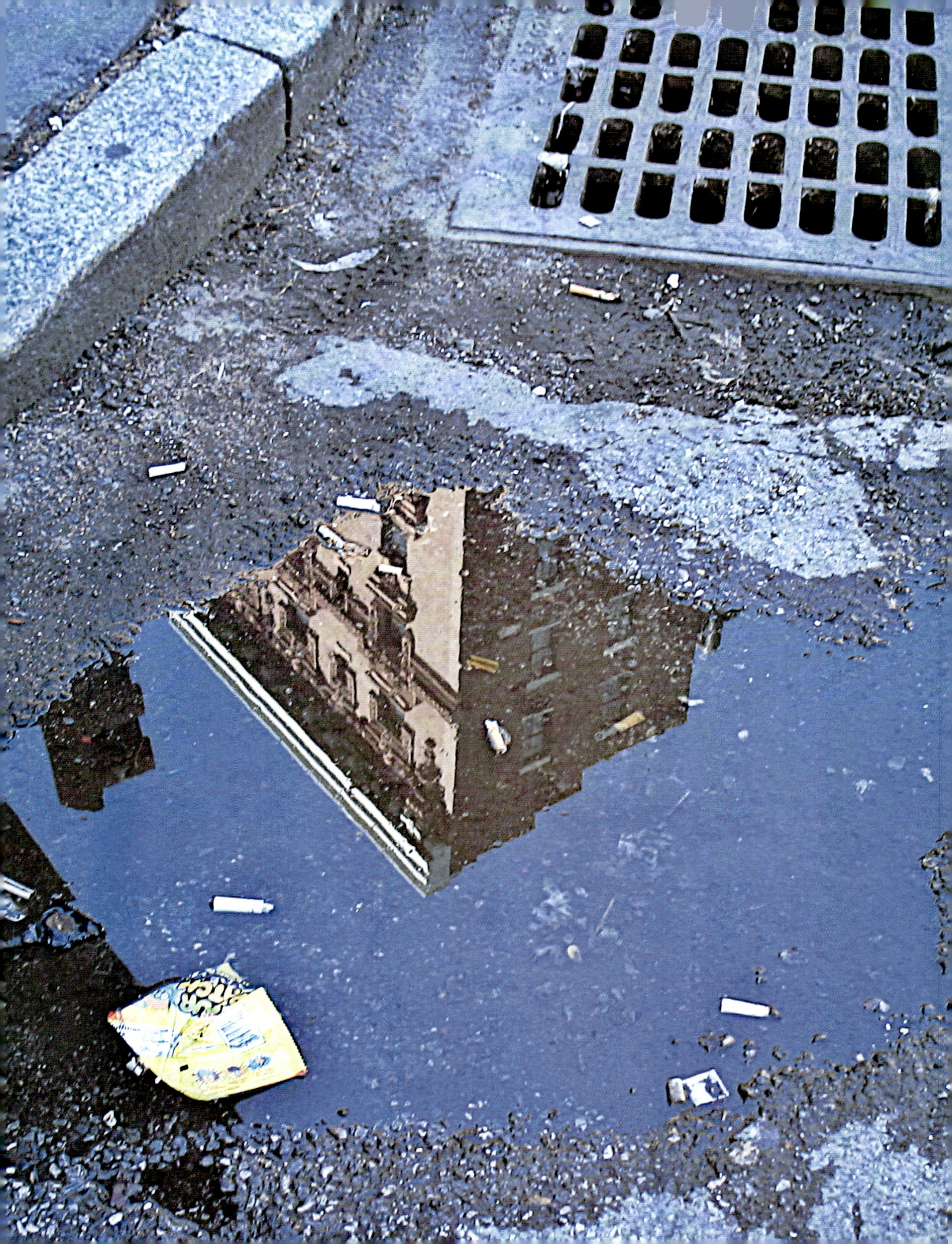

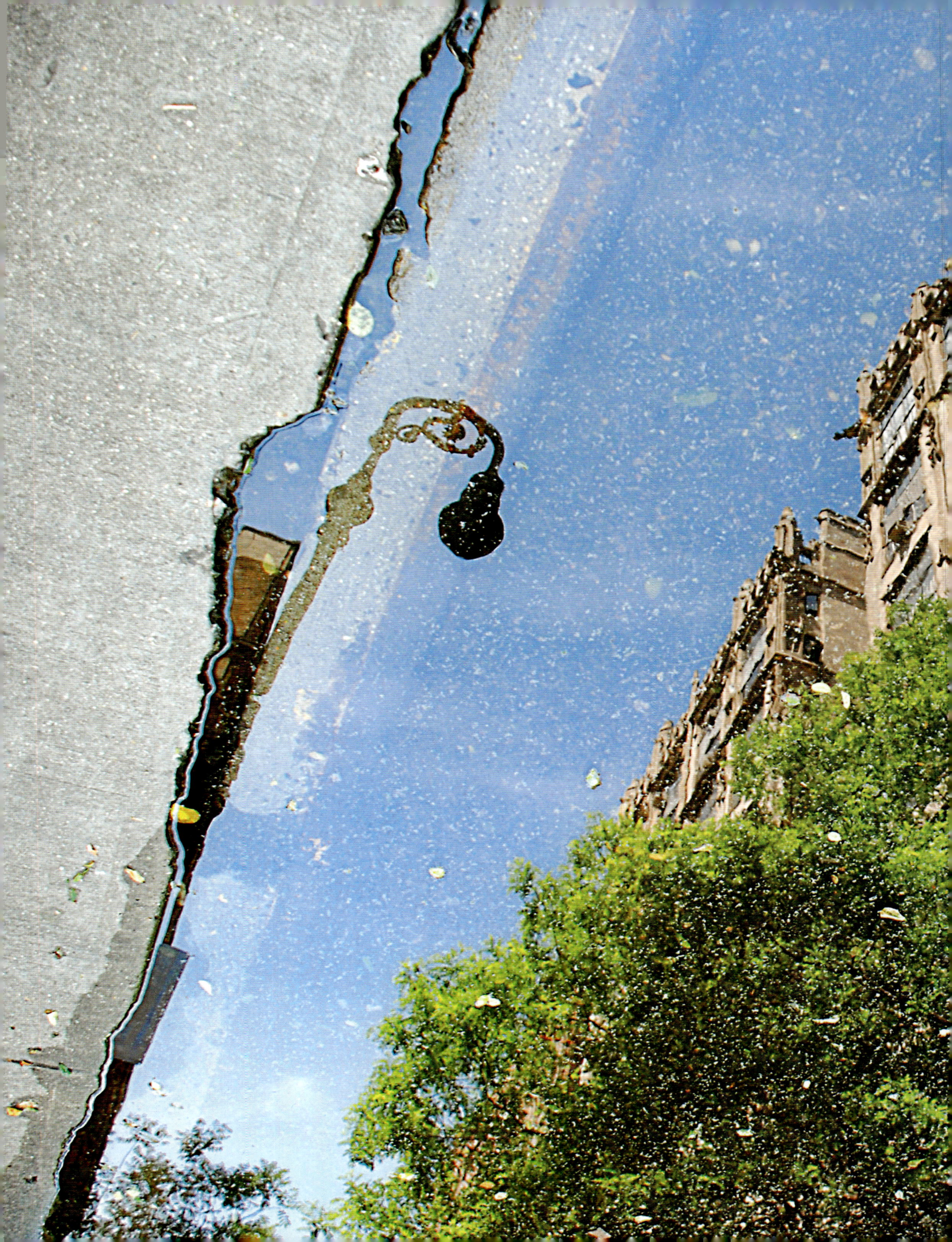

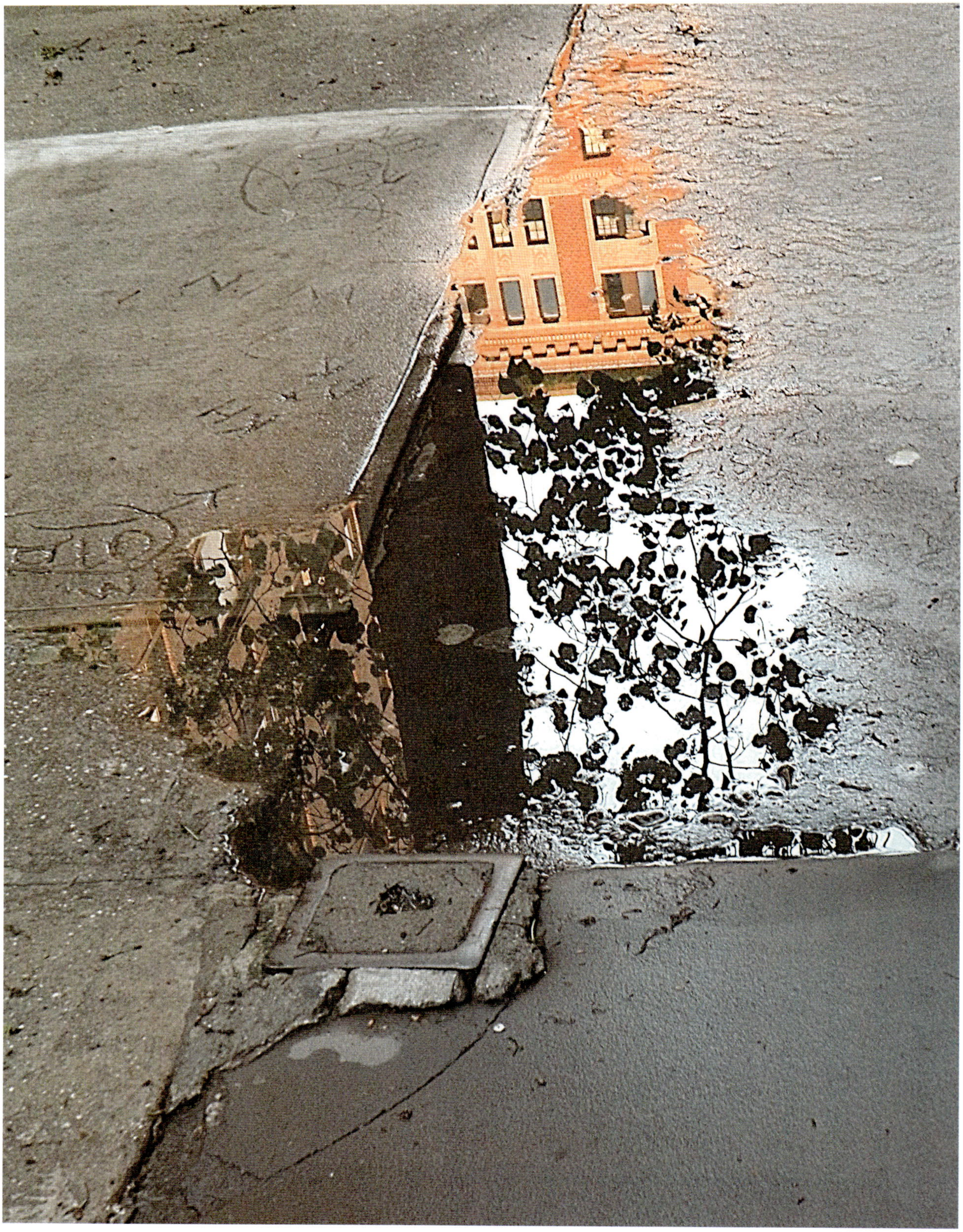

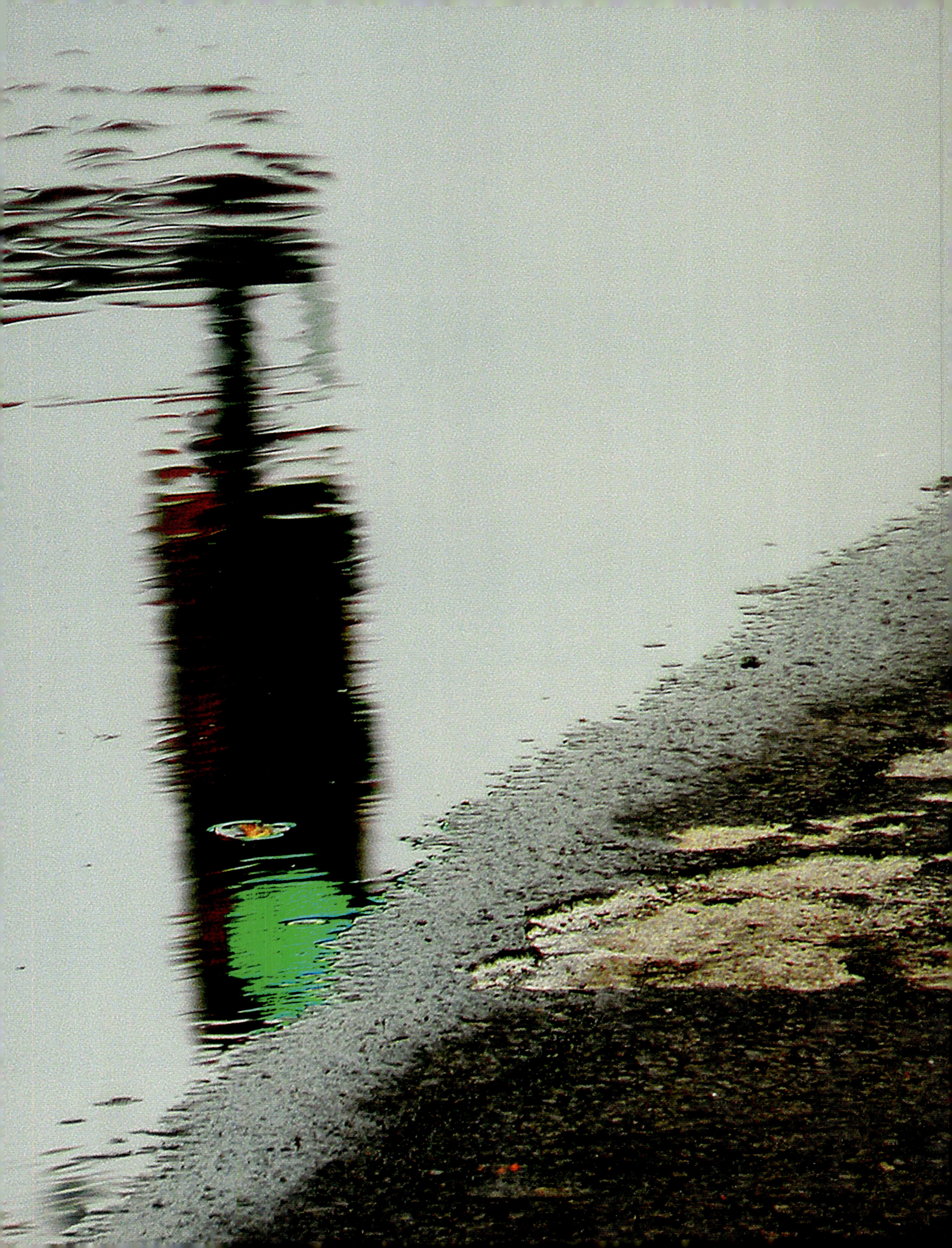

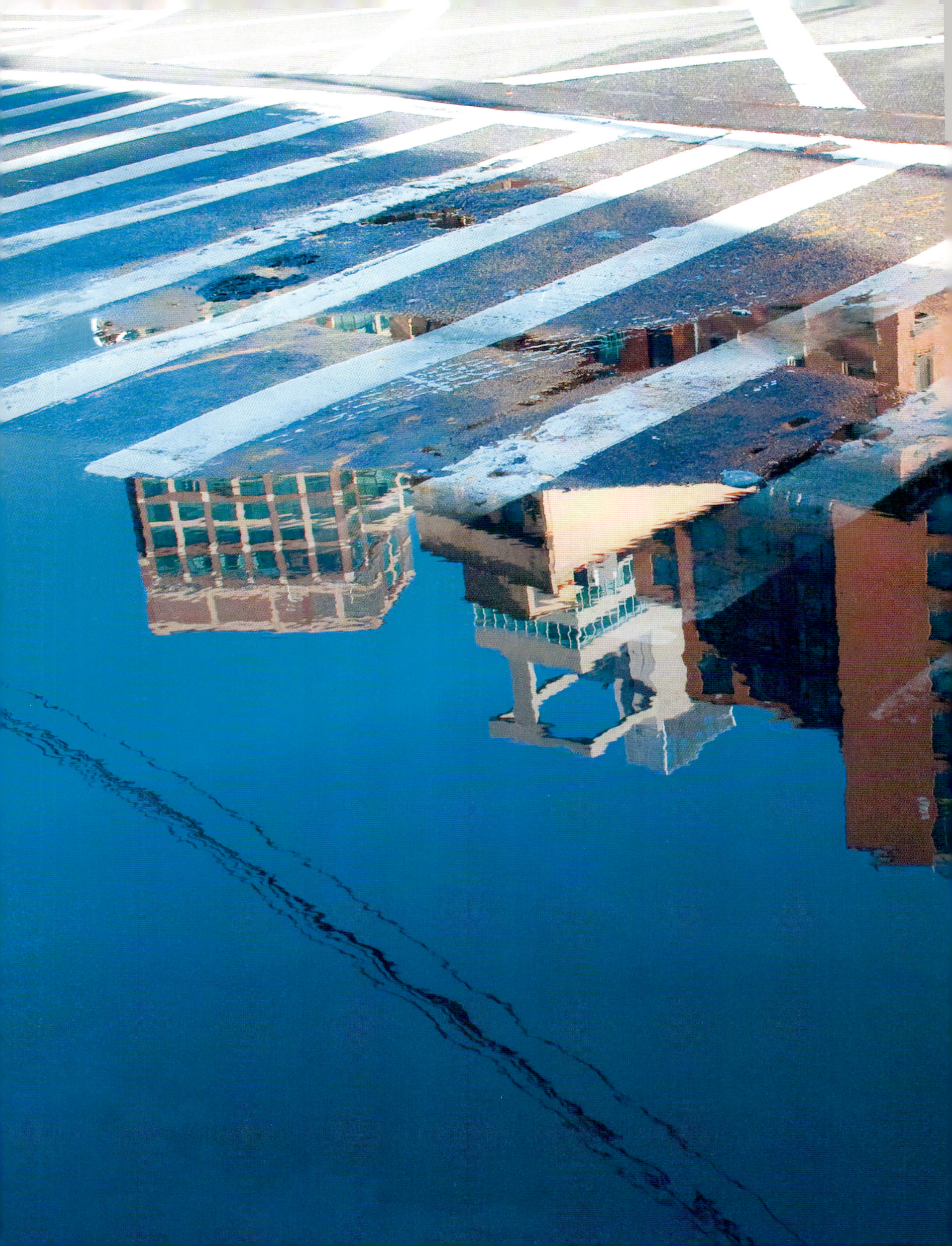

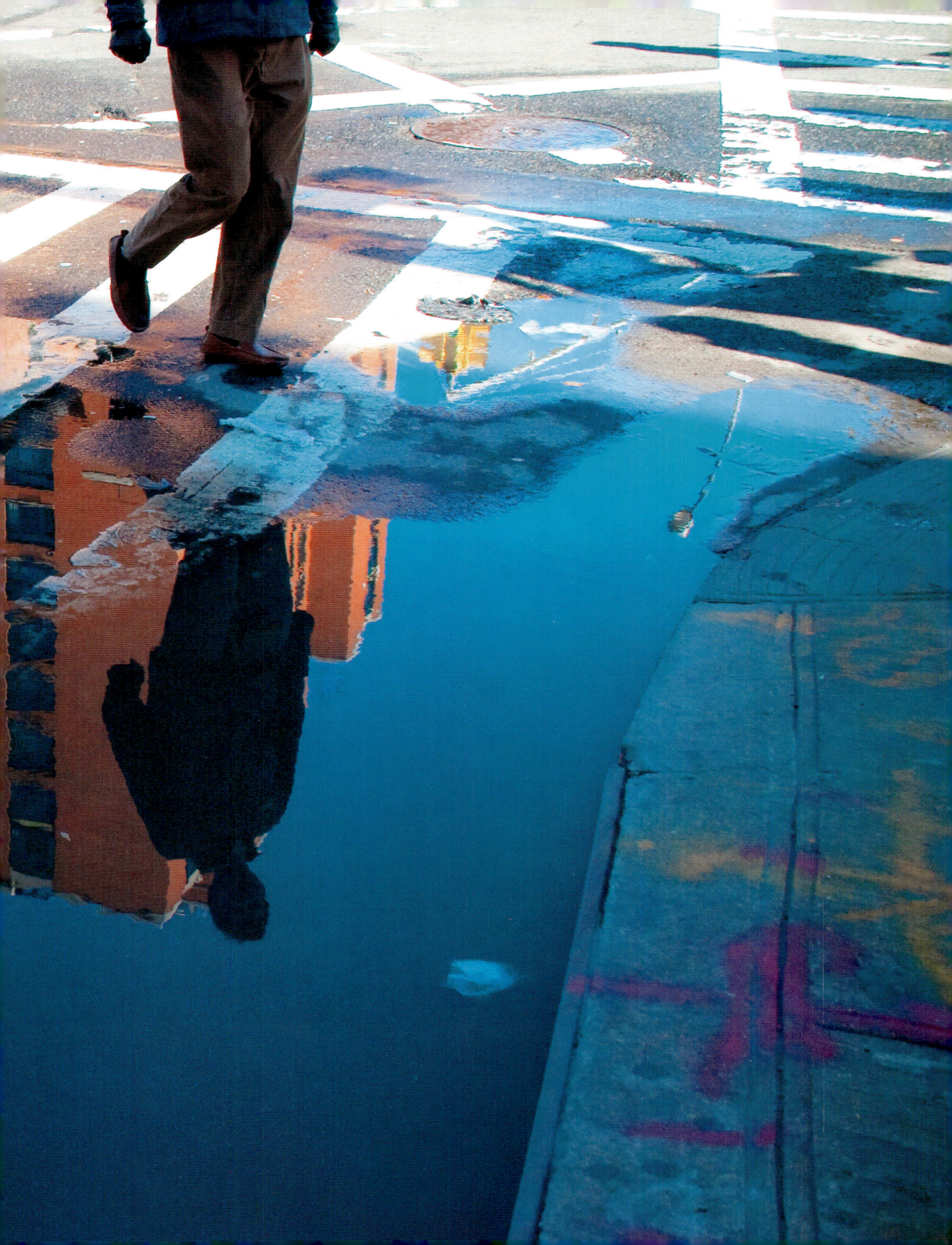

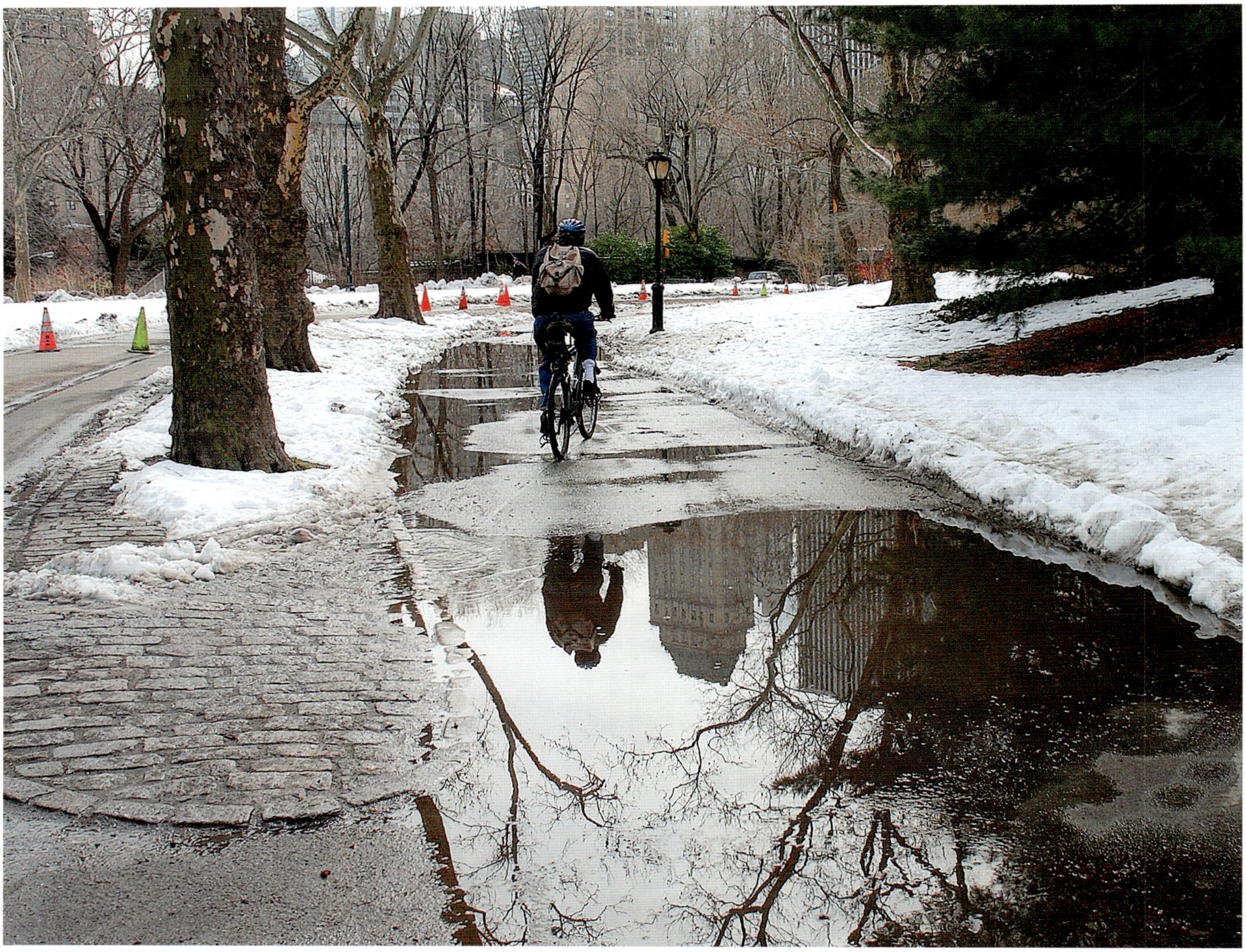

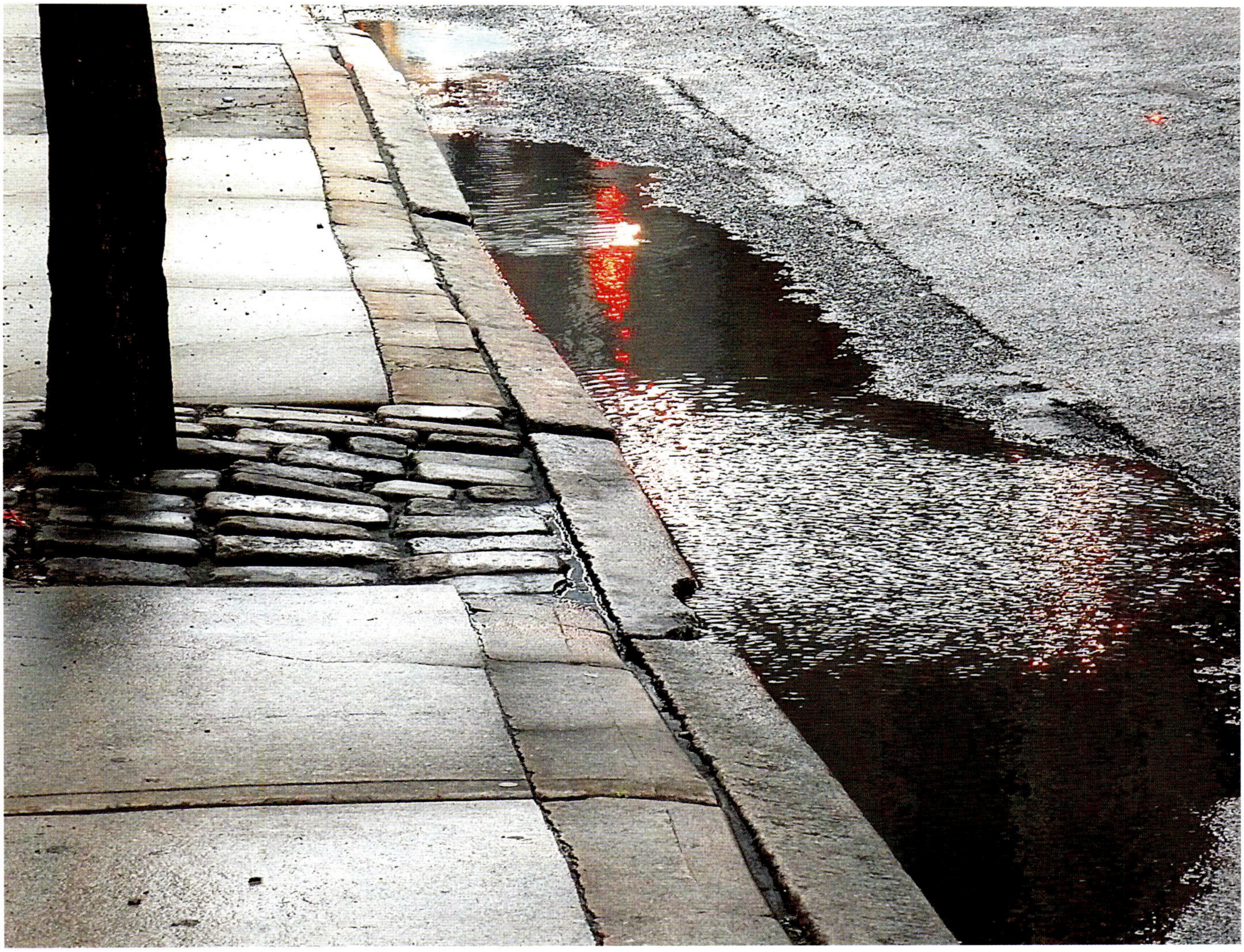

5

construction in **blue, white** & **black**

blue black white
black blue white
black white **blue**

blue:
heavenly
airy cheery
blue:
desolate
dismal dreary
blue:
color of
conflicting moods
blue
beams
blue
broods

poor **blue**
schizoid hue
split in two
like me & you

black white **blue**
white **black** **blue**
white **blue** **black**

black:
absence of all light
black:
paragon of blight
black sheep **black** list
black ball **black** hole
black flag **black** plague
macabre shade
desirable nonetheless:
e.g.
in the **black**
the indispensable
little **black** dress

white **black** **blue**
black white **blue**
black **blue** white

white:
purity
goodness
virginity
white:
old age
terror
dead skin

black white **blue**
each its own contradiction
blue white **black:**
exemplars of split personality
or models of rare versatility?

blue

white

black

{out}

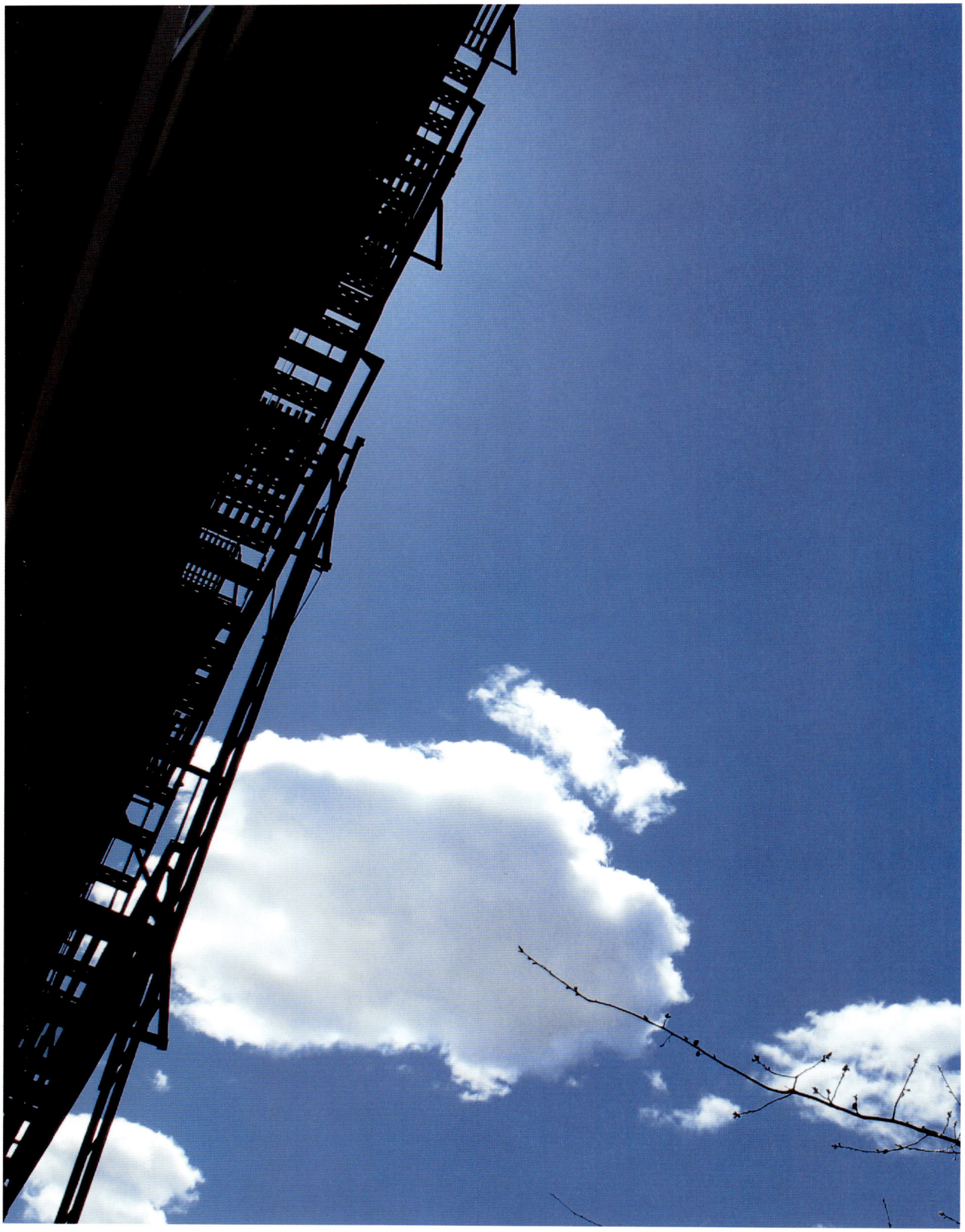

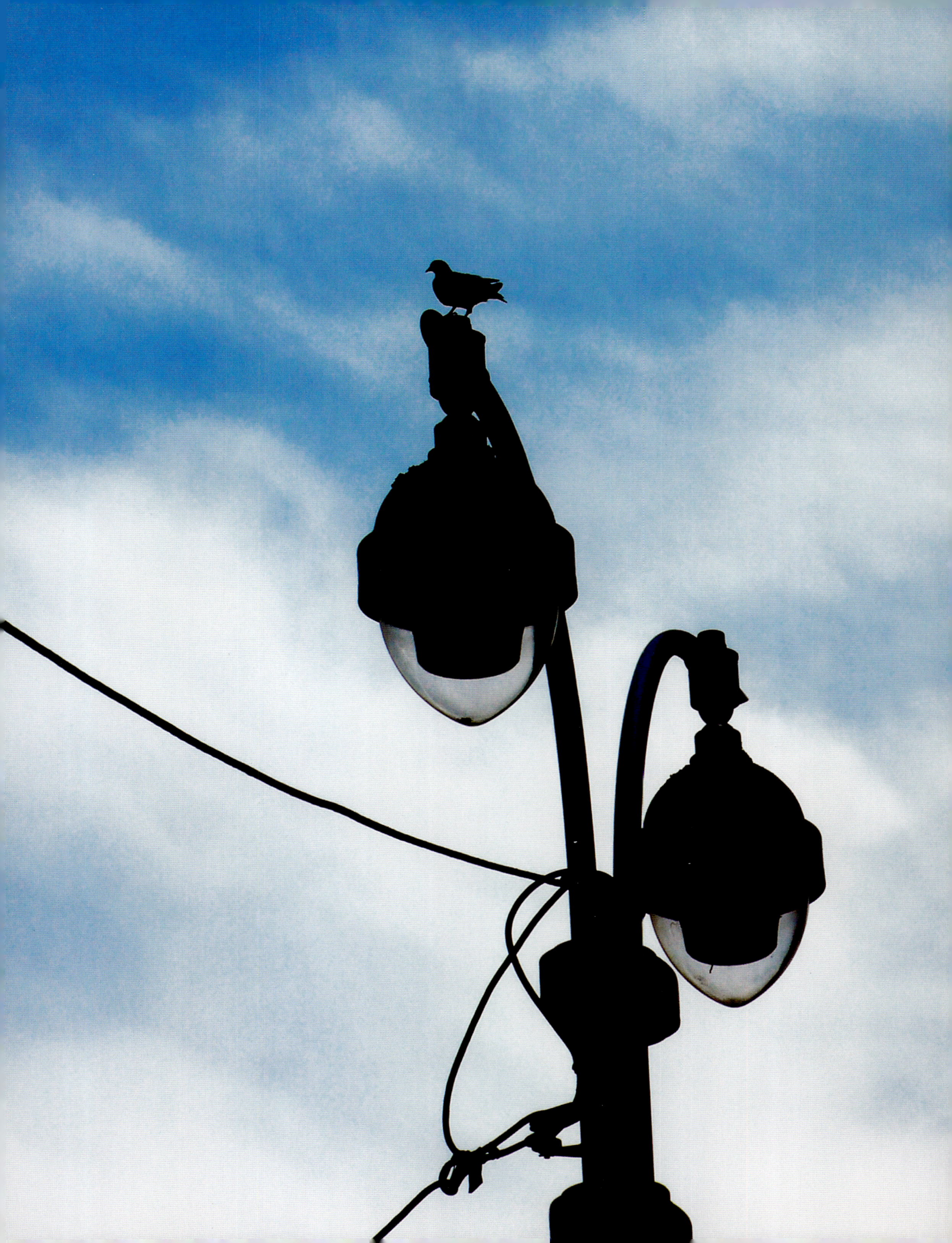

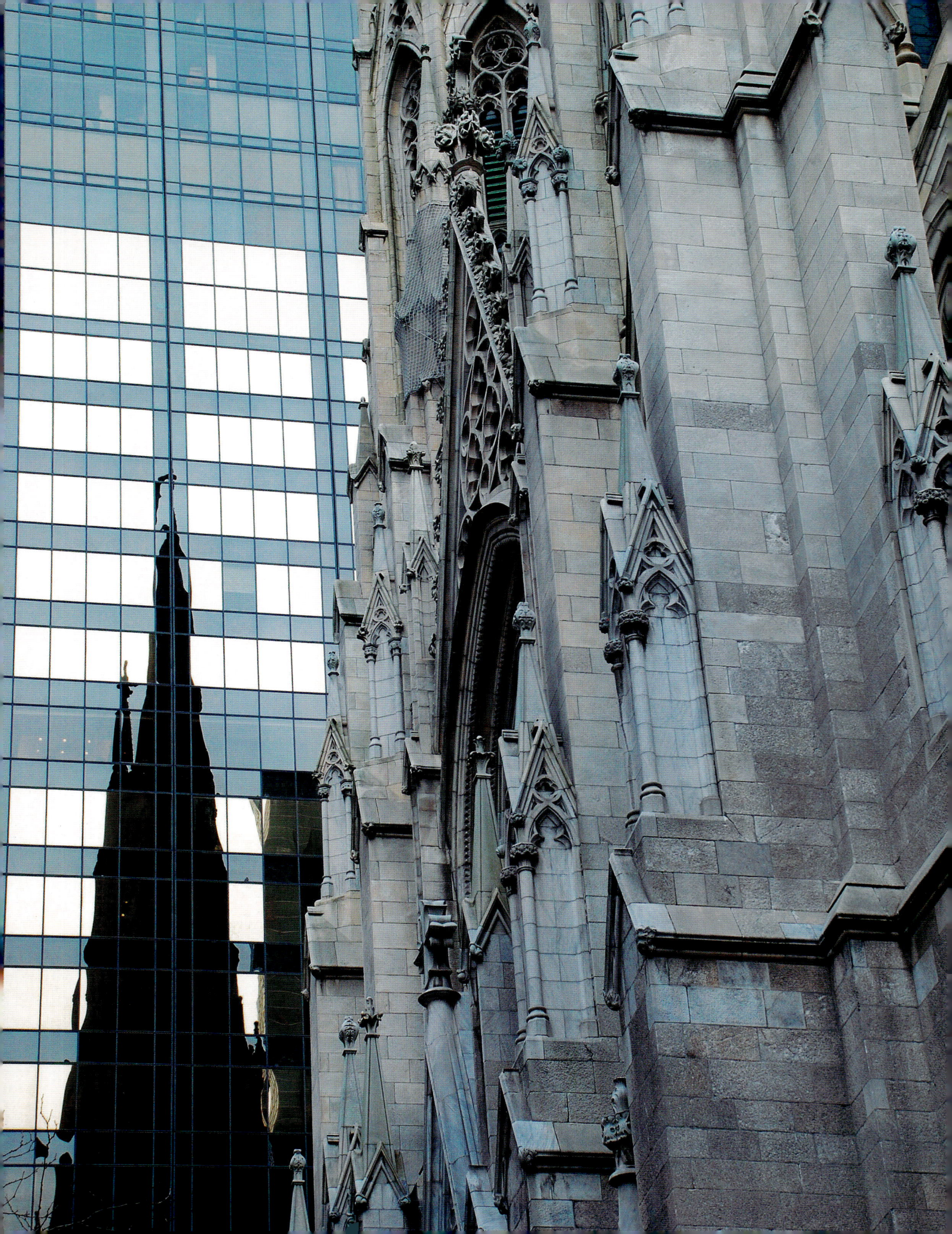

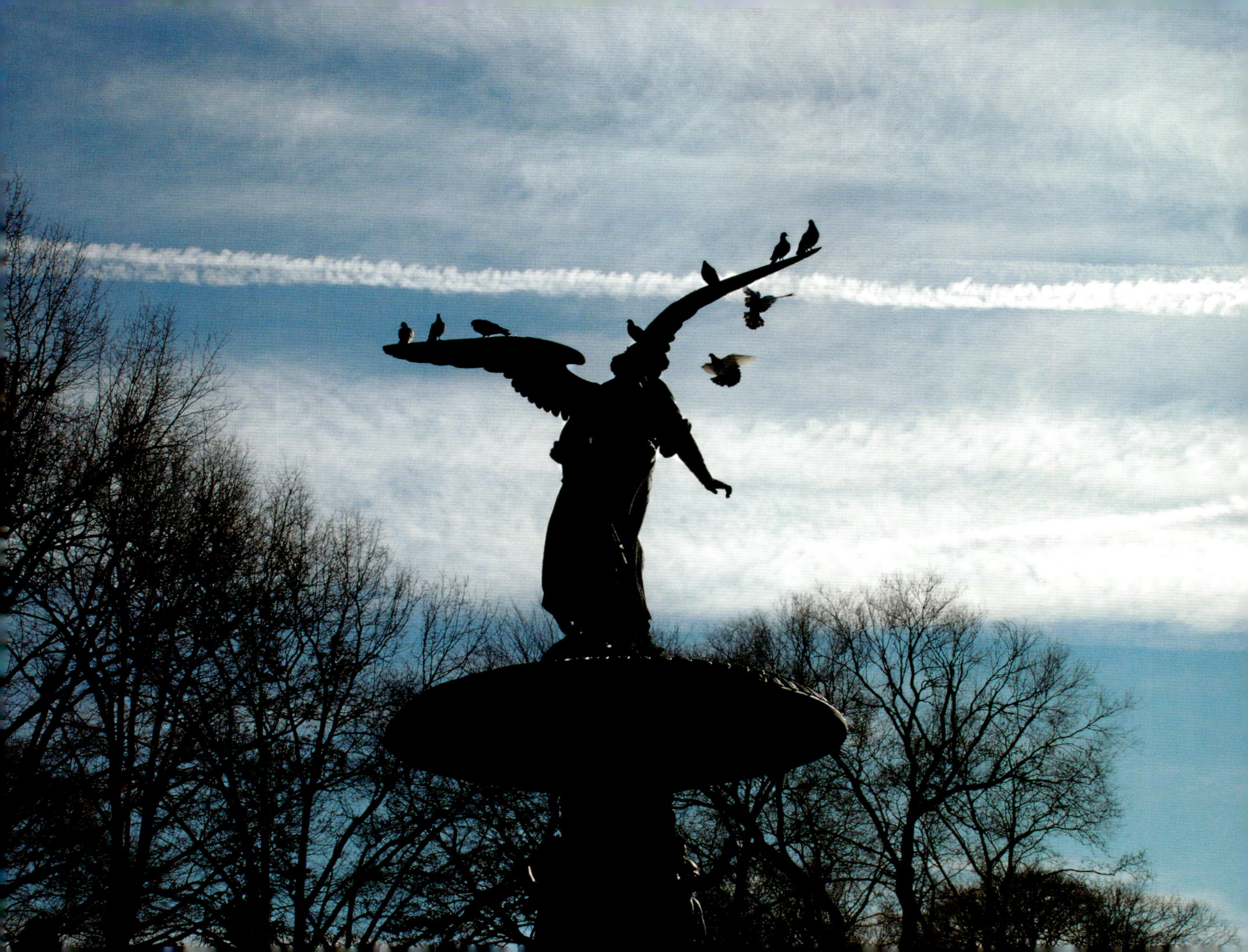

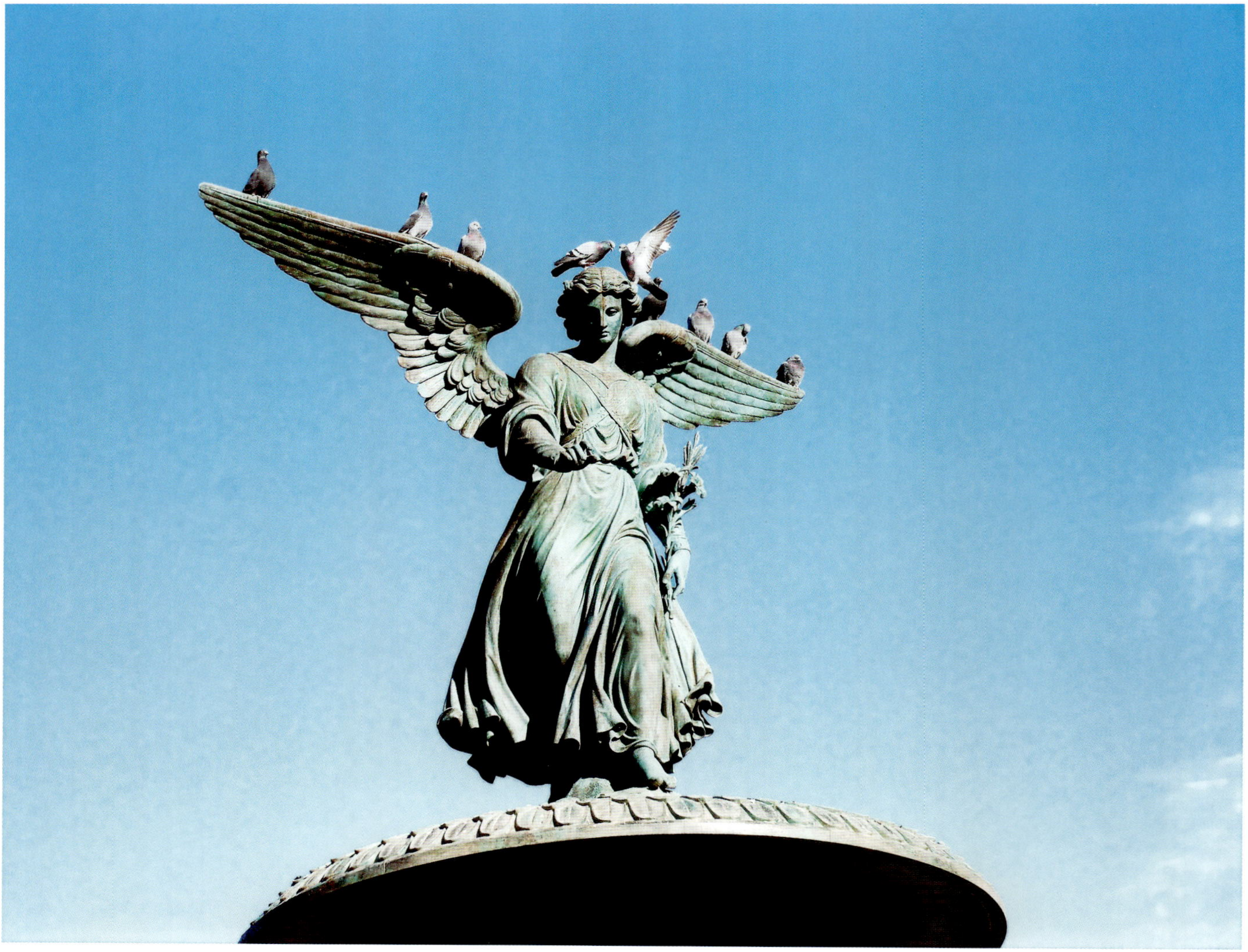

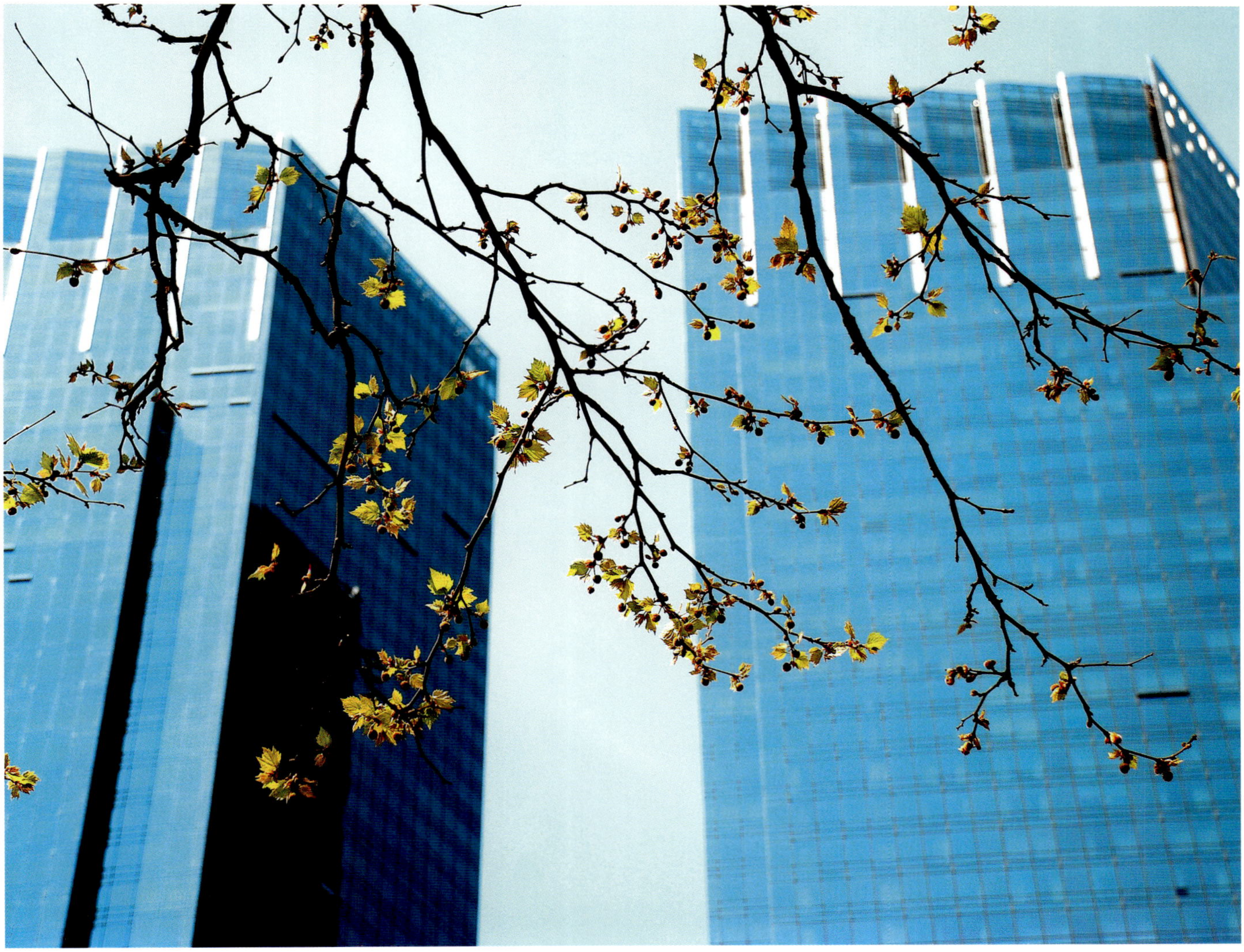

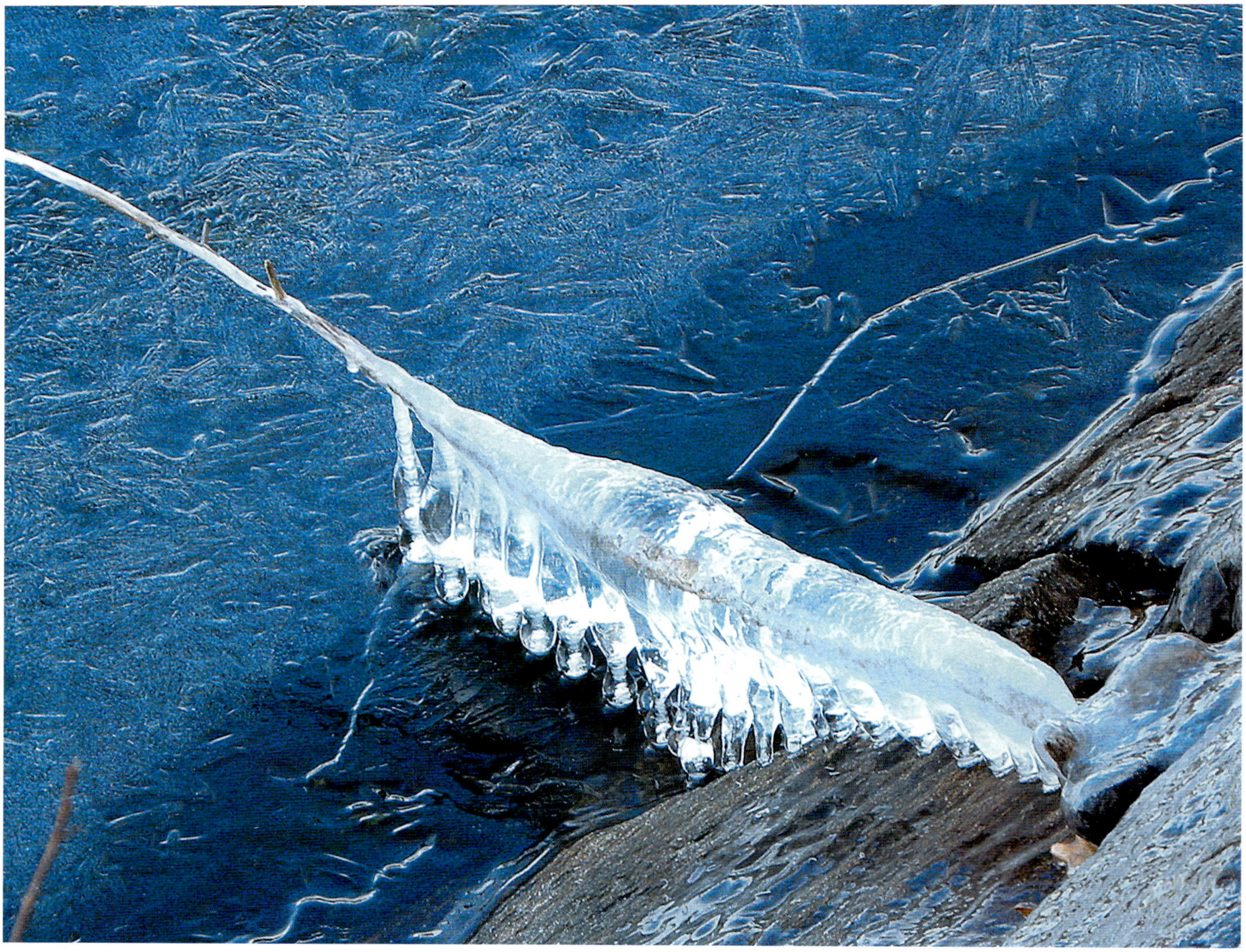

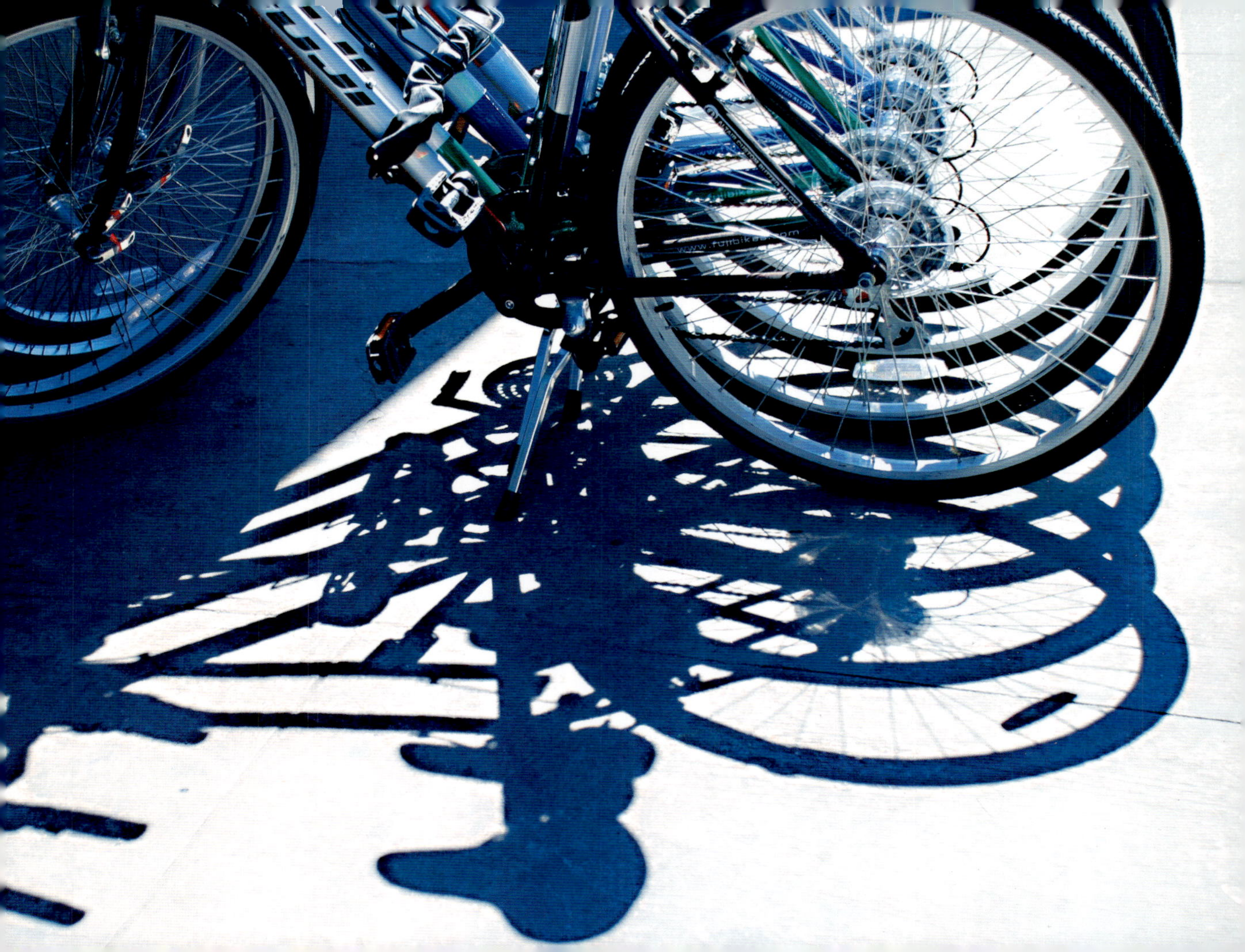

6 FIREWORKS

I

Fireworks is a singular word.
Coined in the reign
of the Virgin Queen,
what, quite literally,
does it mean?

(A) **Fireworks**
as in
waterworks?
Earthworks?
Hardly.

(B) **Fireworks**
as in fire labors?
Maybe.
Considered in a certain light,
the meaning fits.
(Well, no, not quite.)

(C) **Fireworks**
using "works"
as in
the works of Shakespeare
(or, perhaps, more apt: Stravinsky.)
Now we're getting somewhere.
Fireworks
as in
Works of Fire!
Or (in prose, suitably pyrotechnical)
Incendiary Visions Fashioned
by the Iridescent Firegod Himself!

II

To me:

(A) **Fireworks**
are celestial graffiti.

(B) **Fireworks**
are glittering visual poetry.

(C) **Fireworks**
are the sights and sounds
of shells and rockets
raining death
on some imagined battlefield
but cleansed of battle's terror.

(D) **Fireworks**
turn the night sky
into a magical abstract-expressionist
canvas
pulsing with burning colors
and fanciful forms
in vibrant motion.

III

(A) The splendor of the stars inspires awe
But stars do not belong to us.
Those incandescent gems
Adorn the Heavenly Host
As light years overhead they float,
Magnificent, indifferent,
Eternal and remote.

(B) But **fireworks** inspire sheer delight.
Mankind's invention, they belong to us.
Unlike the stars, they're near at hand.
Unlike the stars, they aim to please.
And, most unstarlike, sad to say,
(Like most things linked
With mankind's poignant story)
They're born and swiftly perish.
Therefore all the more
Should we cherish their brief glory.

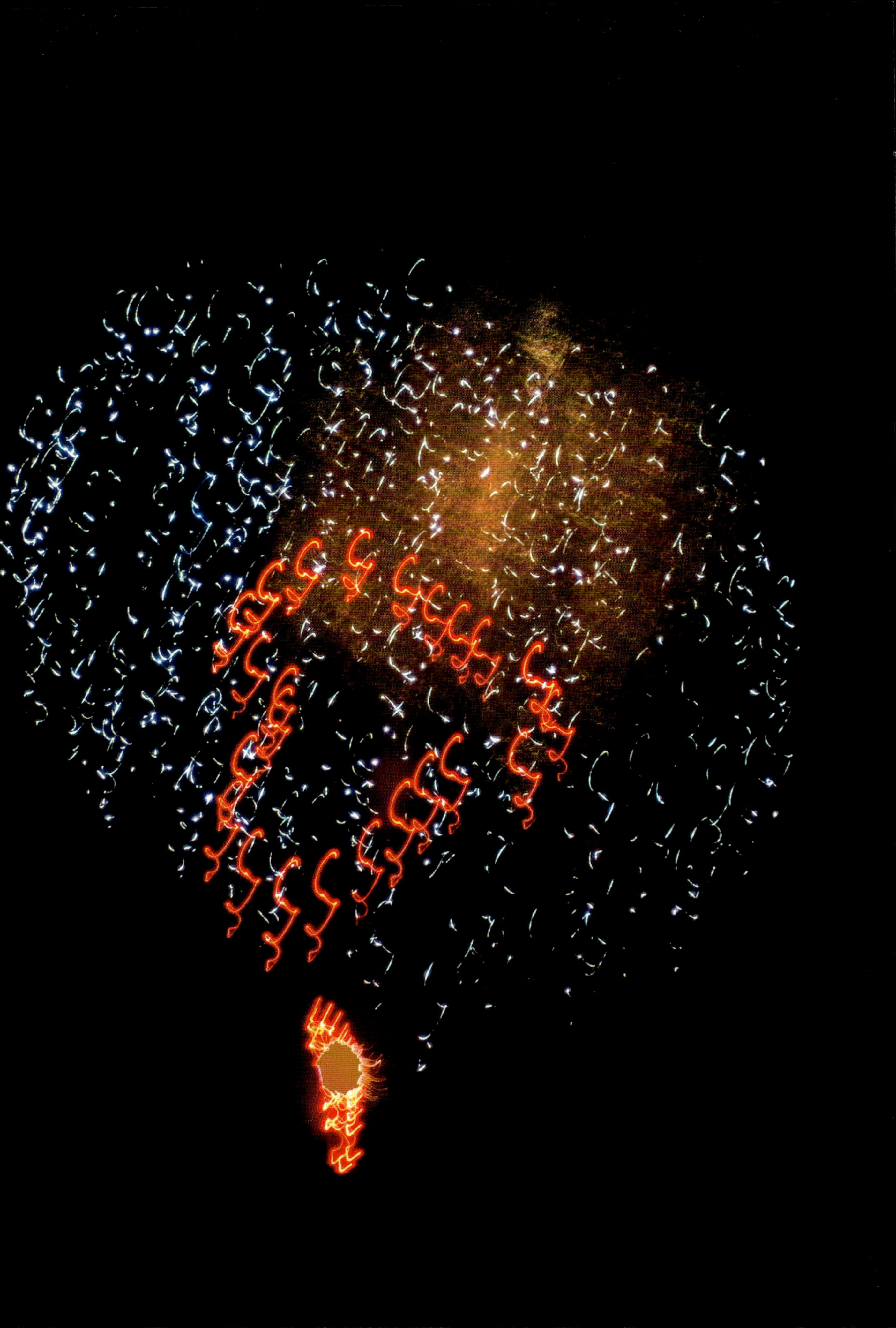

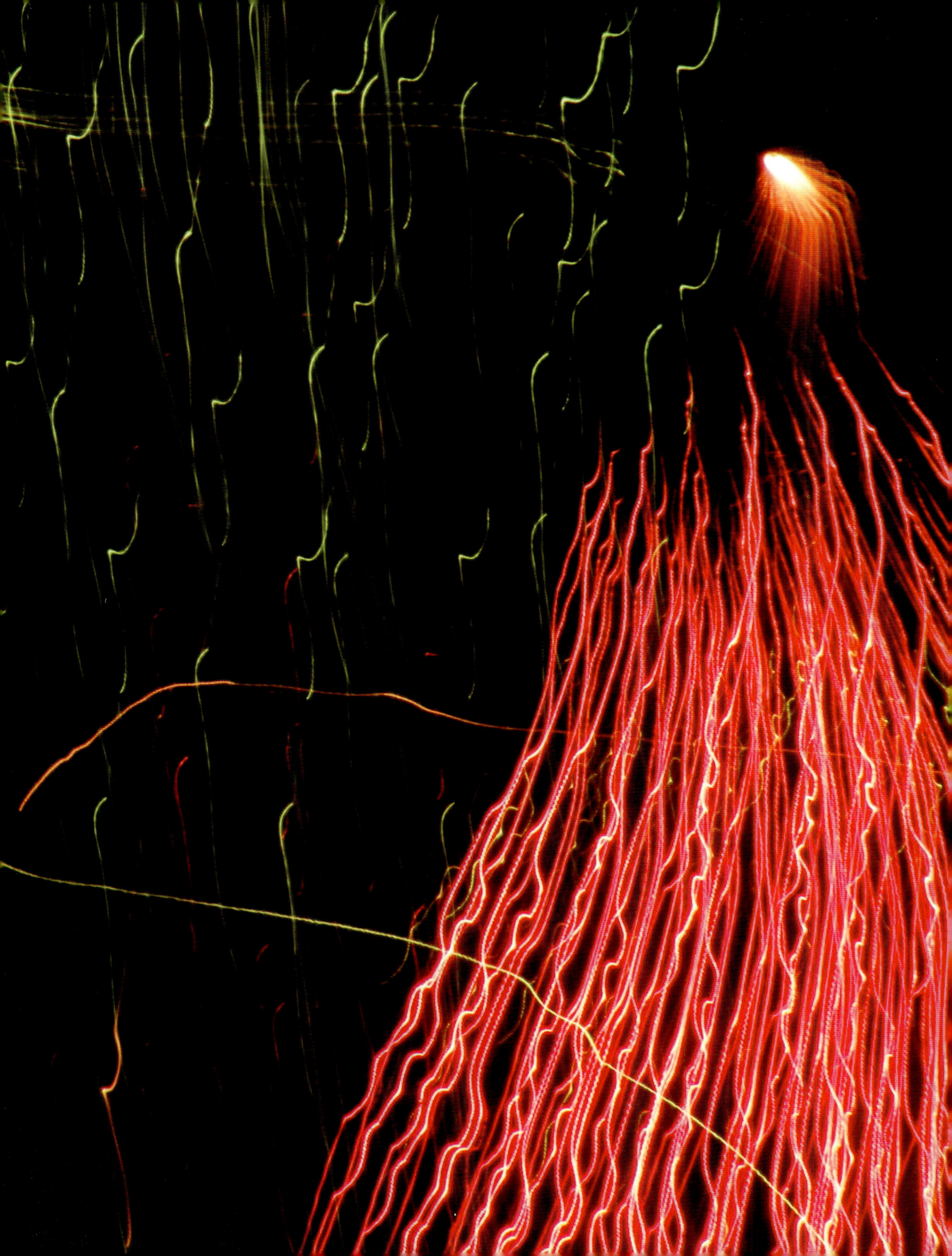

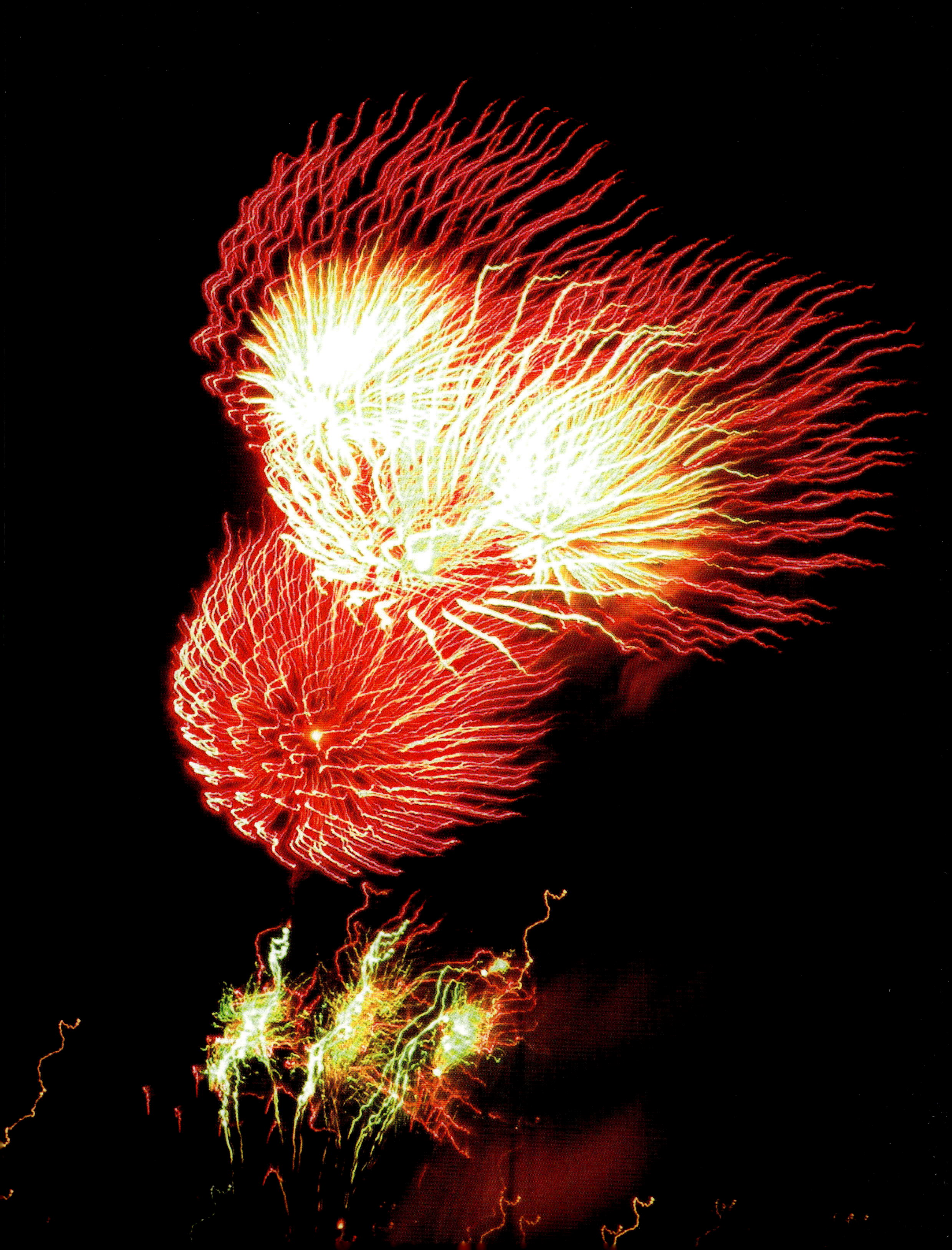

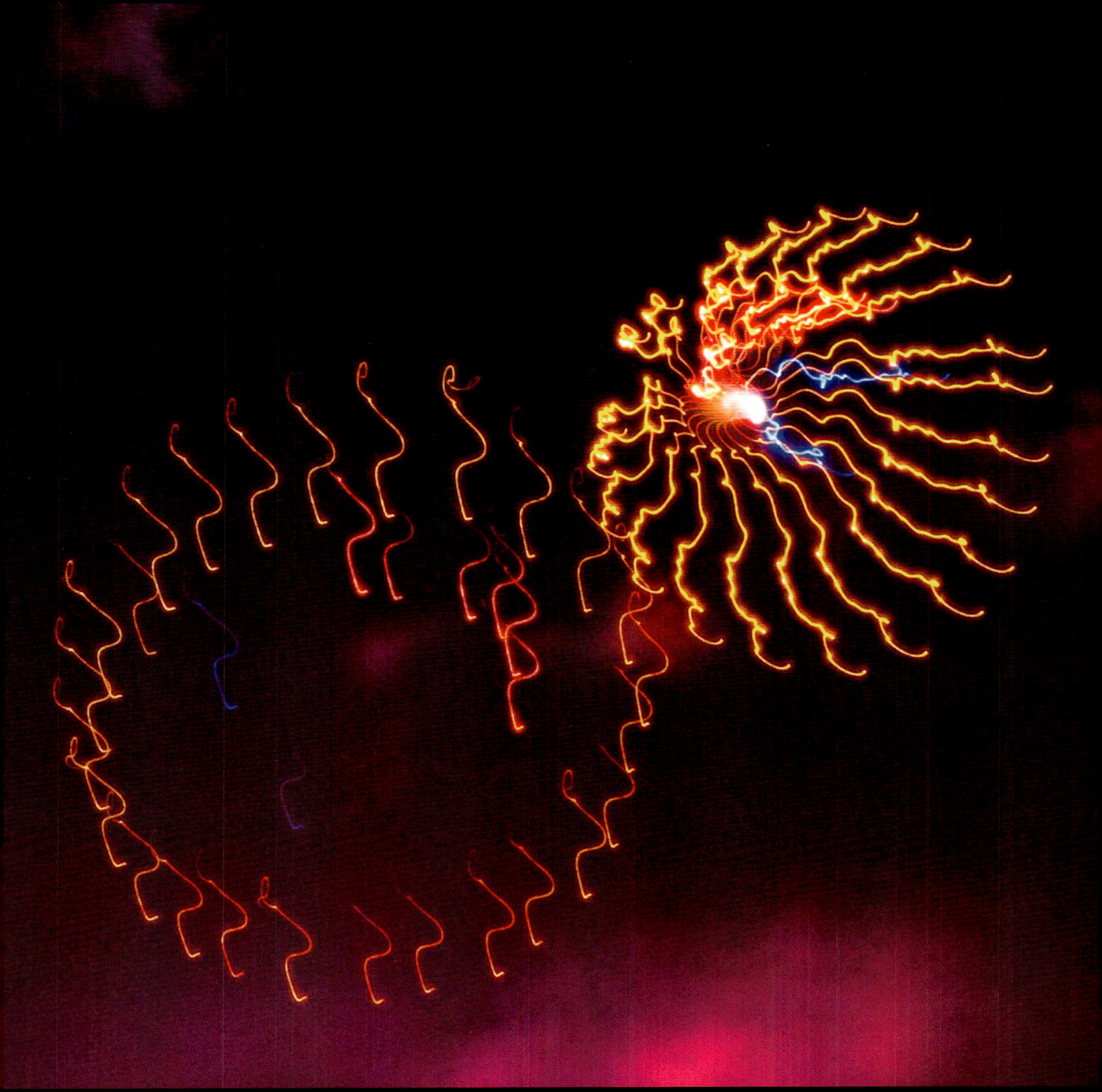

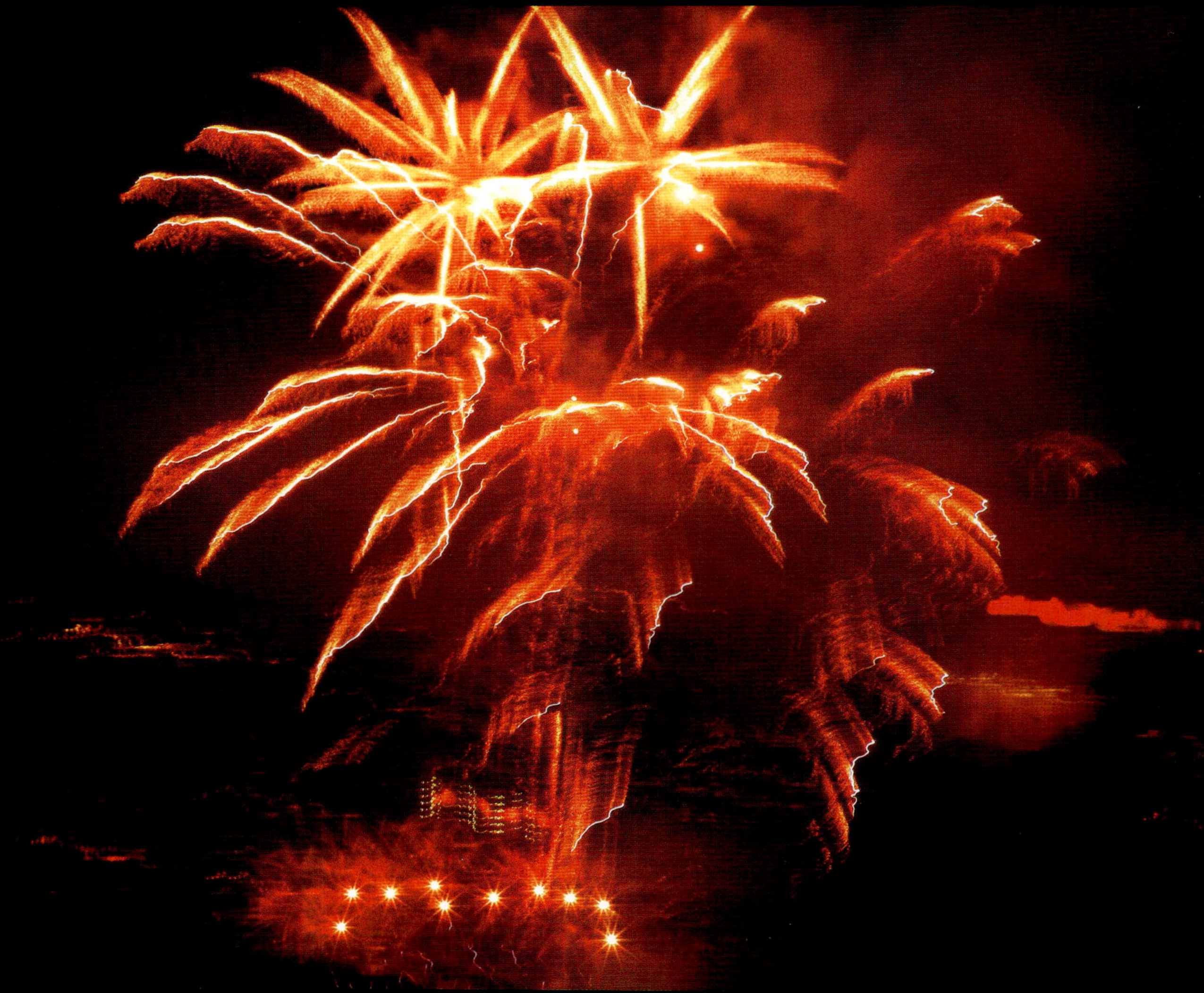

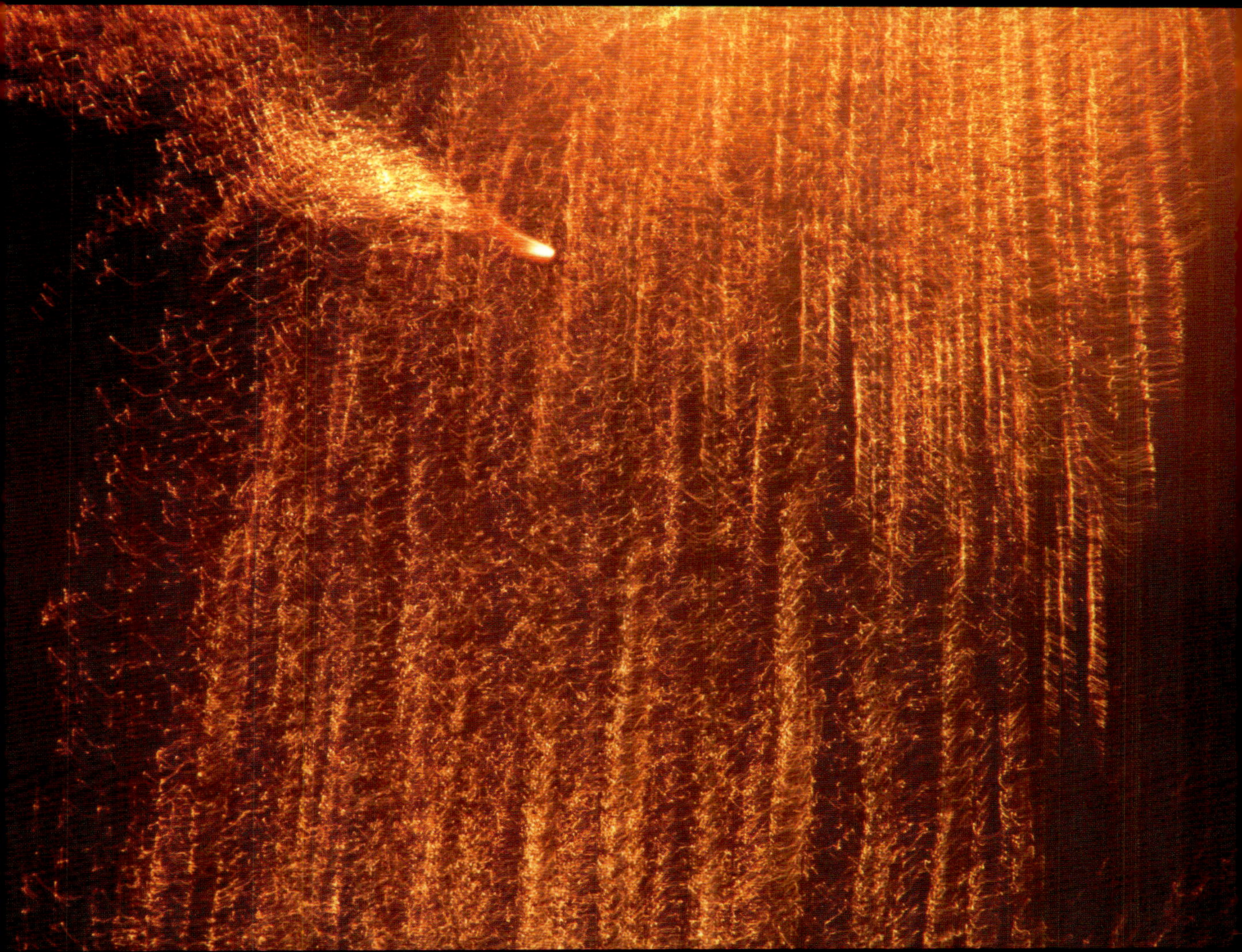

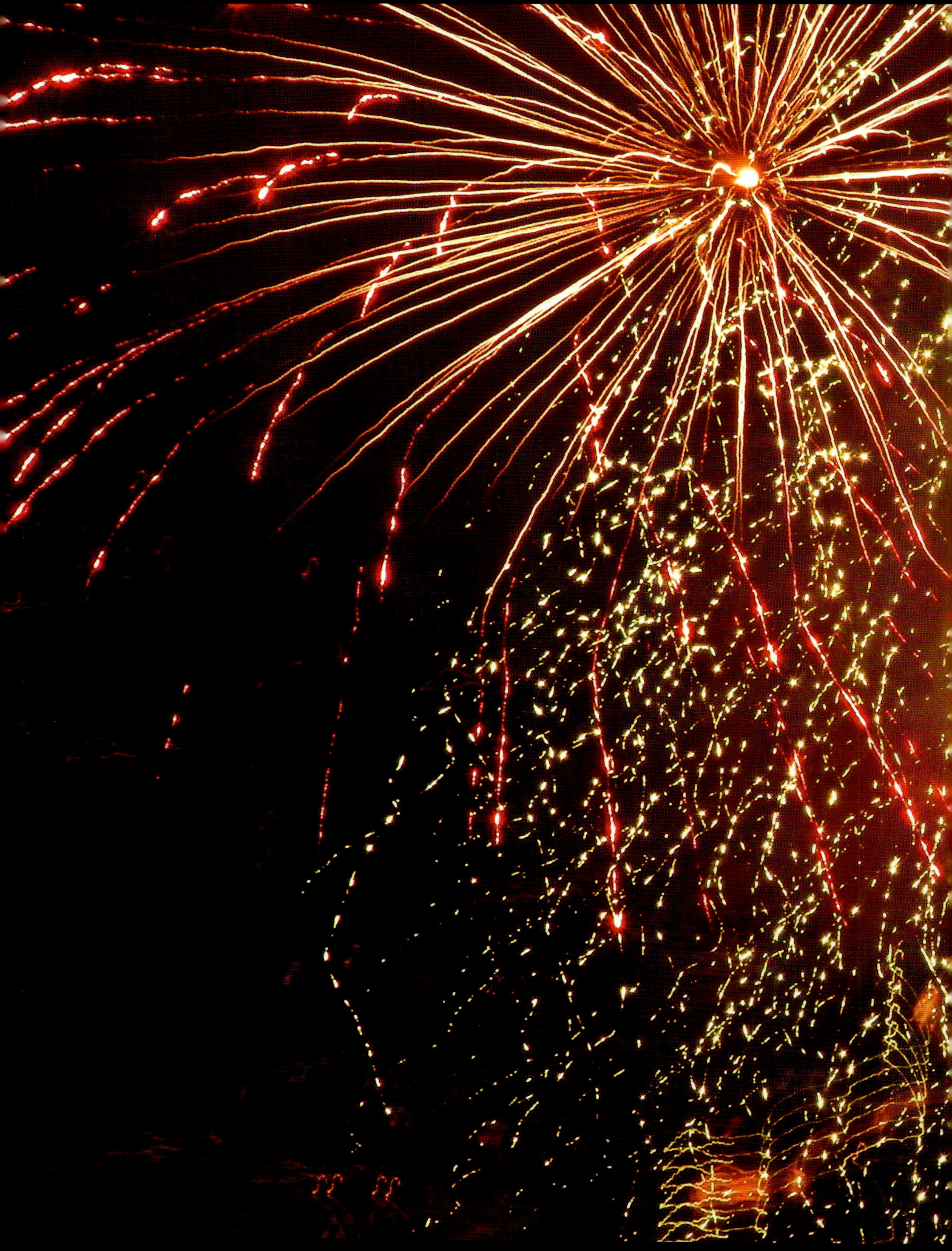

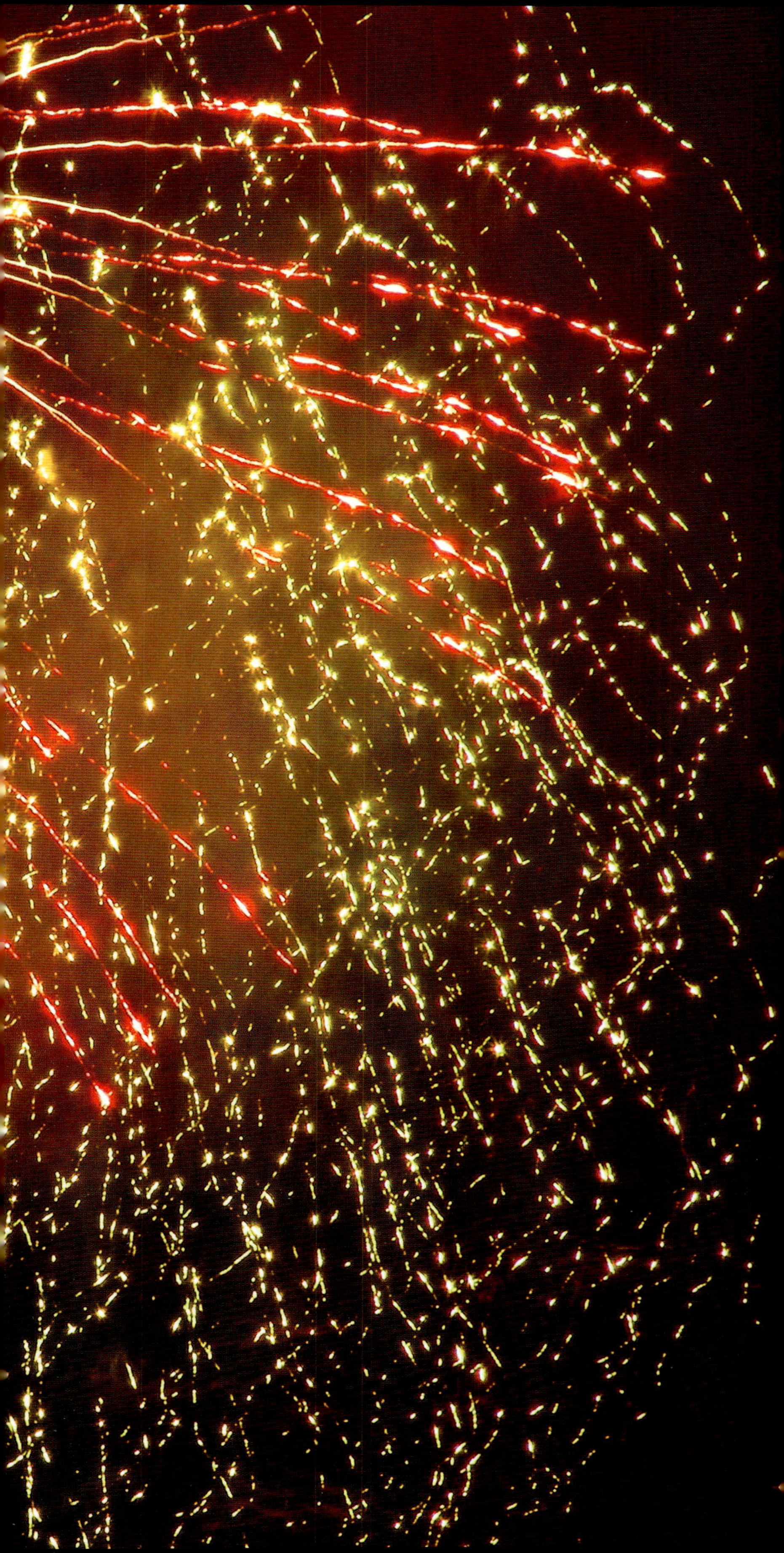

7

A CAR LOOKS AT MANHATTAN (and my wife looks at a car)

When people stop
  to stare at a car,
struck by the elegant contours
  of its hood,
the arresting geometry
  of its headlights
or the brazen theatricality
  of its taillights . . .
when people, as I say,
  stop to stare at a car,
  what they see is a car.
When my wife stops
  to stare at a car,
she sees what the car sees.

WHAT DOES A CAR SEE

when its hood, headlights, taillights
  and assorted body parts
  gaze at Manhattan?
A city no one has ever seen:
  a surreal world
  of melting buildings . . .
silhouettes of spectral trees
  hurrying who knows where . . .
gleaming emblems
  of curiously intricate machinery
  doing who knows what . . .
a magic lantern show
  of phantastical shapes,
  colors, patterns and designs . . .
this is what a car sees.

WHAT DOES MY WIFE SEE

when she looks at a car?
  She sees what the car sees.
Kaleidoscopic visions drift
  towards her waiting camera
and float through her surrogate eye
to be observed, sifted and appraised
  by her eye's mind,
soon to sprout as printed images,
ports of entry to this mystic universe.

MY WIFE HAS A REMARKABLE EYE

When my wife looks at a car,
  she sees what the car sees.
The question is:
  what does she see
  when she looks at me?

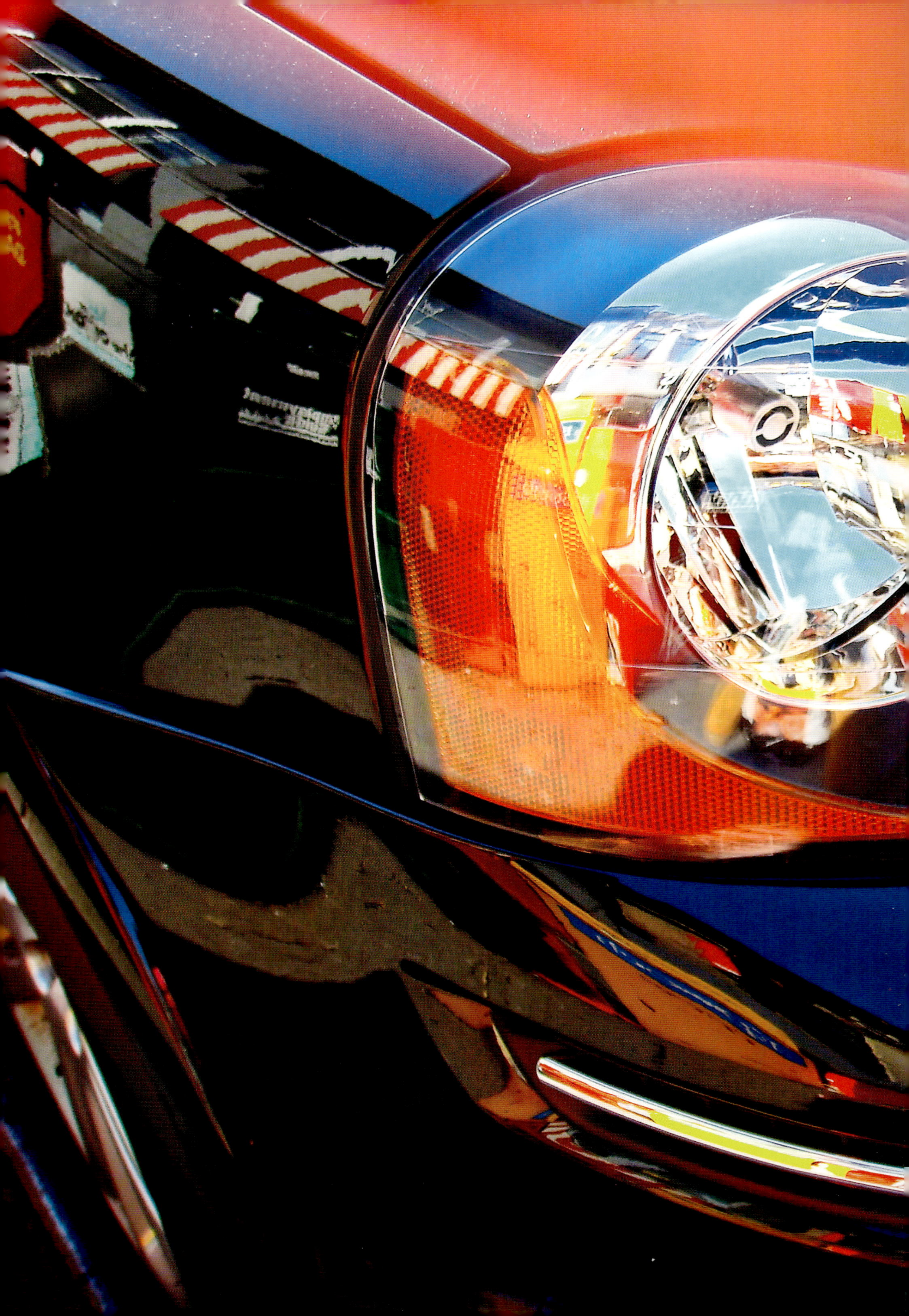

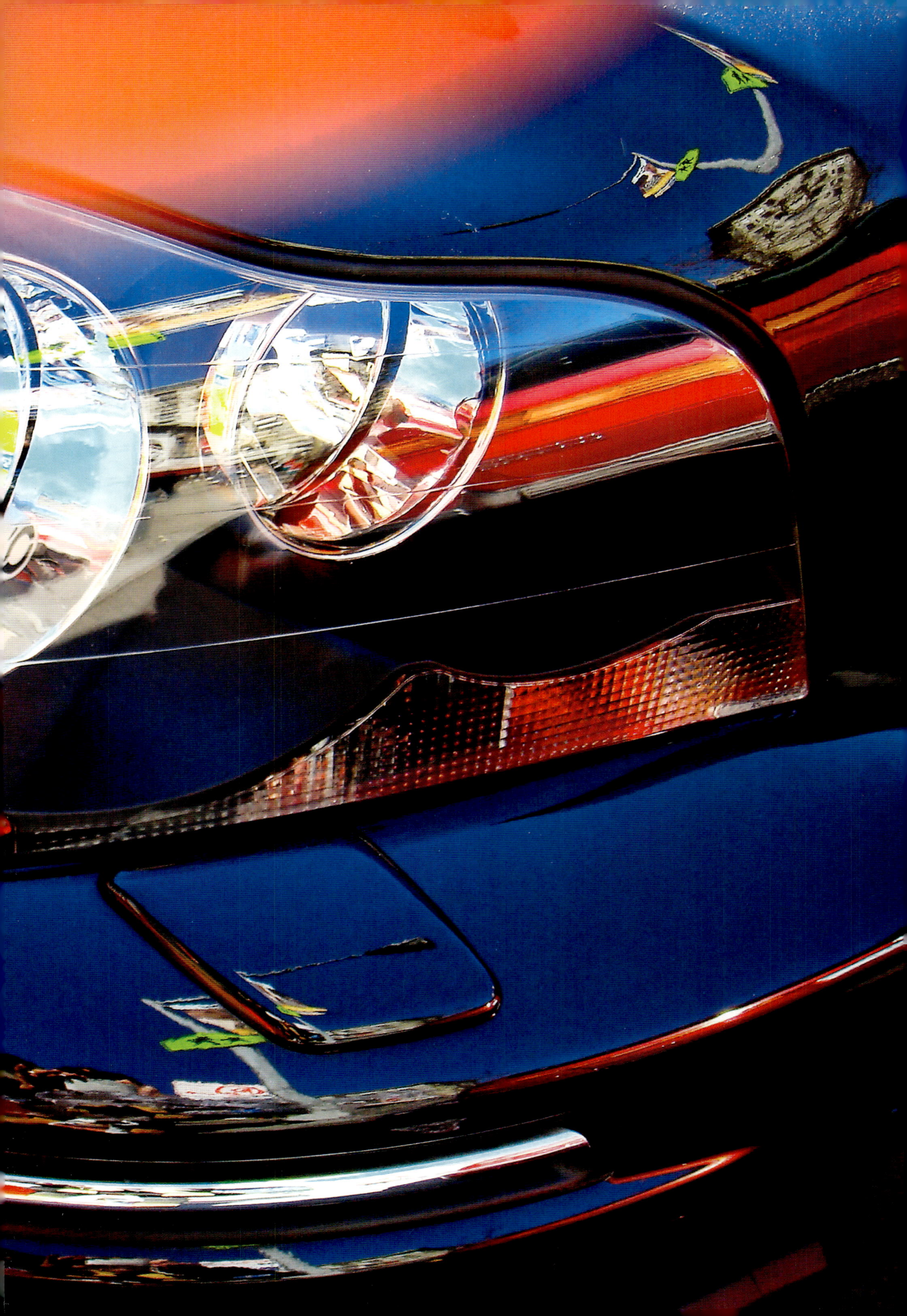

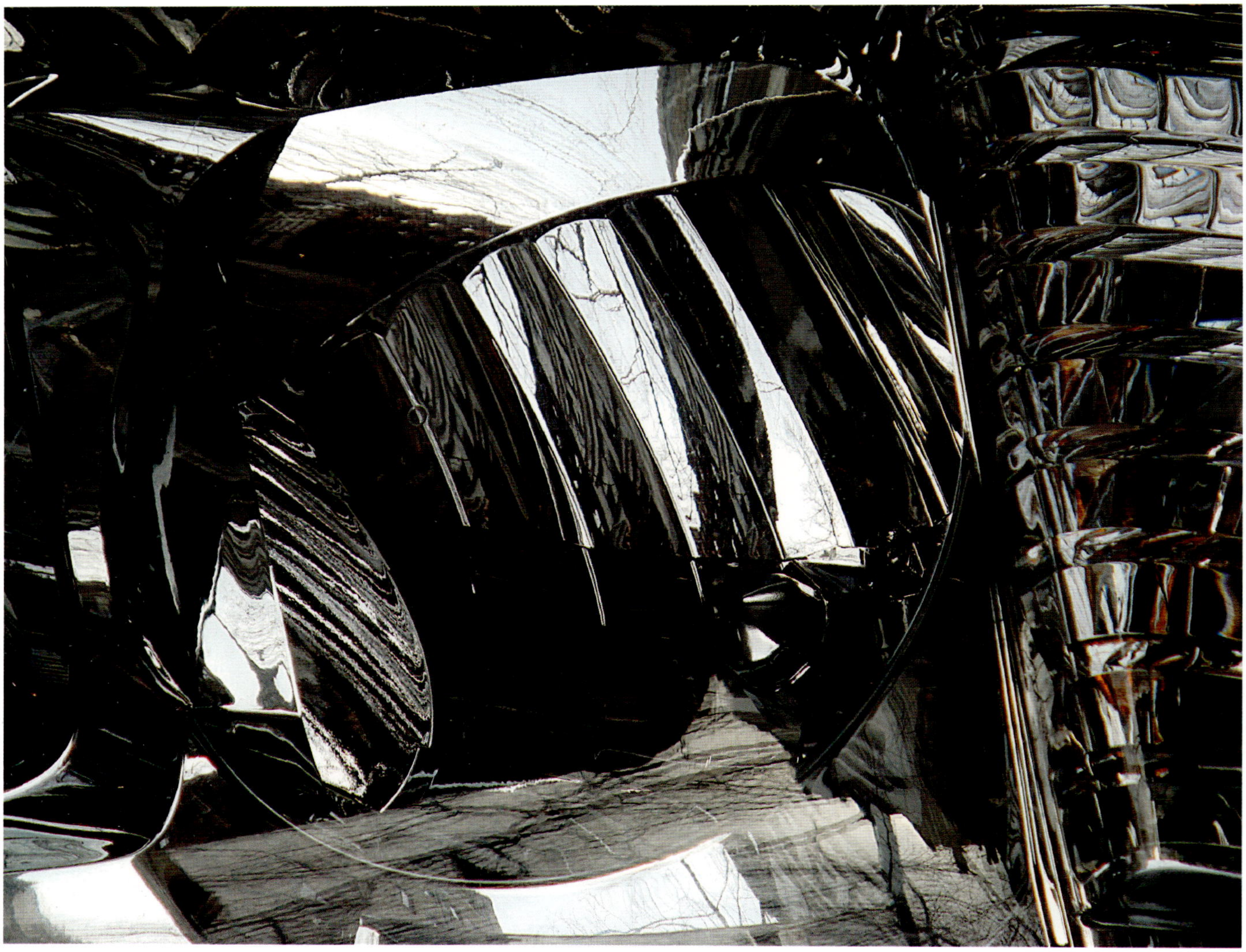

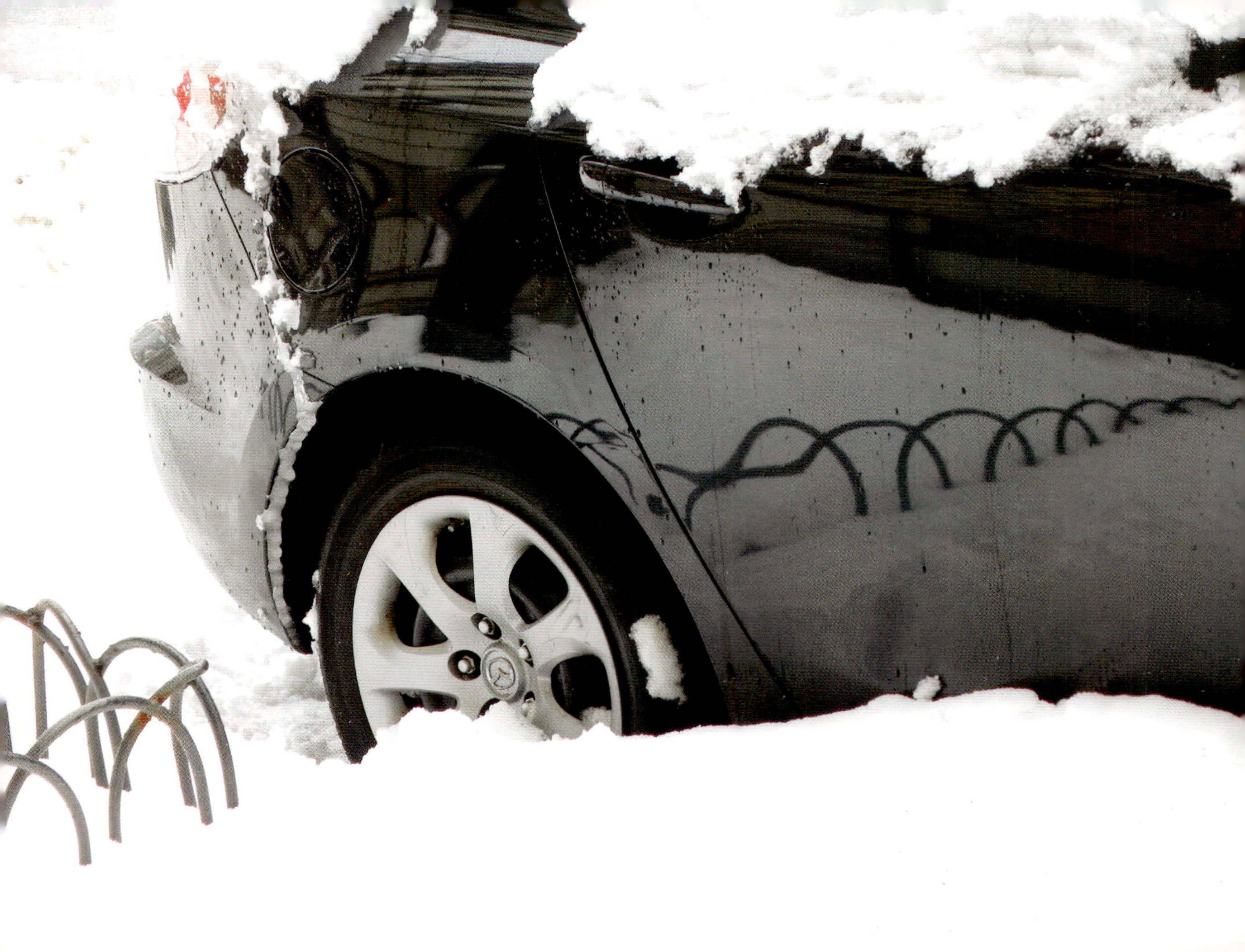

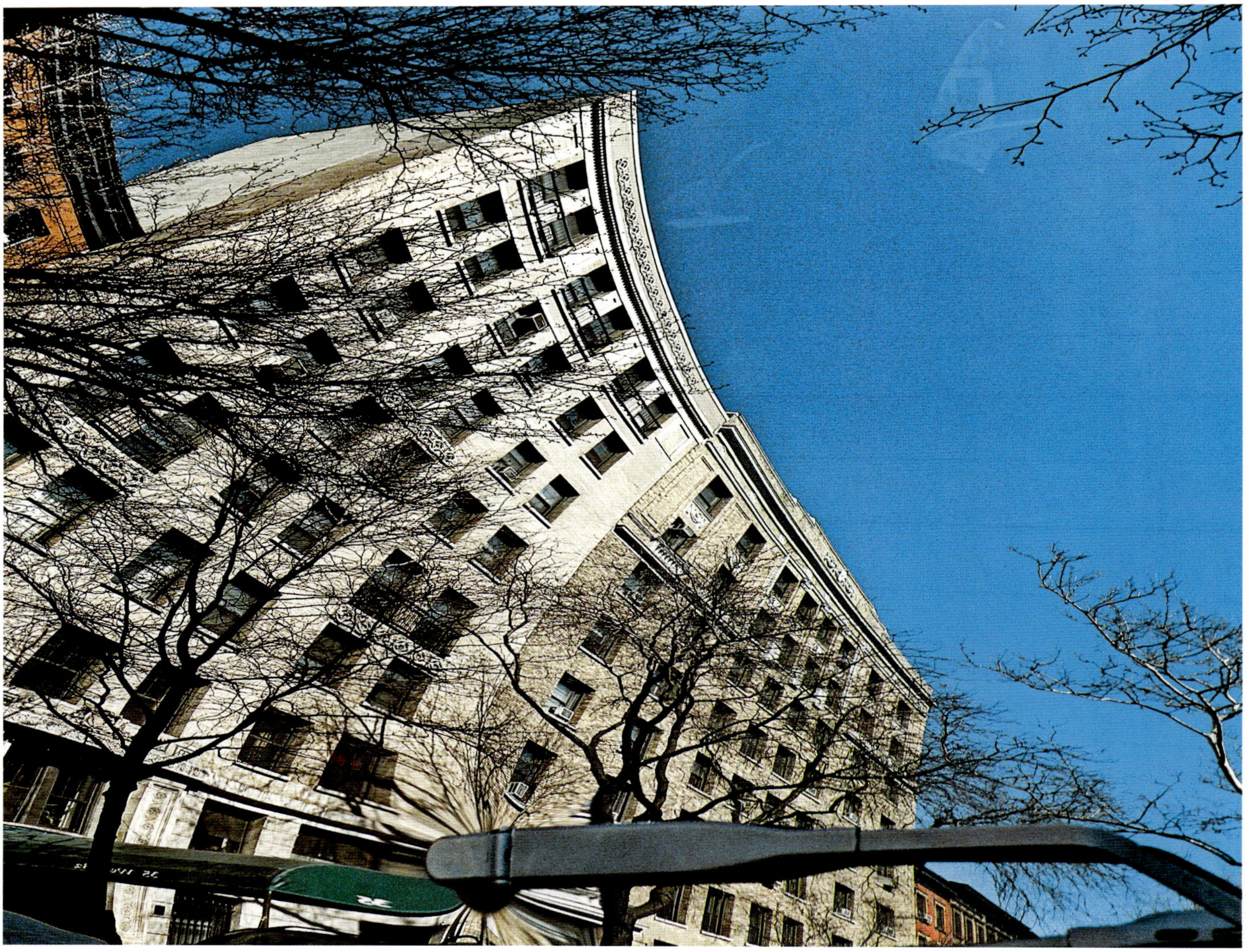

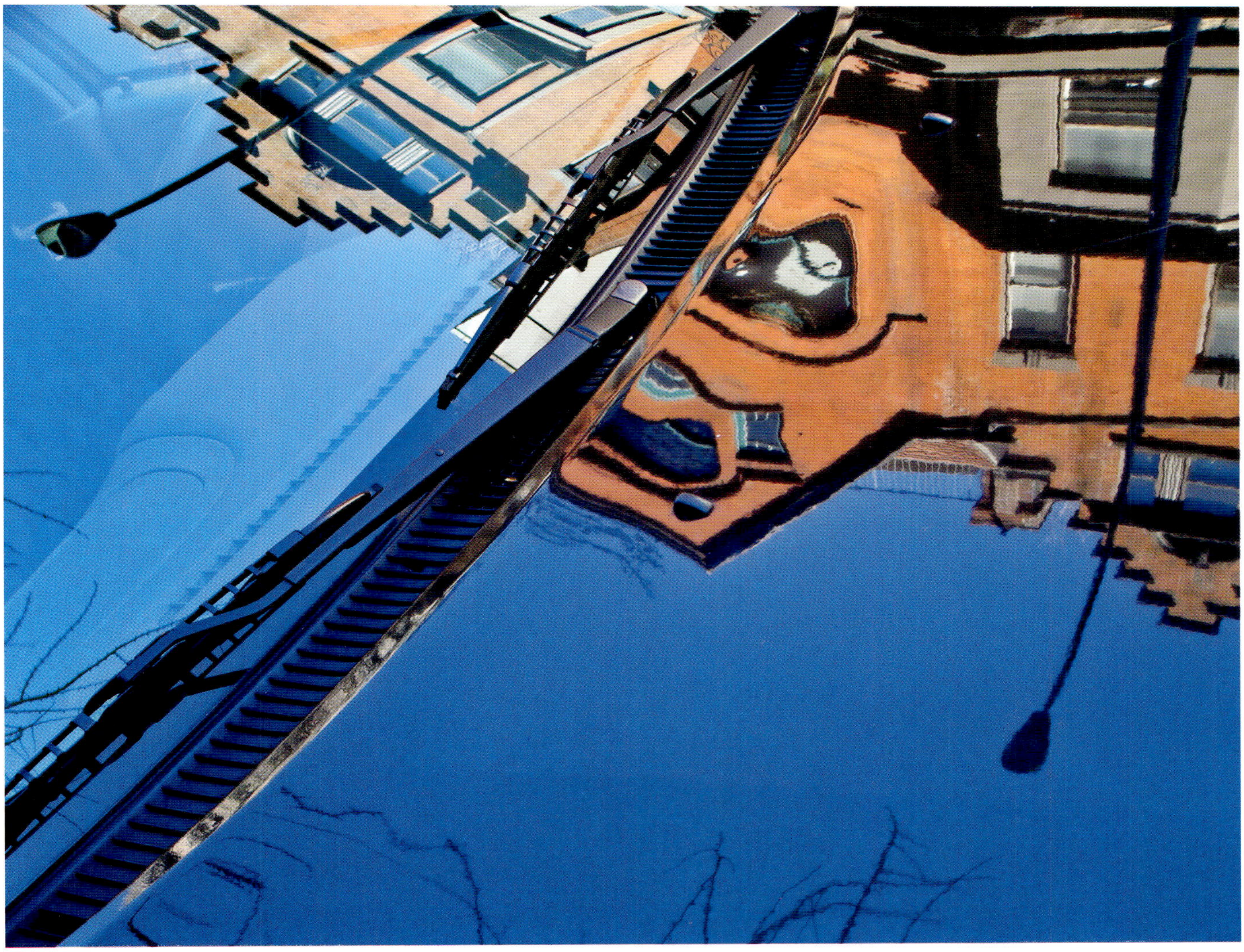

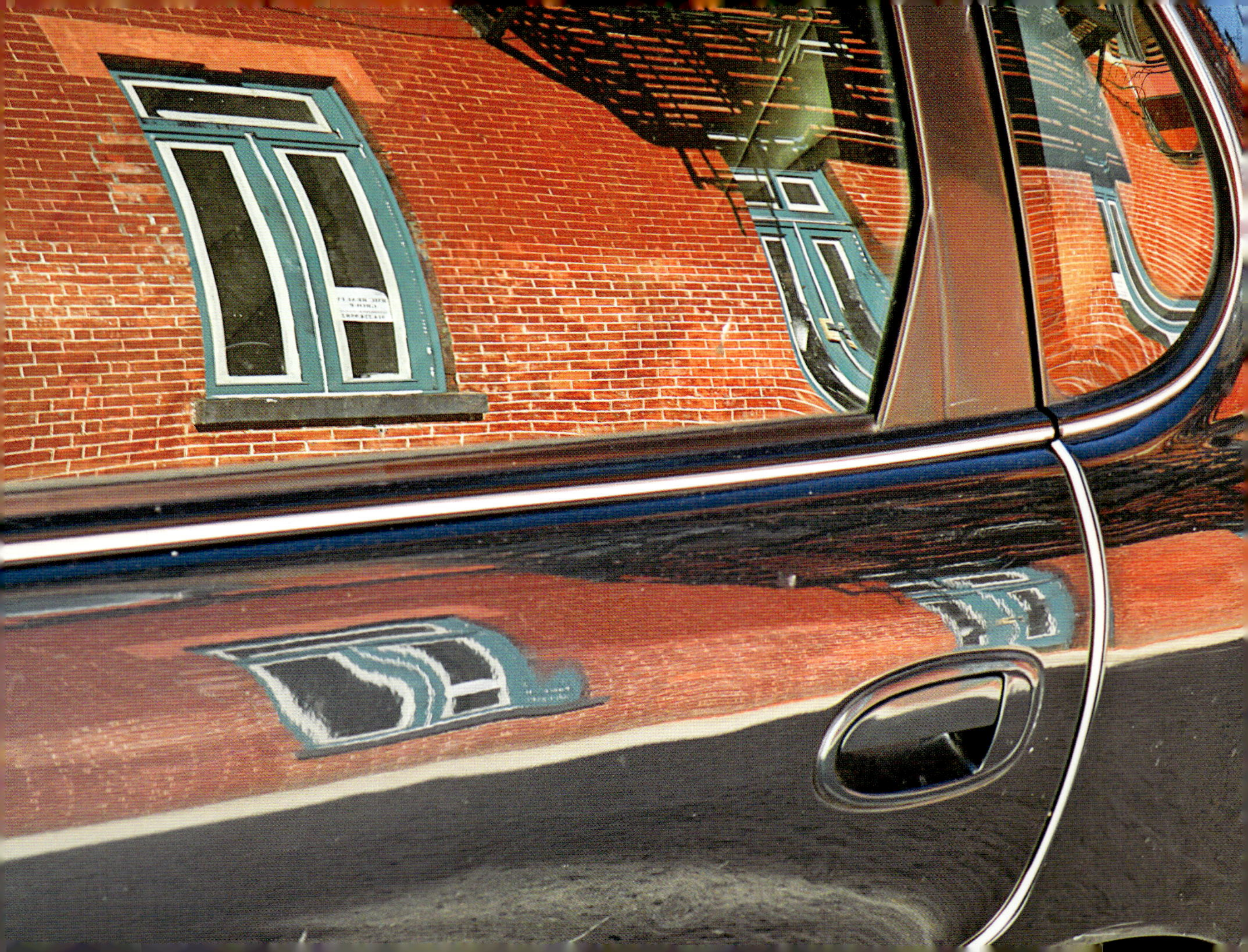

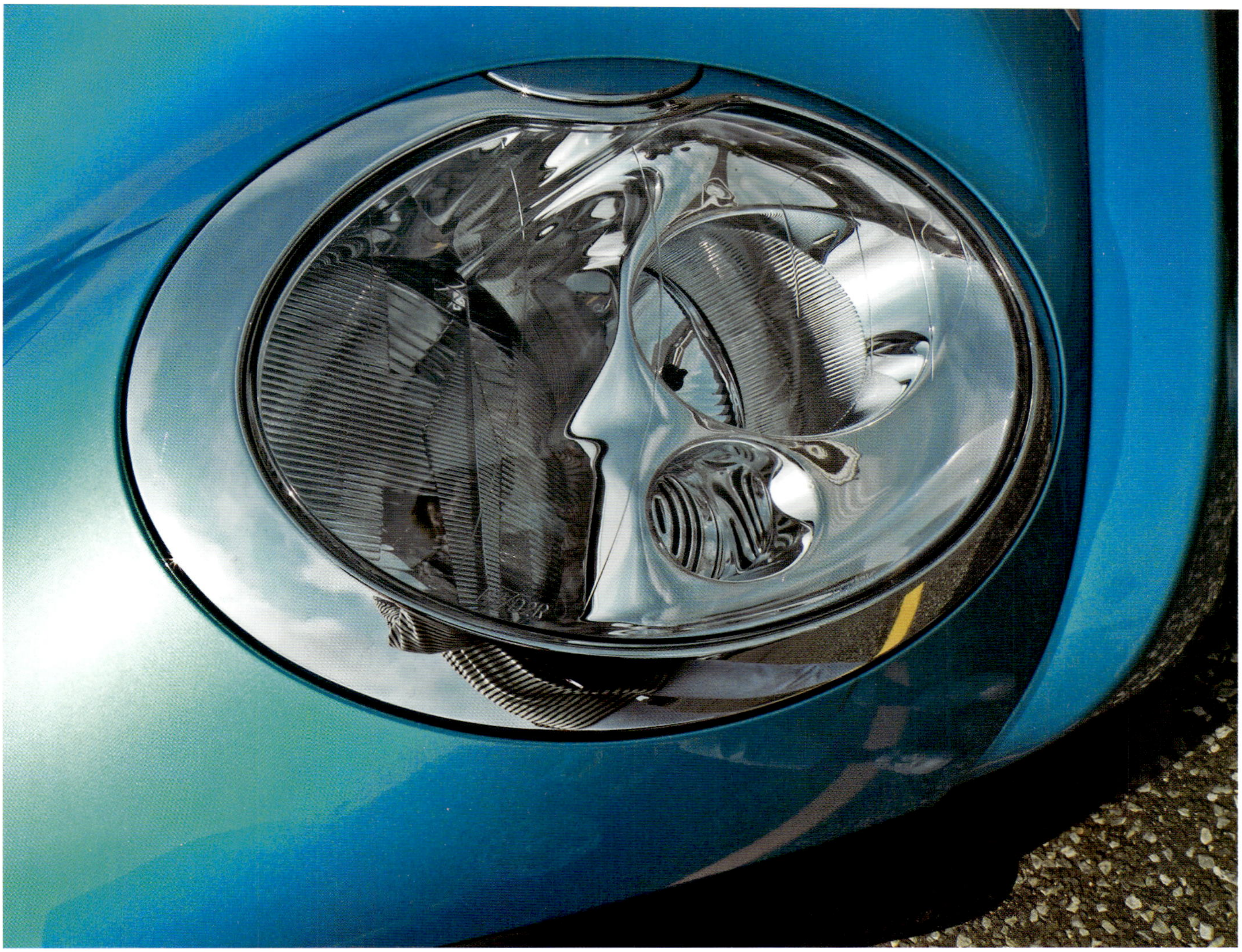

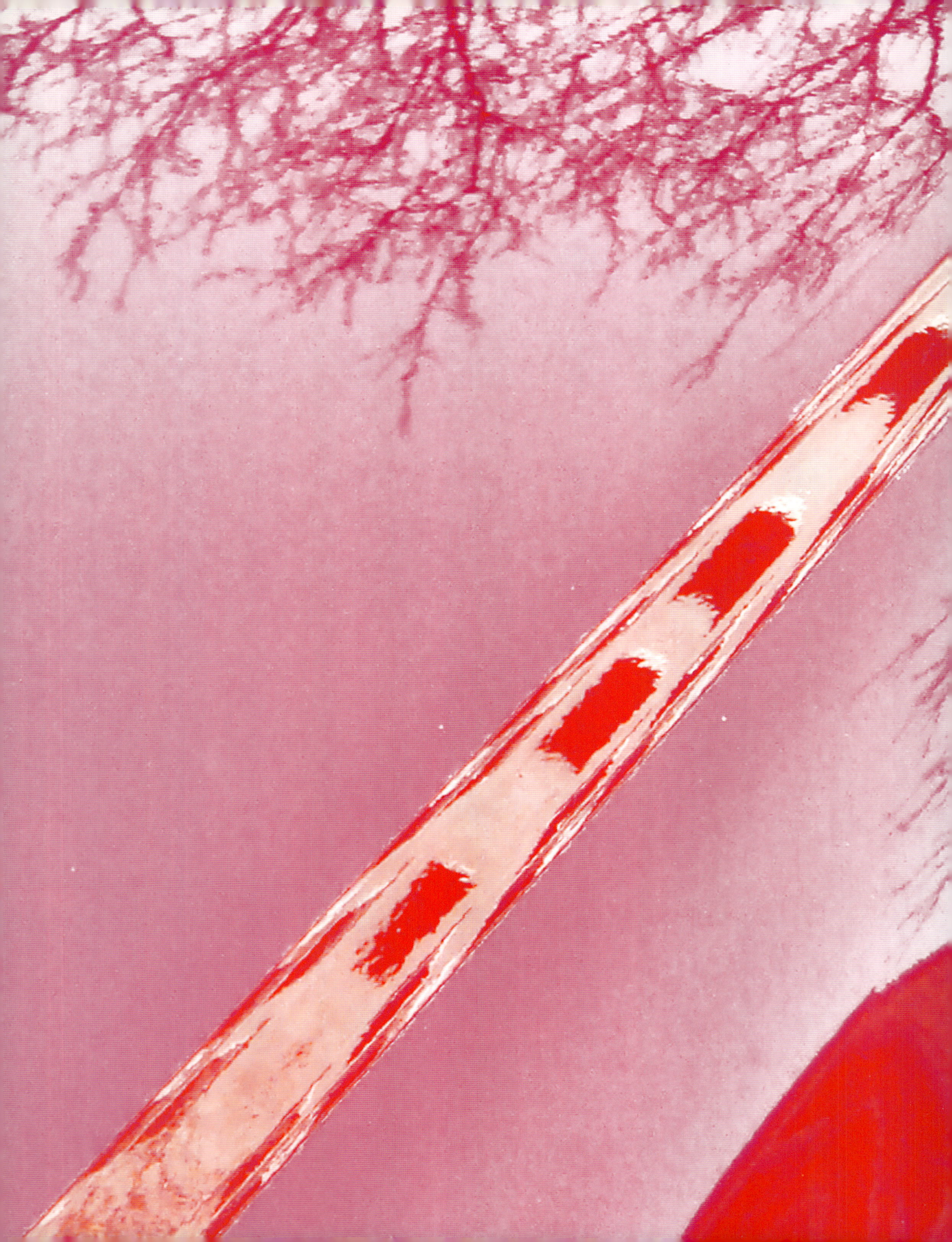

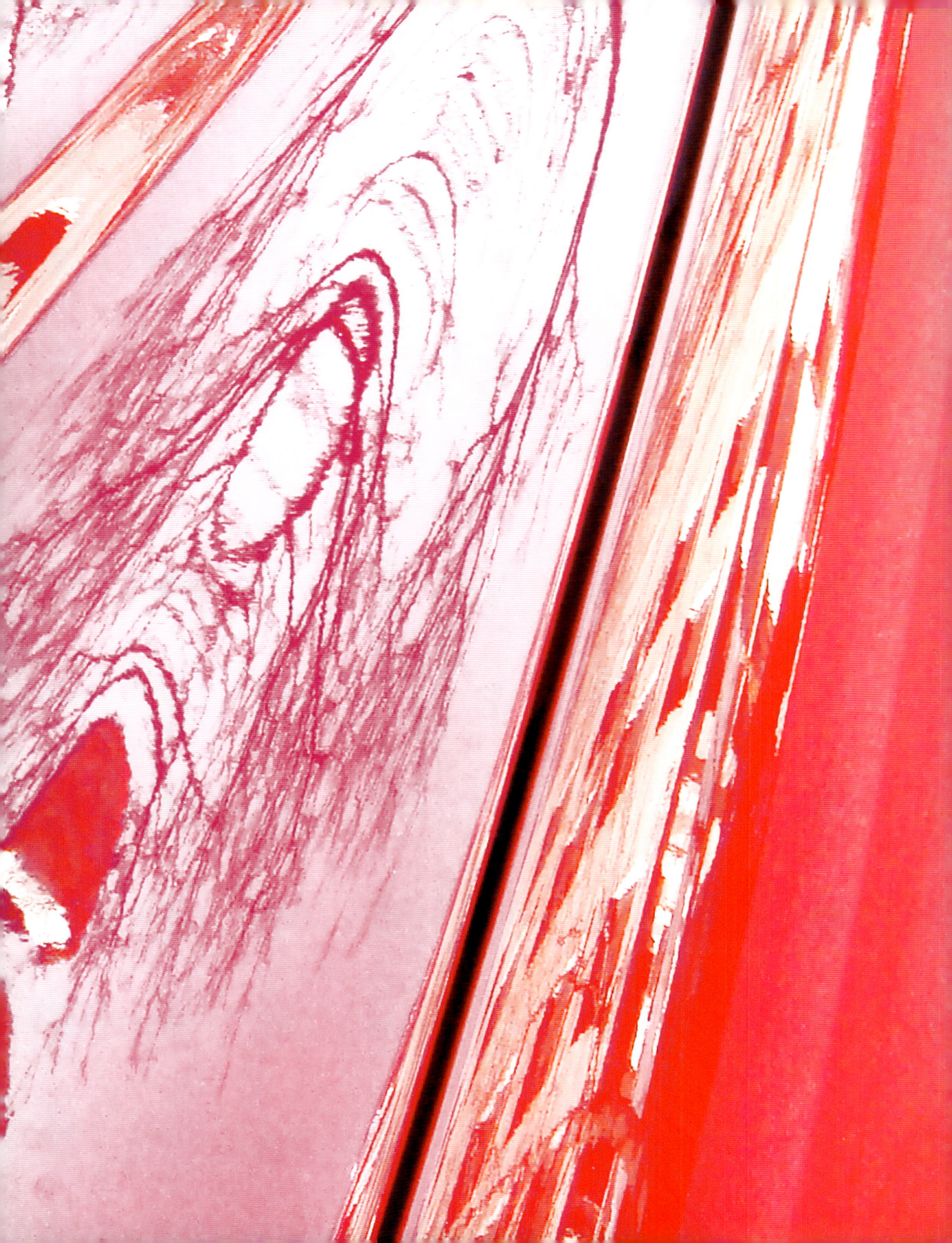

8
SWONNET

'Tis time to air my feelings, pro and con,
regarding that beguiling bird, the swan:
descendant of a proud and stately race,
epitome of calm, unstudied grace.
Its supple neck is awesome to observe
as, gently, it uncoils each flowing curve.
In short, the swan is amply blessed with pros.
As for the cons, let's take a look at those.

One major fault is all we need pursue;
great beauties, so I'm told, may have it too.
Both swans and sirens, being what they are,
'tis best to view their beauty from afar.
To cull a quote from Mother Nature's script:
"Who comes too close may get severely nipped."

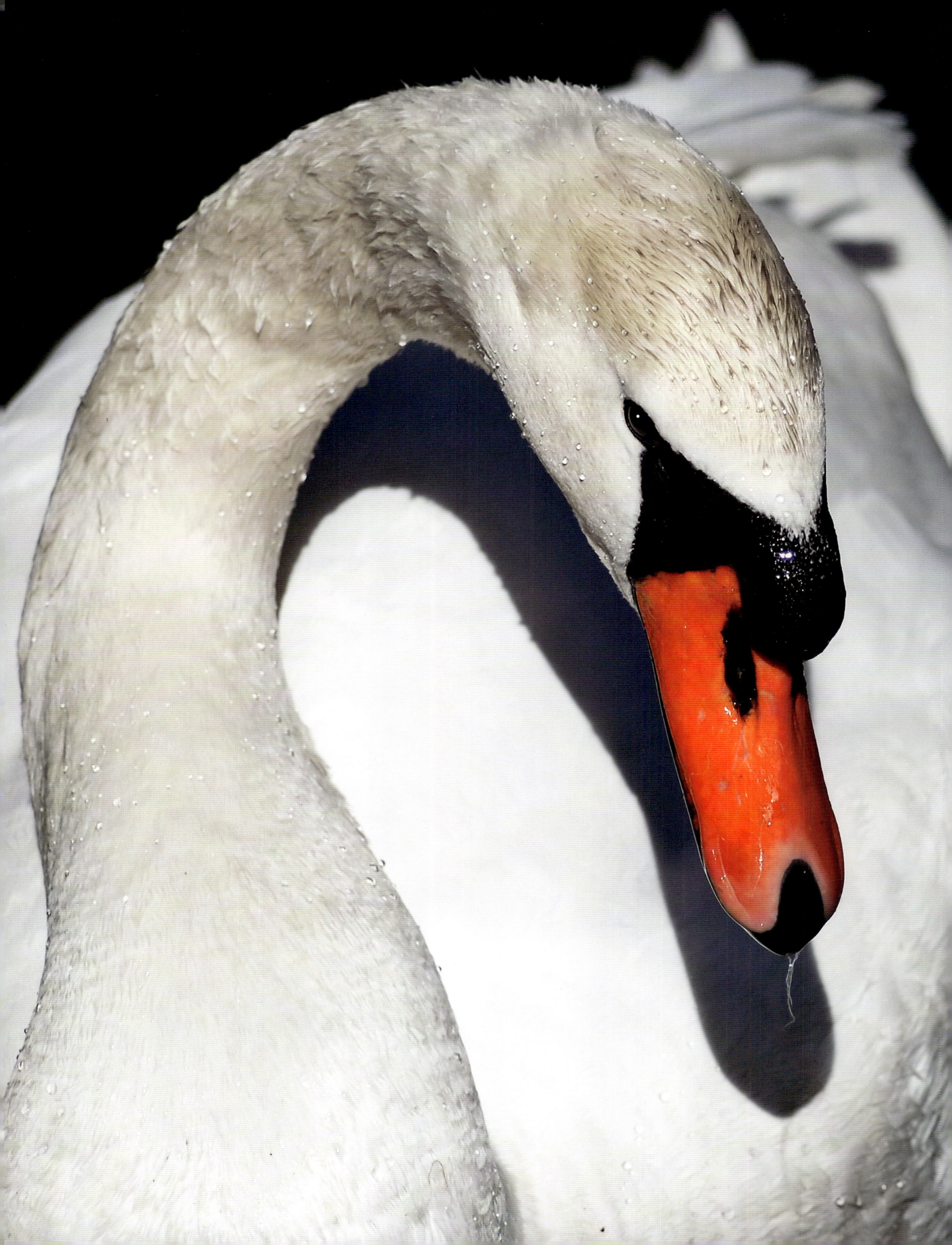

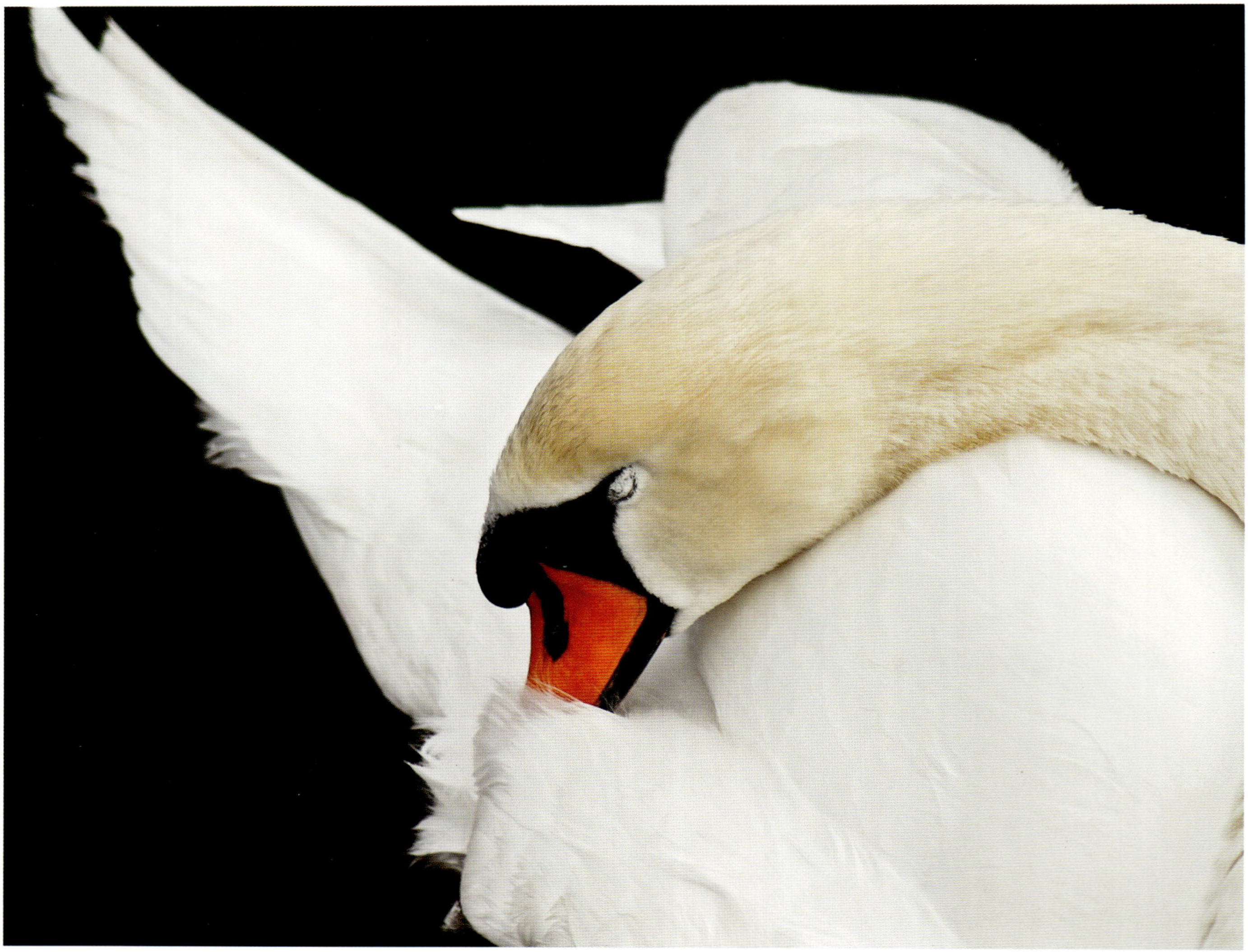

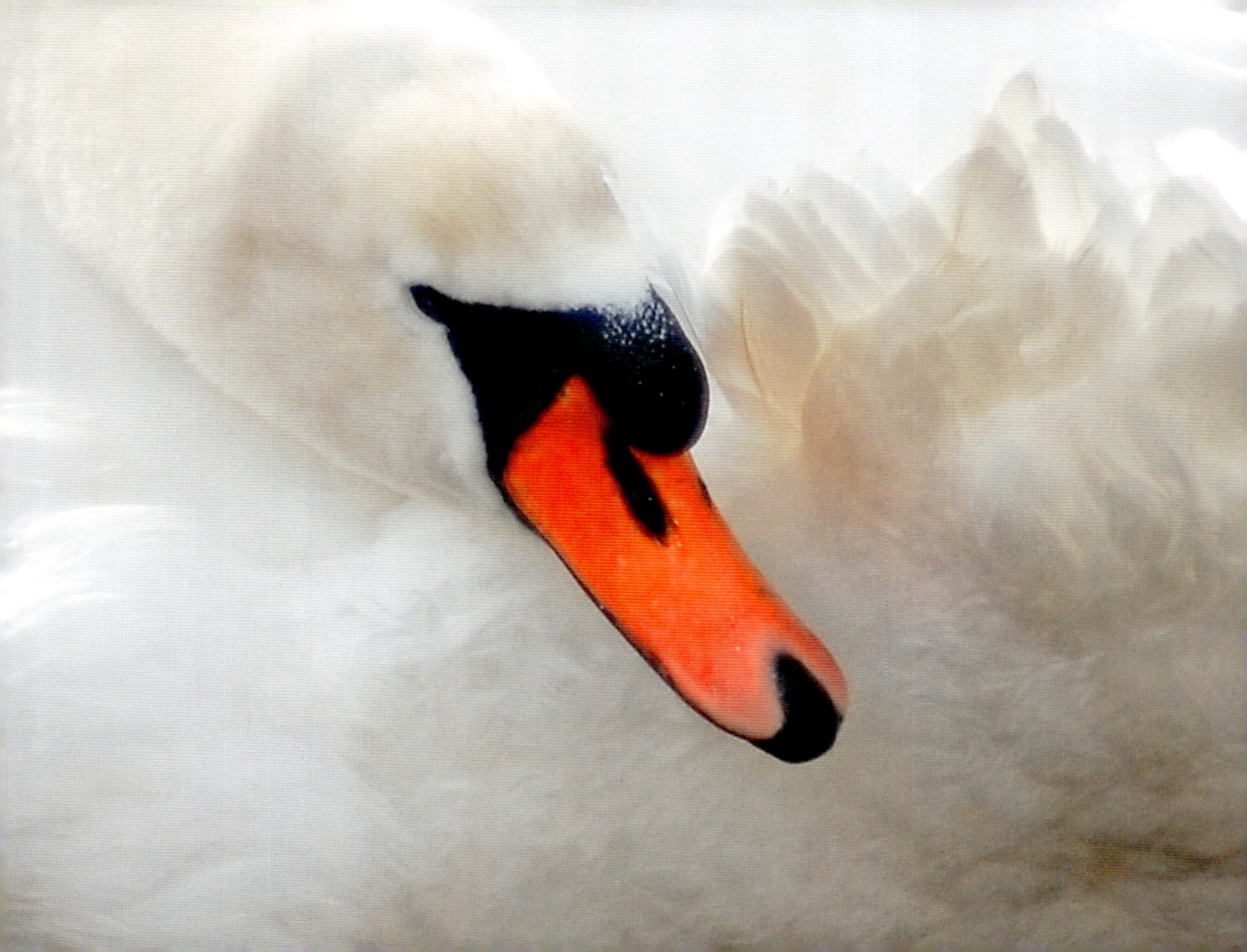

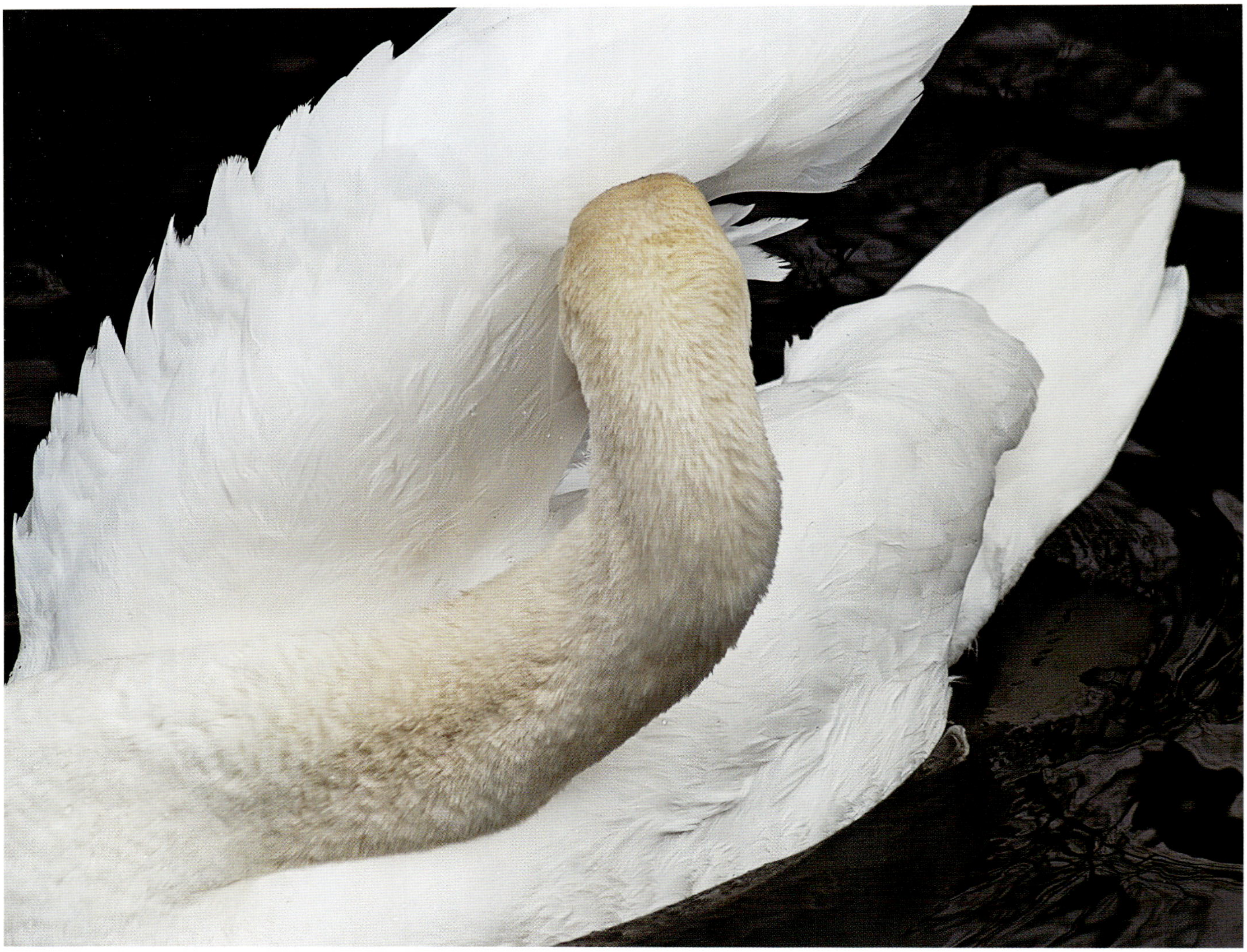

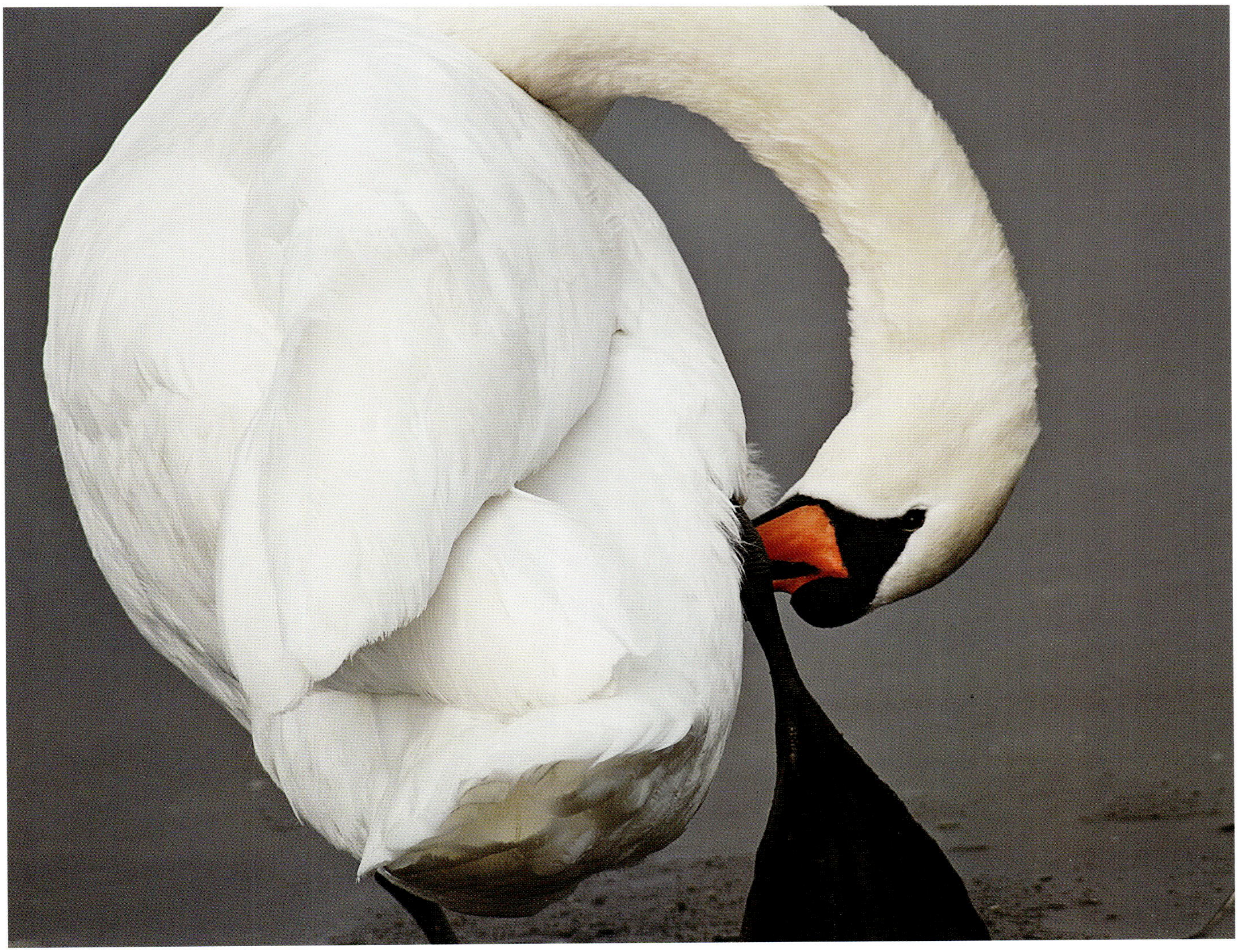

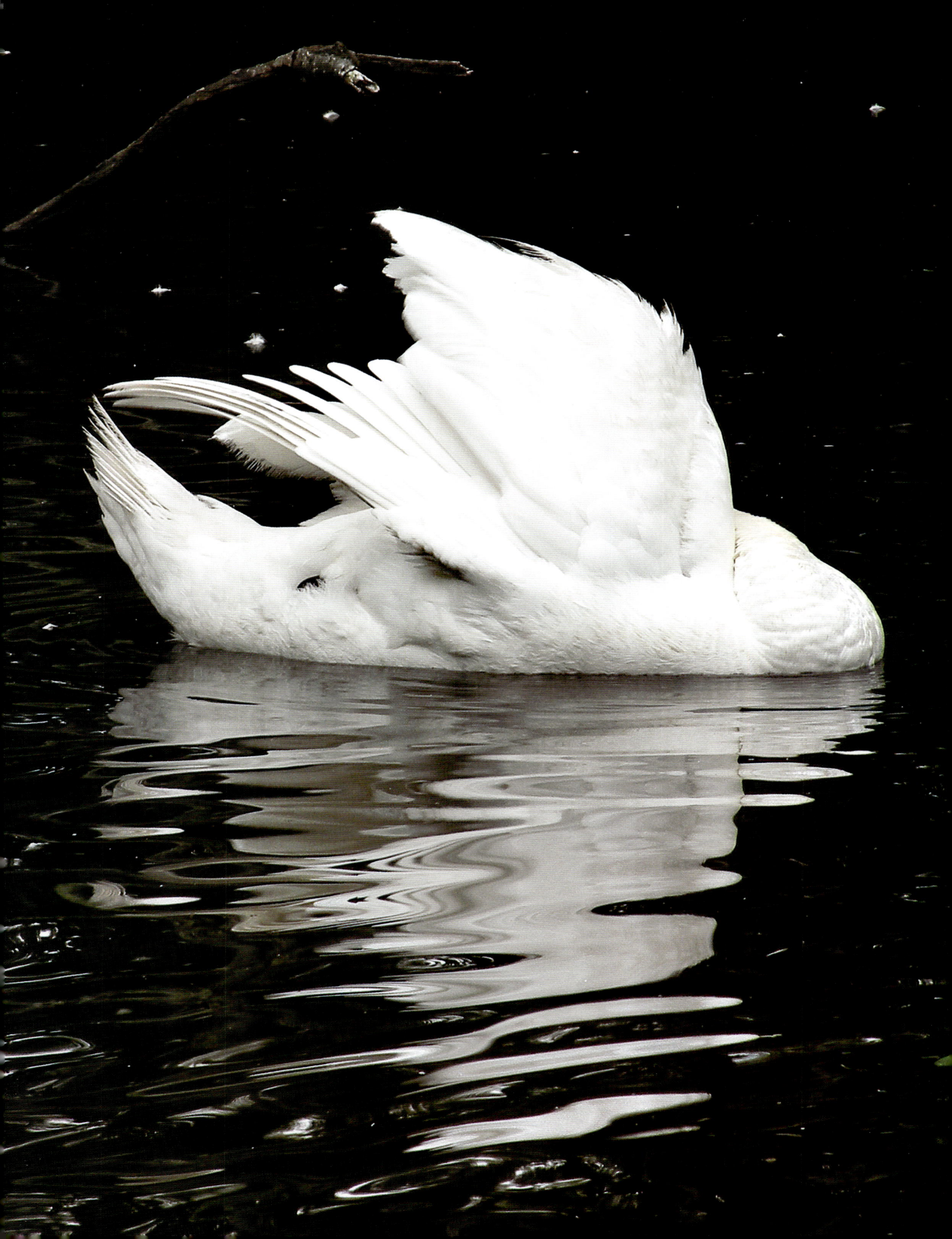

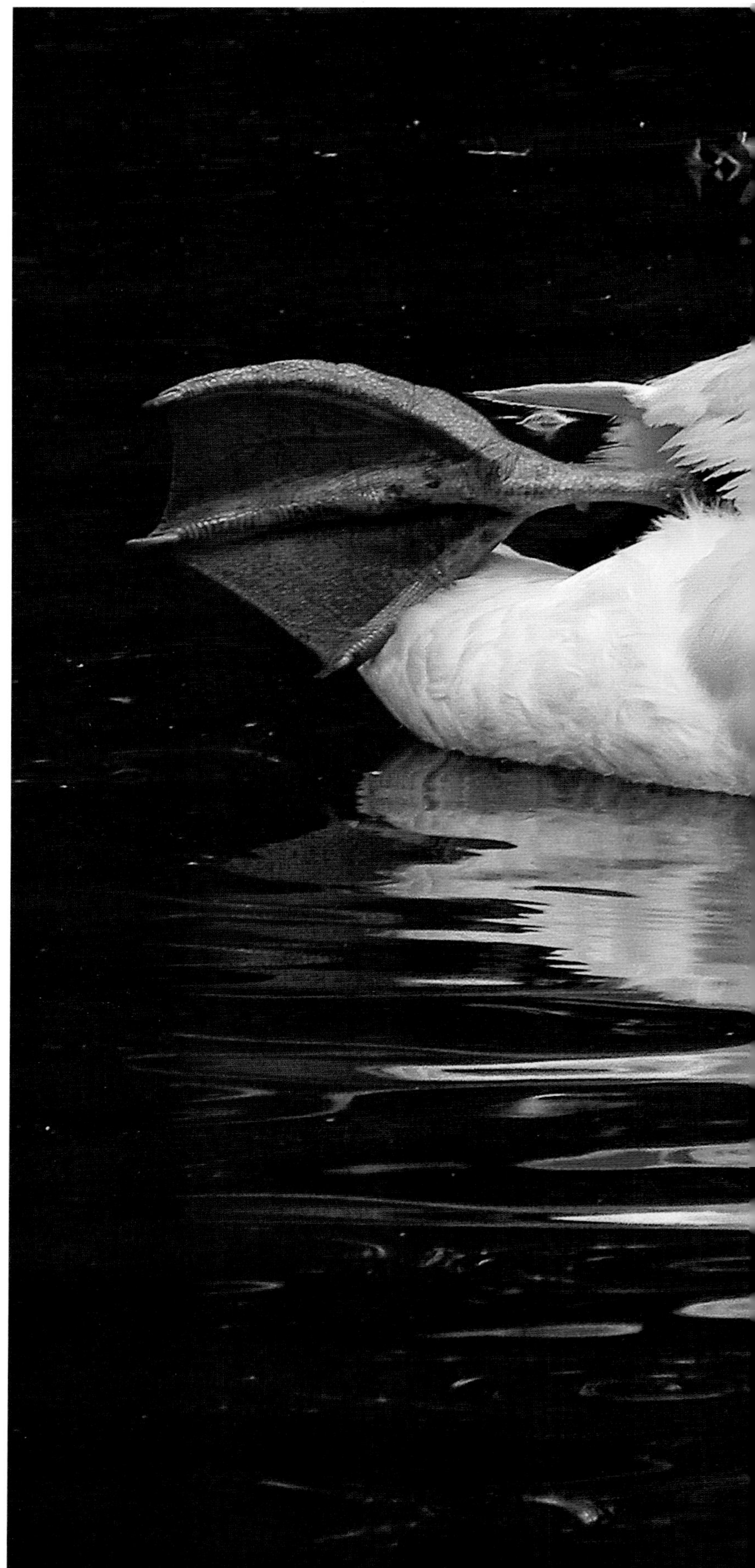

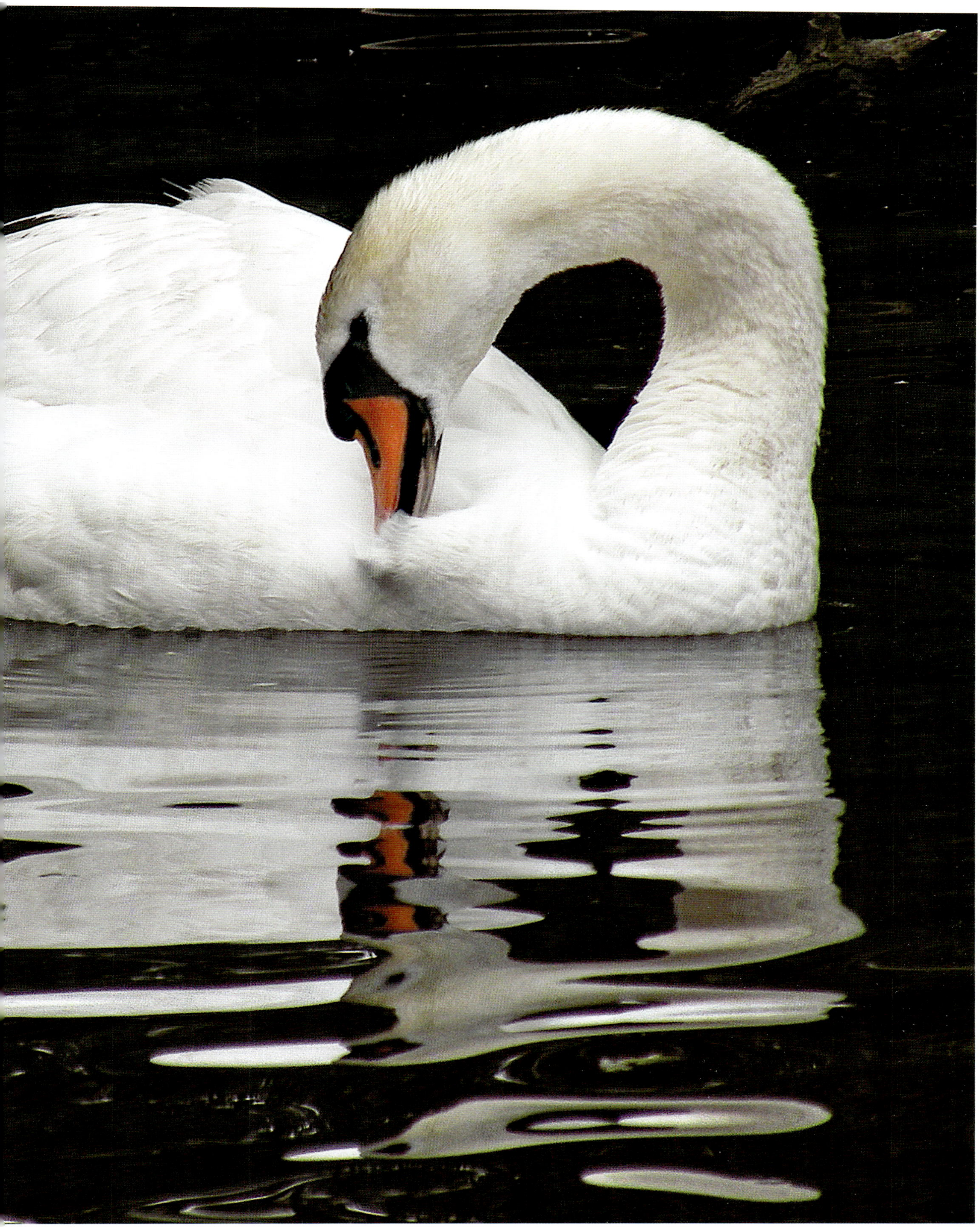

9

QUESTIONS

Who are they . . .
these castoff men and women . . .
these silent shapes
sleeping on sidewalks . . .
in doorways . . .
anywhere and everywhere?
Who are they?
Where did they come from?
Did they have a childhood?
Did they show their first crude drawings
to their proud, smiling parents?
Did they have skates? A bike?
A pencil box?
A best friend?
Were they in the high-school band?
The school play?
Did they have a college sweetheart?
A husband, a wife,
a partner?
Children?
Did they have a home?
An apartment?
A furnished room?
A bed, a desk,
a closet?
A telephone number?
Did they have a job?
A bank account?
Dreams?
What happened?
Did they fall through a hole in life?
When did they became castaways?
Human snails?
Debris?
Could this happen to me?
Who are they?

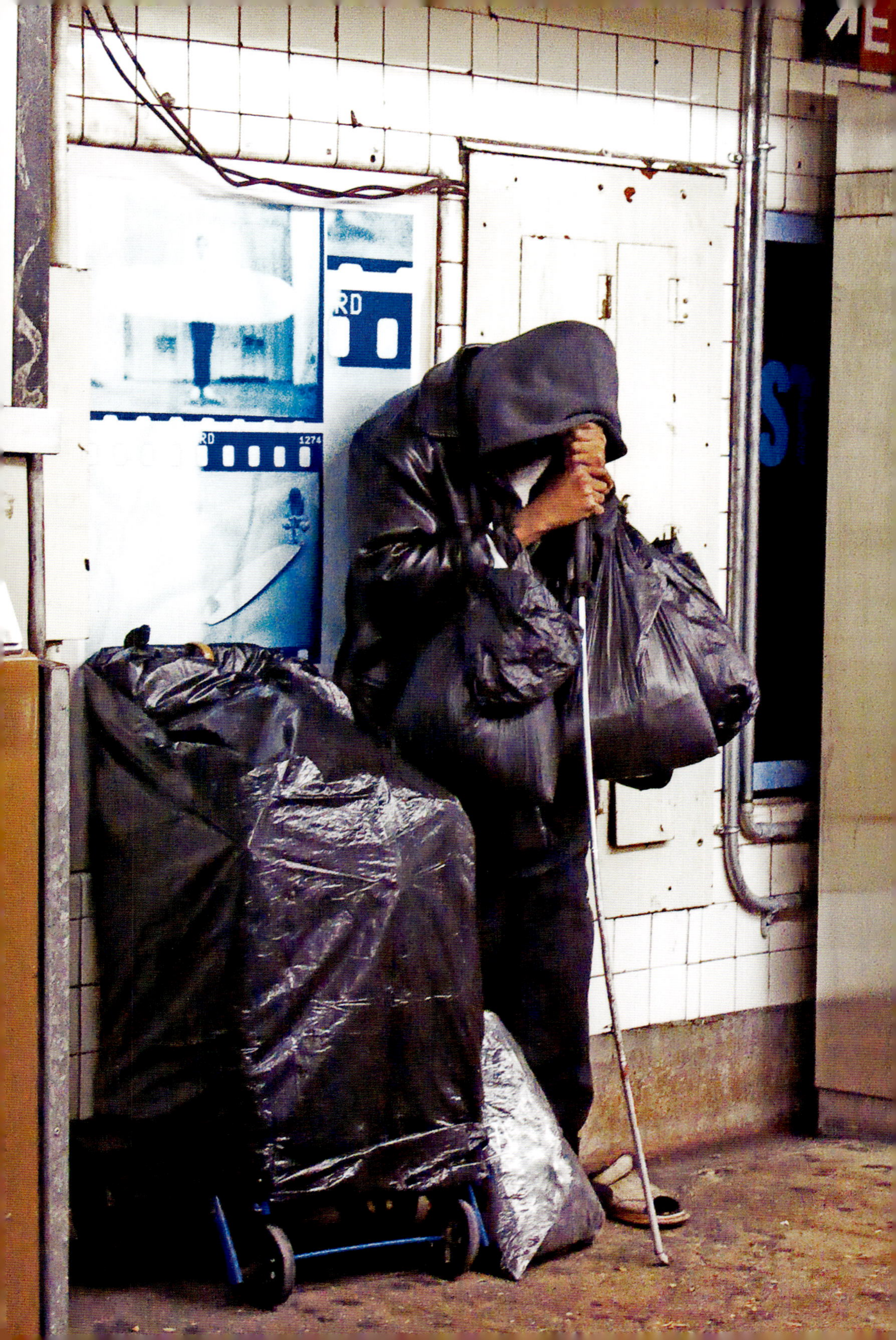
1274

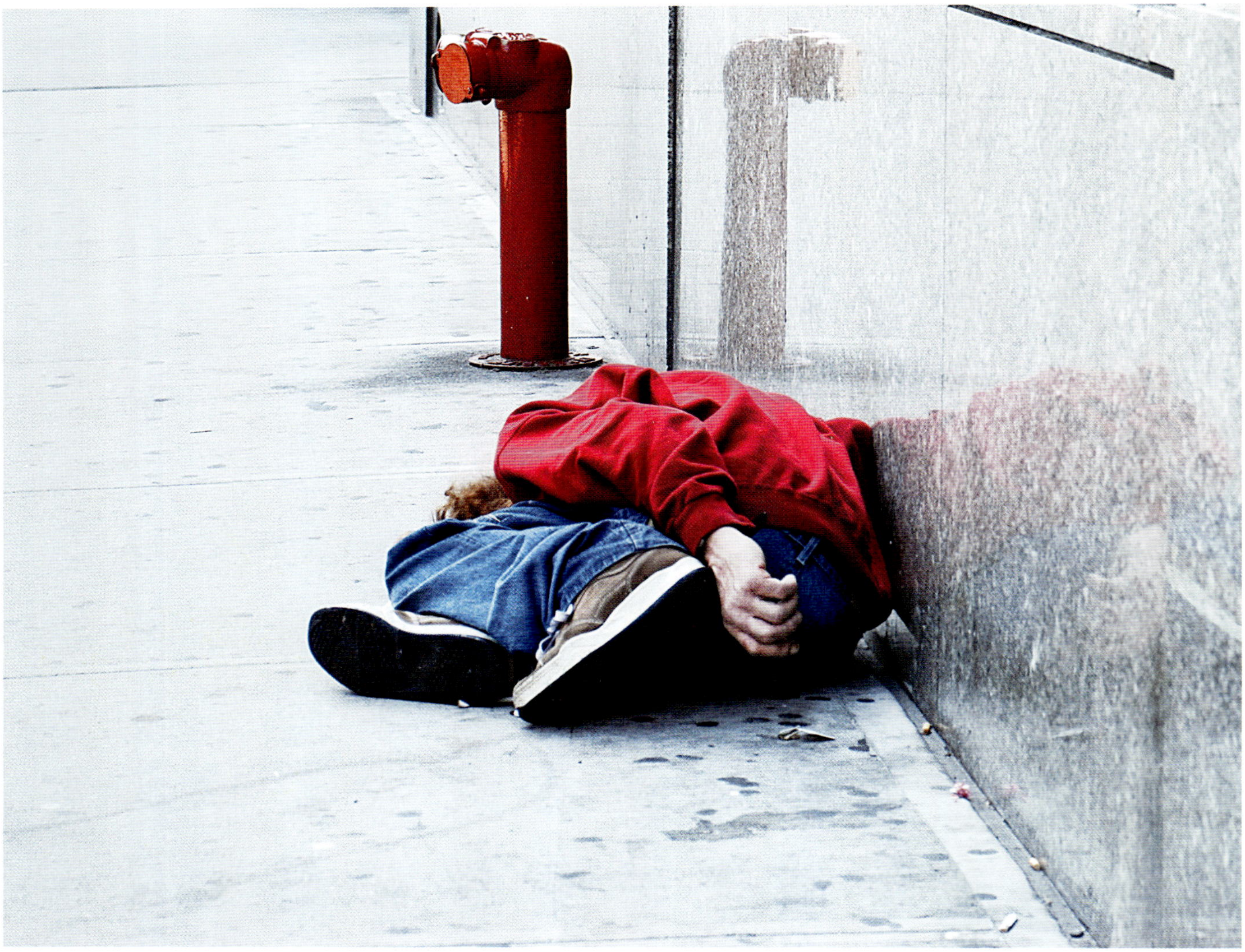

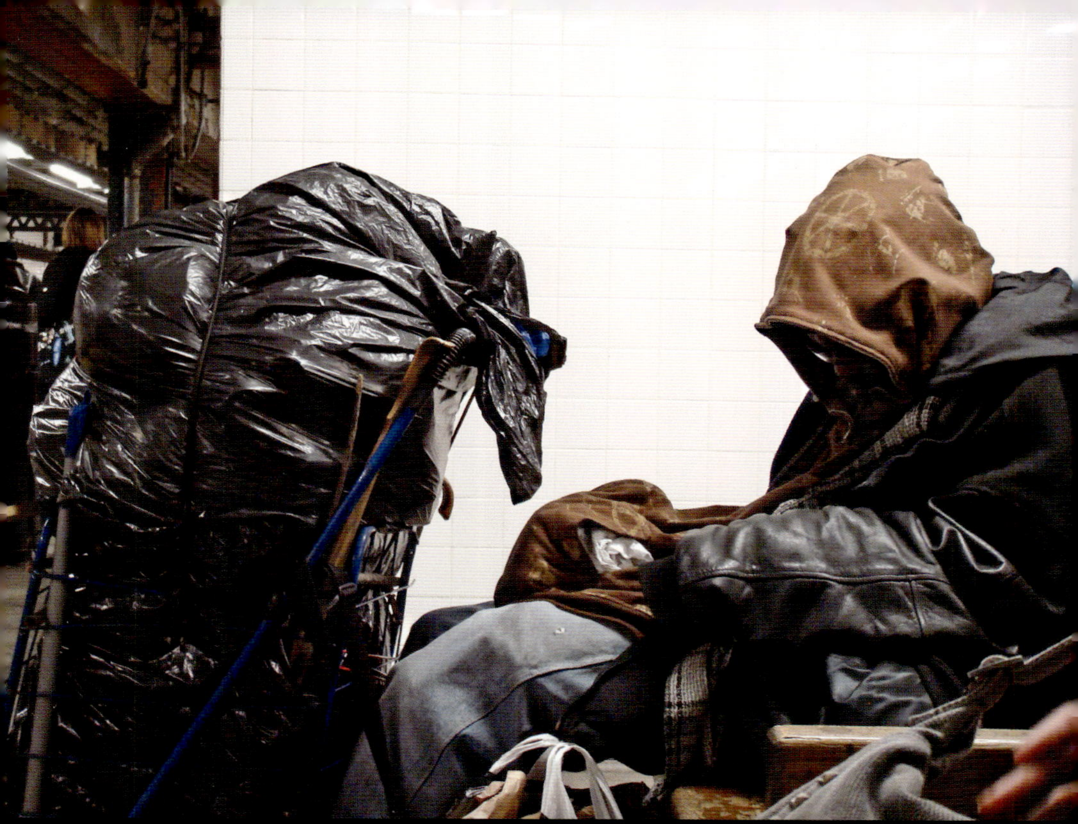

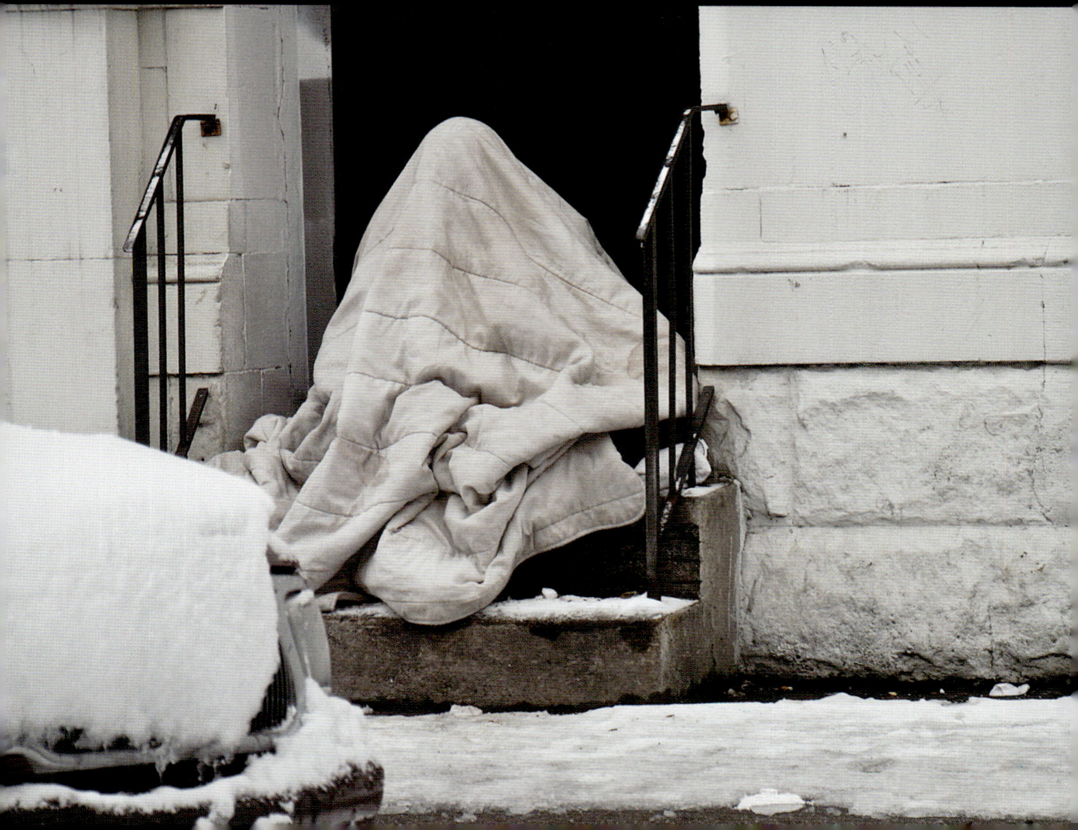

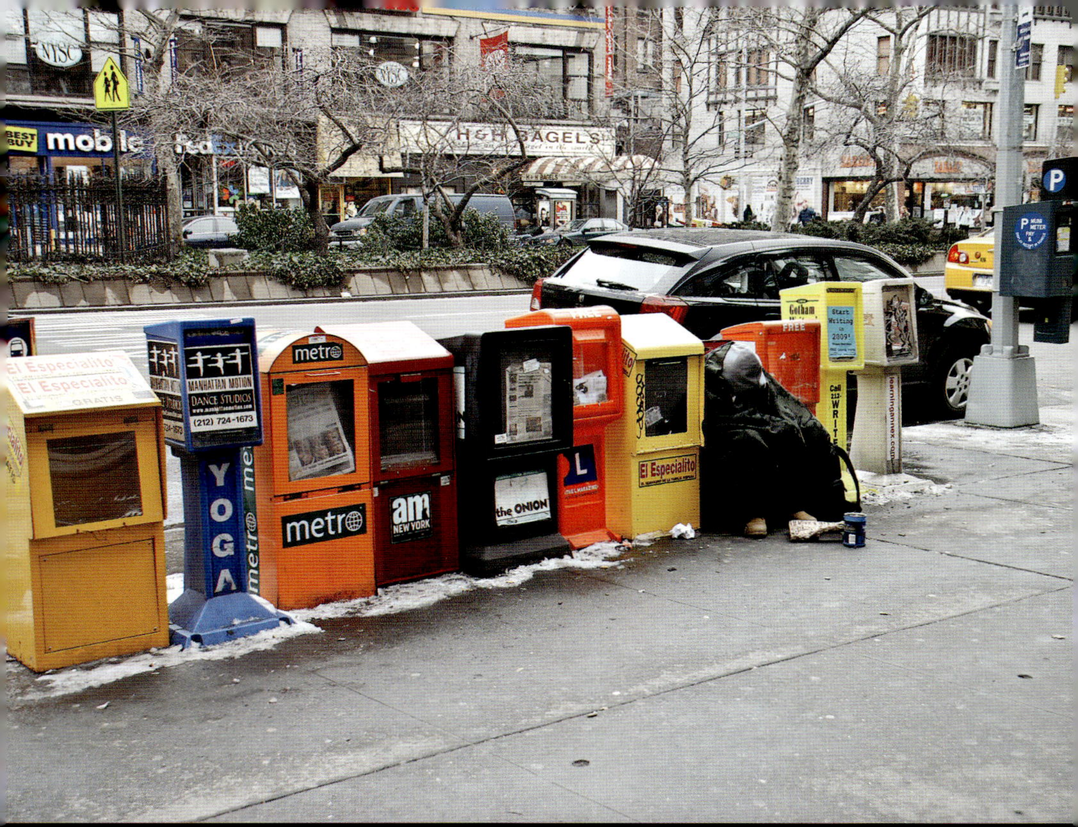
NYSC
BEST BUY
mobile
H&H BAGELS
El Especialito
El Especialito
GRATIS
MANHATTAN MOTION
DANCE STUDIOS
(212) 724-1673
YOGA
metro
metro
am
NEW YORK
the ONION
FREE
El Especialito
Gotham
Start Writing in 2009!
FREE
Call 212-WRITE

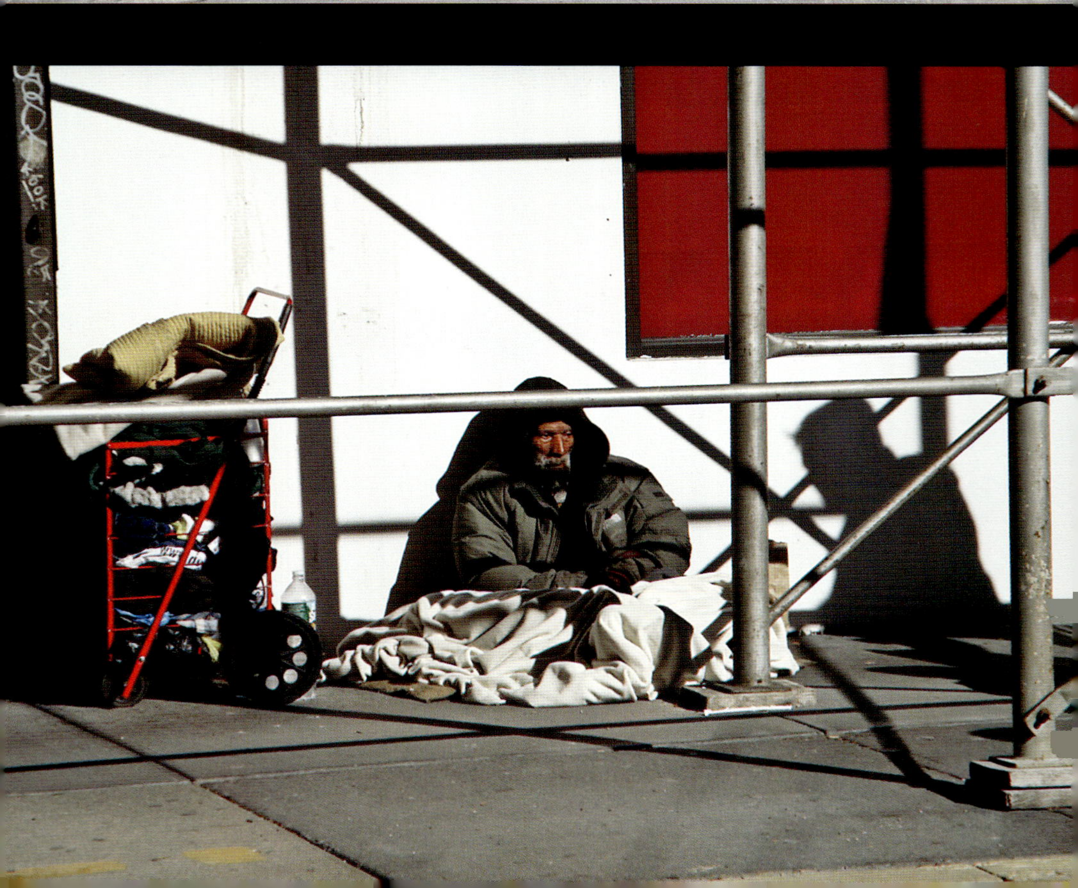

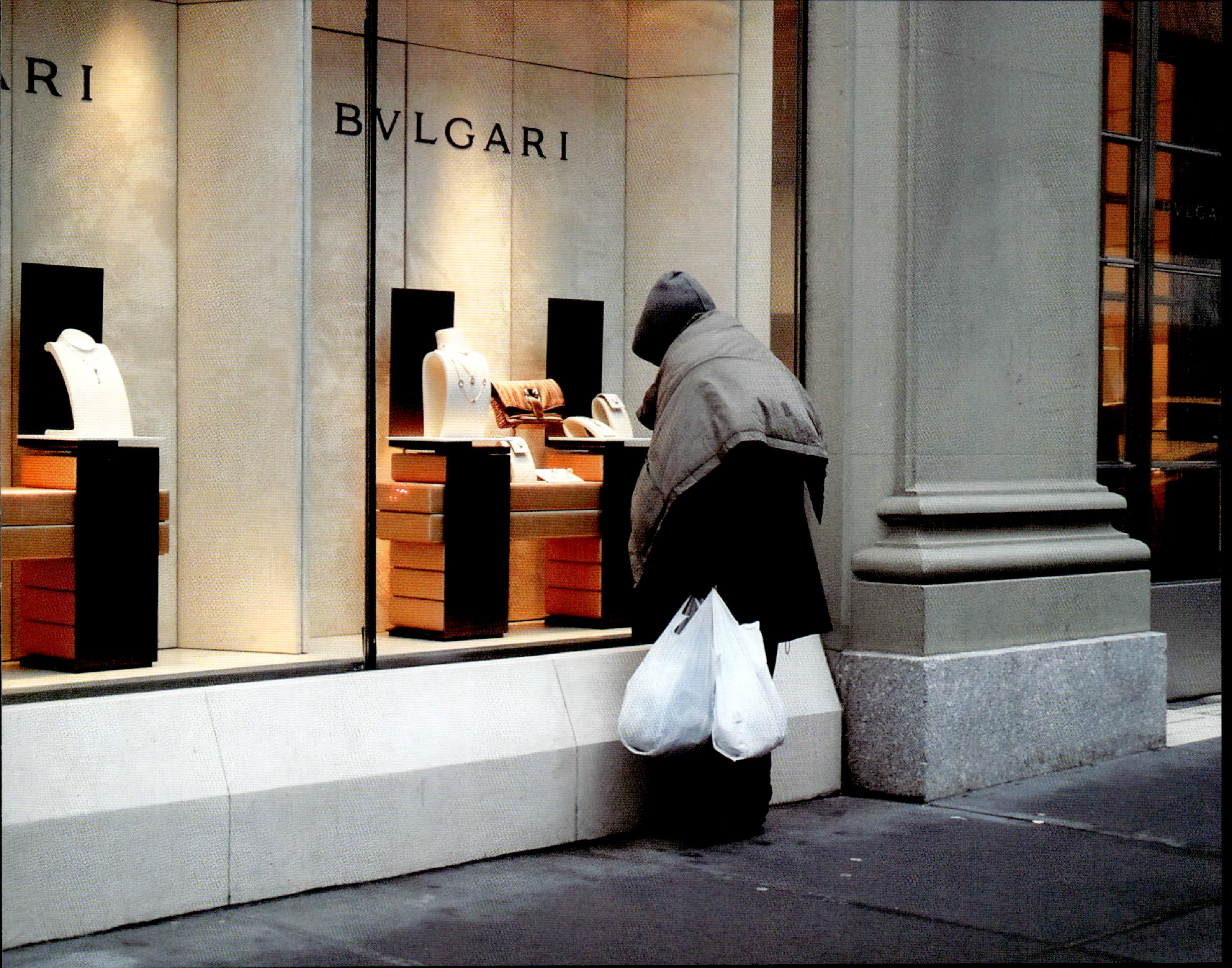
BVLGARI

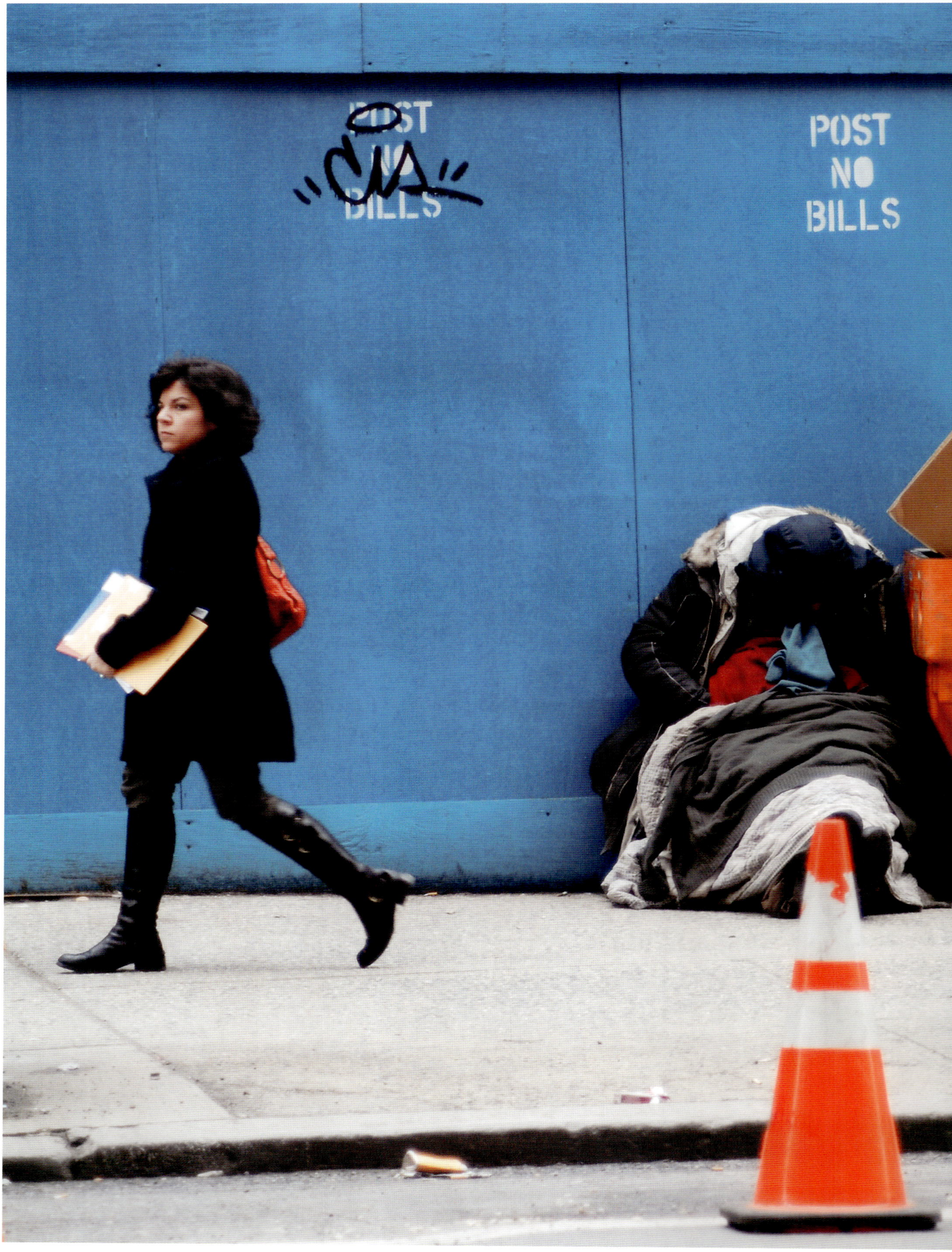
POST
NO
BILLS

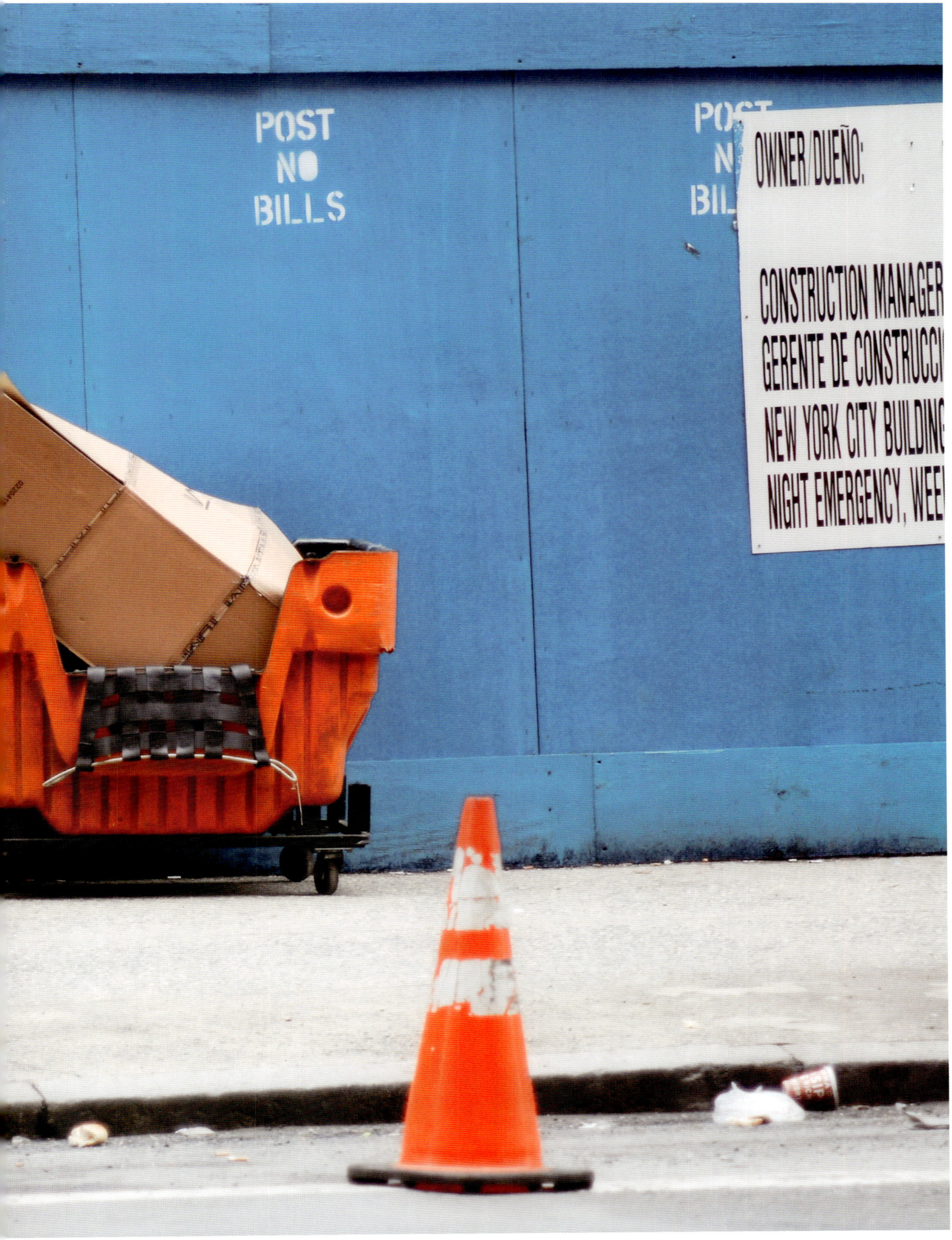
POST
NO
BILLS
OWNER/DUEÑO:
CONSTRUCTION MANAGER
GERENTE DE CONSTRUCC
NEW YORK CITY BUILDING
NIGHT EMERGENCY, WEE

10

THIS ALIEN RACE

1.

When did they land,
this alien race?
We saw no massive ships
from outer space
hovering overhead.
No UFOs split the upper air
yet all at once
there they were
everywhere:
some in every borough,
with the greatest concentration
in Manhattan.

2.

Incredibly,
despite the widespread scale
of this invasion,
there was no pandemonium,
no panic in the streets.
Far from rousing epic consternation,
these otherworldly visitors
inspired only awe and admiration,
for they were beautiful,
male and female,
utterly desirable.

The women svelte,
long of limb,
slim and all but hipless,
skin unblemished, cheekbones high,
avatars of glamour.

The men manly,
tall and lean,
perfectly proportioned,
suave, poised,
nonchalant,
models of indifference.

3.

Since they arrived,
I daresay every one of us
at one time or another
has felt compelled to stop and stare
at these enigmatic creatures,
their cool, unearthly beauty
holding us in thrall;
their faces perfect ovals
with strong, well-chiseled features
or, sometimes, none at all.

Intrigued,
we scan each flawless face,
unlined and ever youthful
and wonder whether
Botox was ubiquitous
on that far distant world
from whence they flew.

Their heads,
we also note,
though quite well-shaped,
are often bald
and sometimes black
or mirror-like
or blue.

4.

And though it may be true
that we view with some misgivings
the absence of expression
on every stoic face,
we envy nonetheless,
this alien race,
for when it comes to
knowing what to wear
and how to wear it,
these creatures
are paragons of style.

5.

Is it any wonder
that they choose to dwell
in stores that sell
the raiment that they wear so well:
establishments like Vera Wang
and Hilfiger and Saks;
emporiums like Macy's,
Bloomingdale's and T.J.Maxx.

Some make their homes
within the stores,
while some prefer the windows.
And some—
or do we fancy this?—
manage to pass
through the window glass
into the street
(on well-shod feet).

6.

Our city has a history
of welcoming the tired, the poor,
the huddled masses
yearning to be free.
We've also spread the welcome mat
for banker and aristocrat.
Which is to say
our town has welcomed
every type of émigré,
though none that seemed as strange as these
bizarre, outlandish refugees.

Startled as we were
by these odd, exotic beings,
we did what we have always done:
we took them in and left them free
to make New York their home.
And for our hospitality,
how rich was our reward!

7.

They taught us
all the pretty ways
to wear a scarf
with dash and flair.

And how to pick
a proper hat
and wear it
with a jaunty air.

And how to choose
the clothes we wear
with confidence
and *savoir-faire.*

8.

Without their chic example,
we'd be dowdy and ill-dressed
but now in every mirror
we can see how we've been blessed
by these ultra-stylish visitors
who came from outer space:
this alien race.

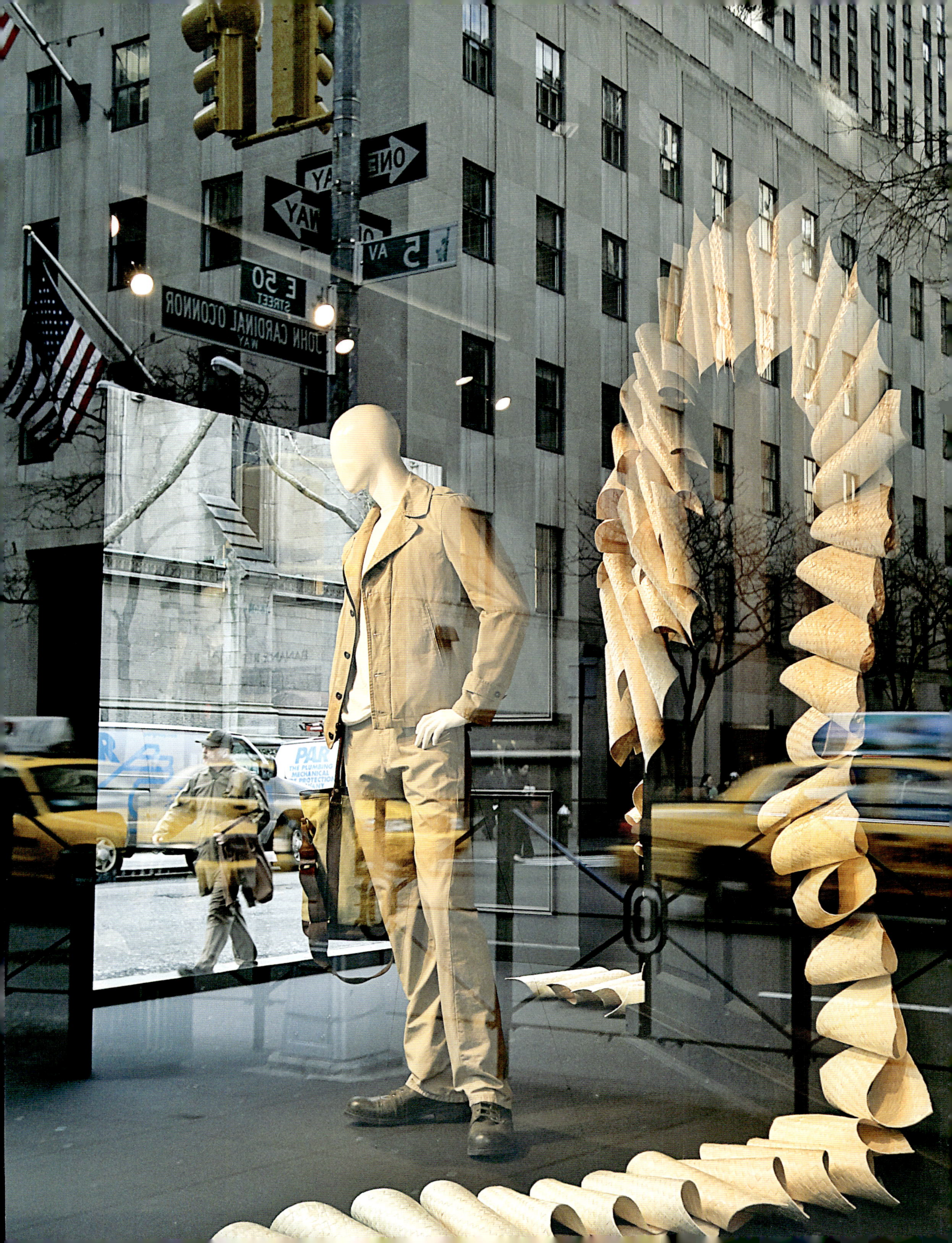
ONE WAY
E 50 STREET
5 AV
JOHN CARDINAL OCONNOR WAY
PAR
THE PLUMBING
MECHANICAL

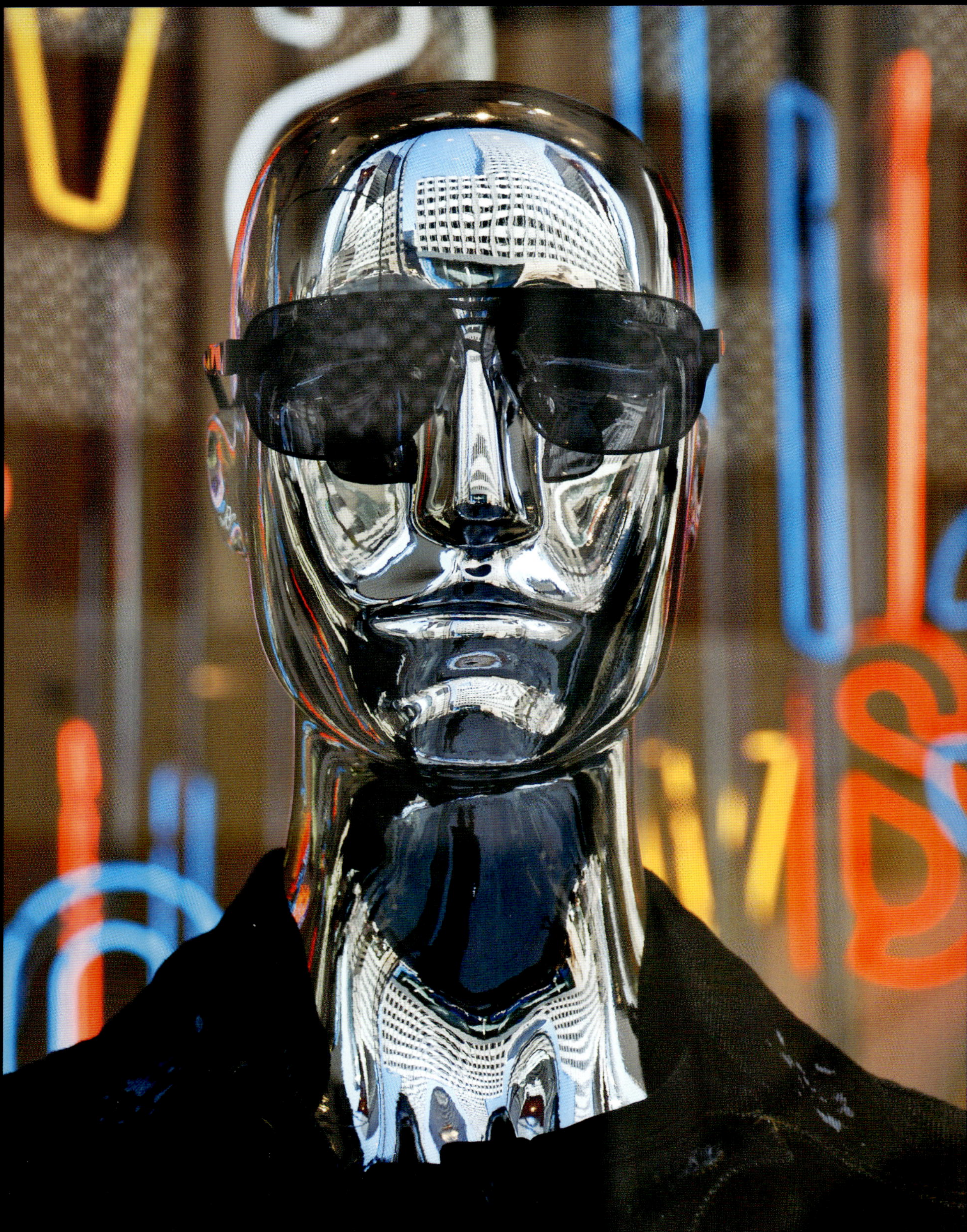

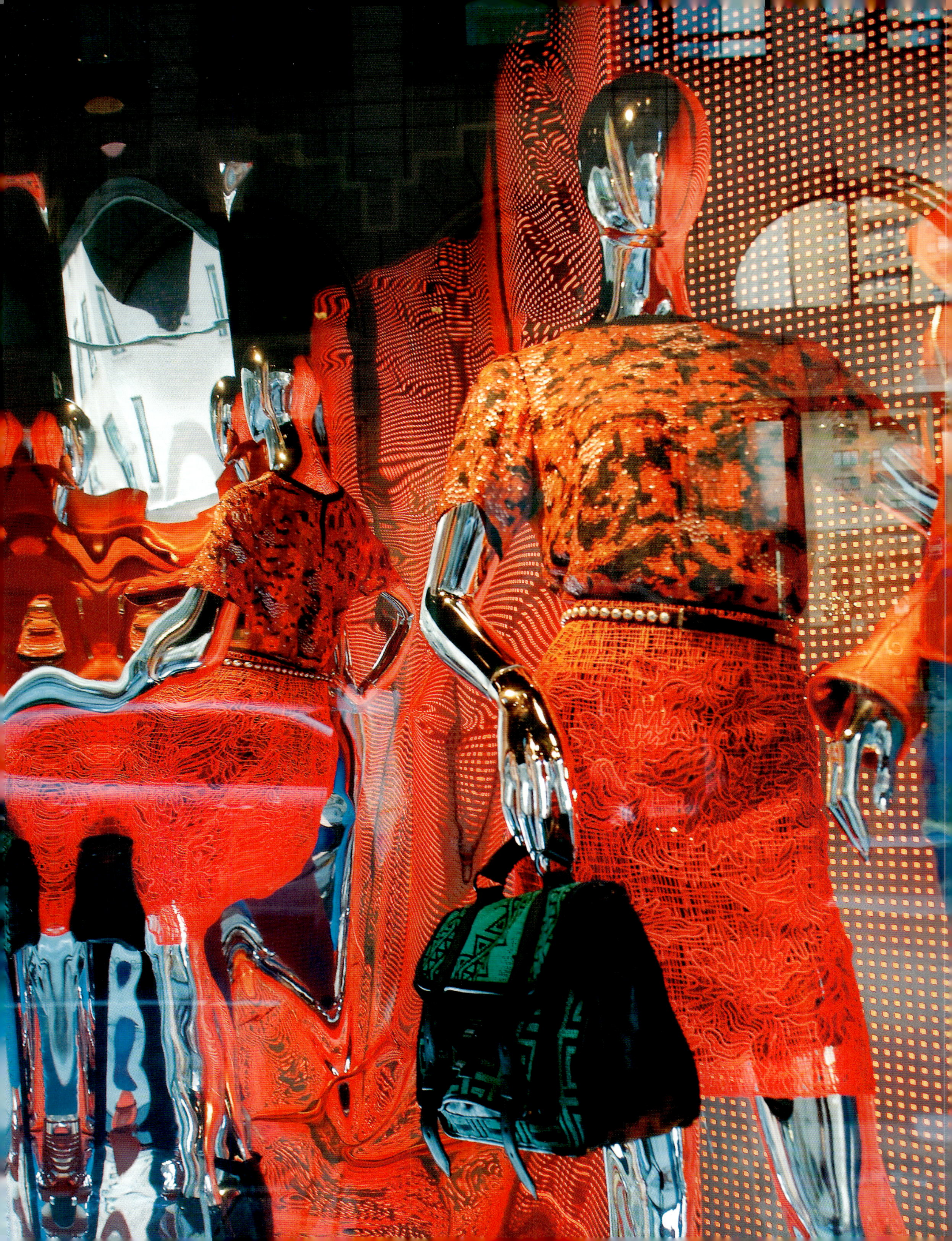

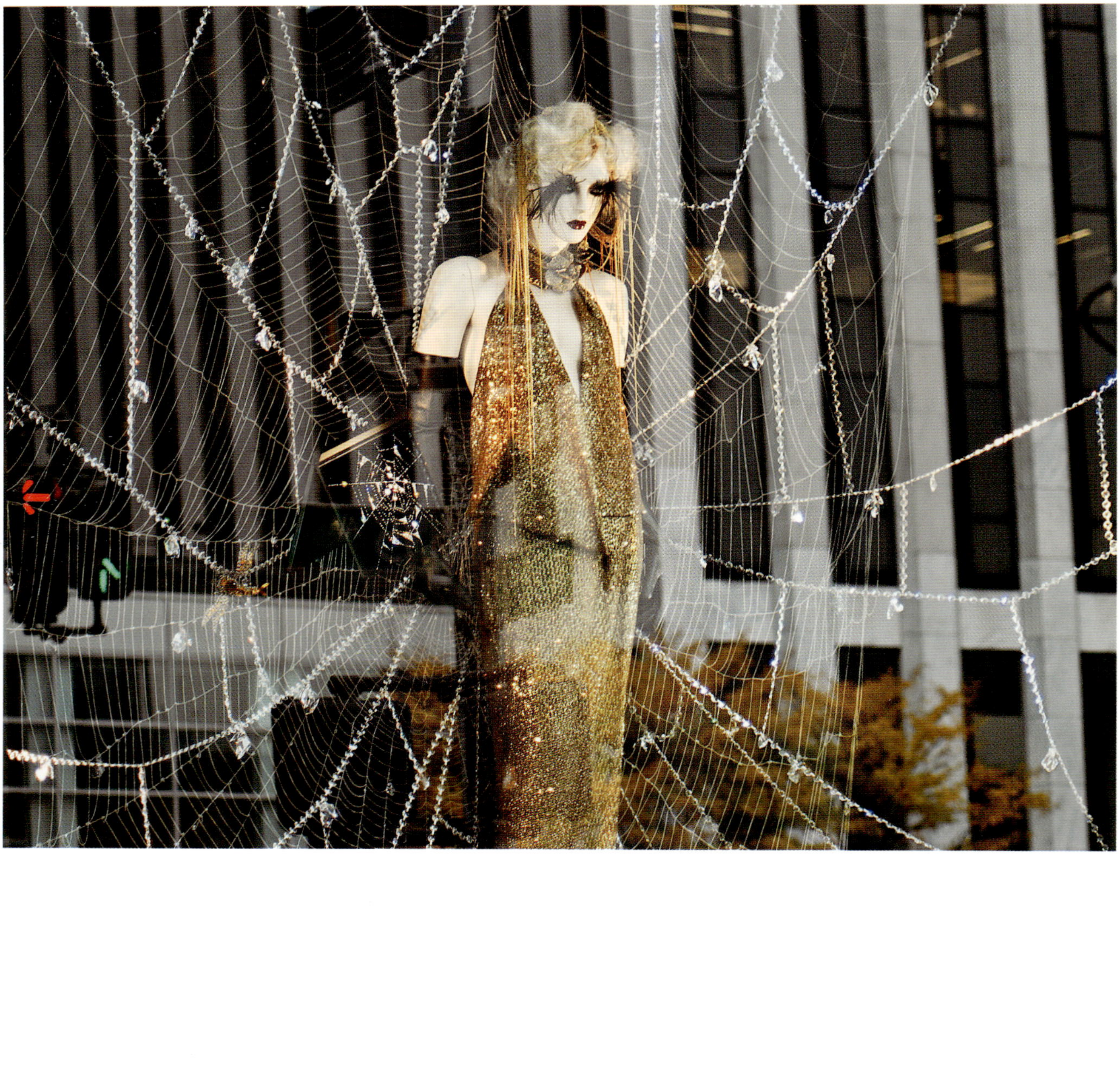

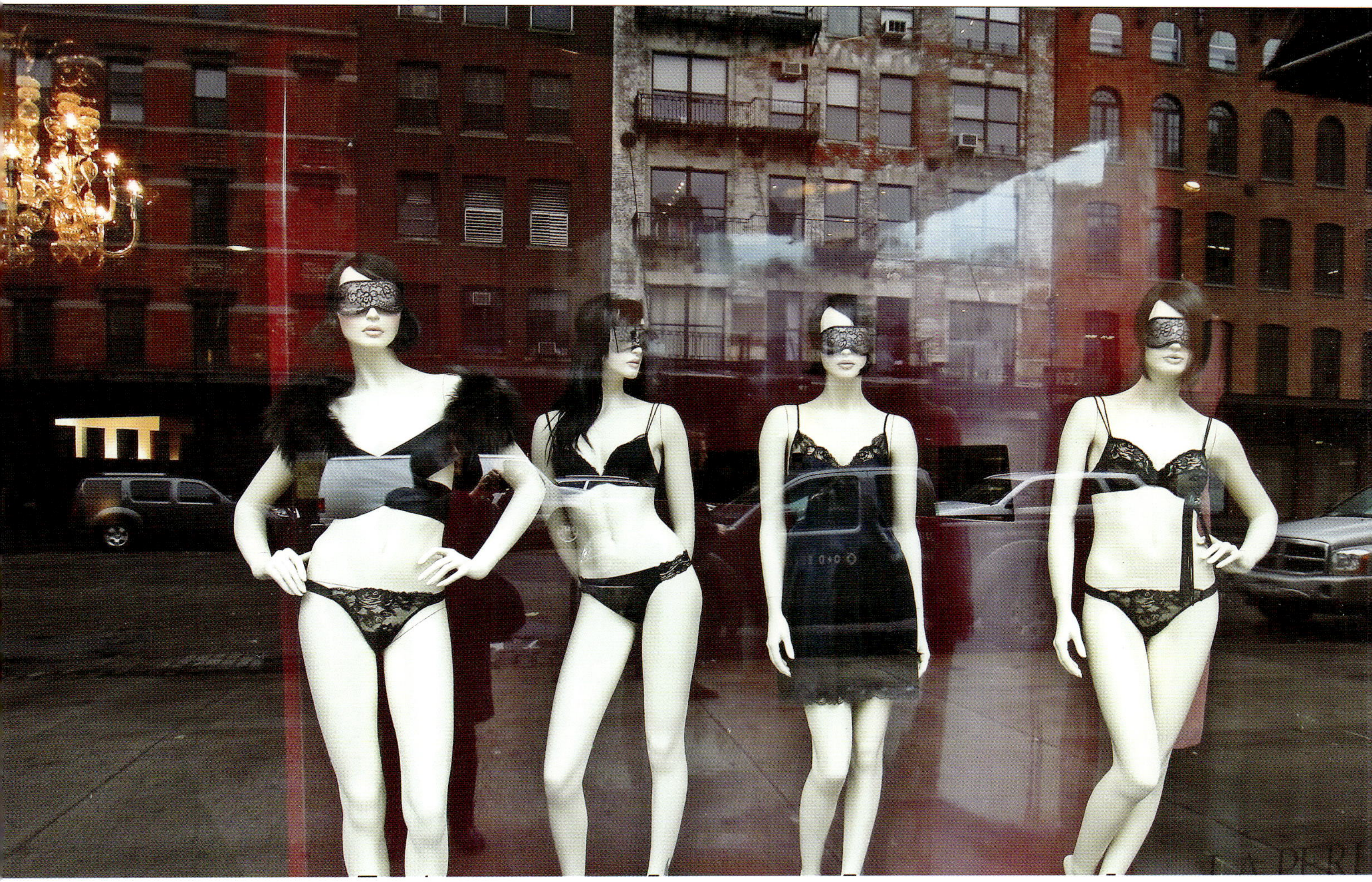

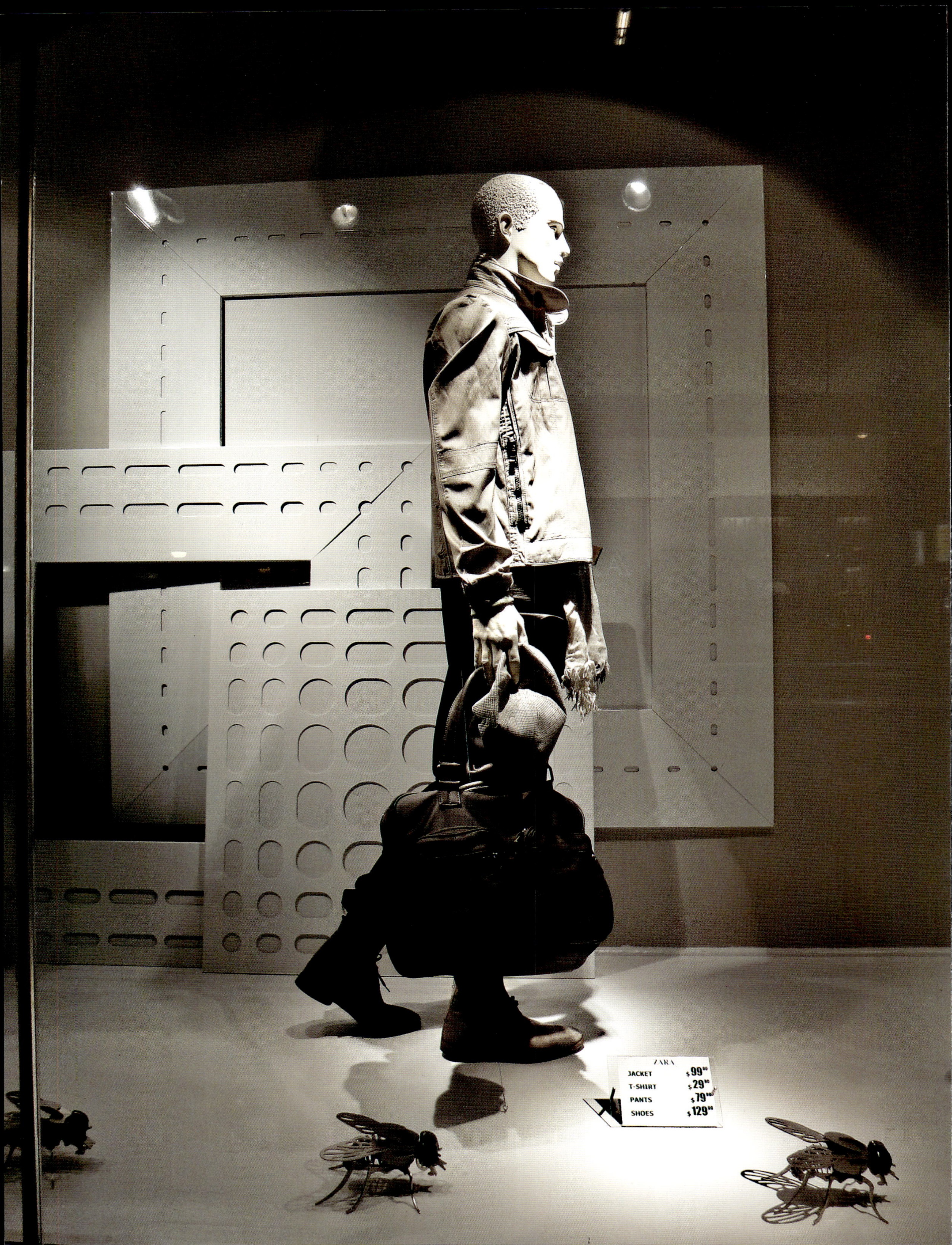
ZARA
JACKET $99.90
T-SHIRT $29.90
PANTS $79.90
SHOES $129.90

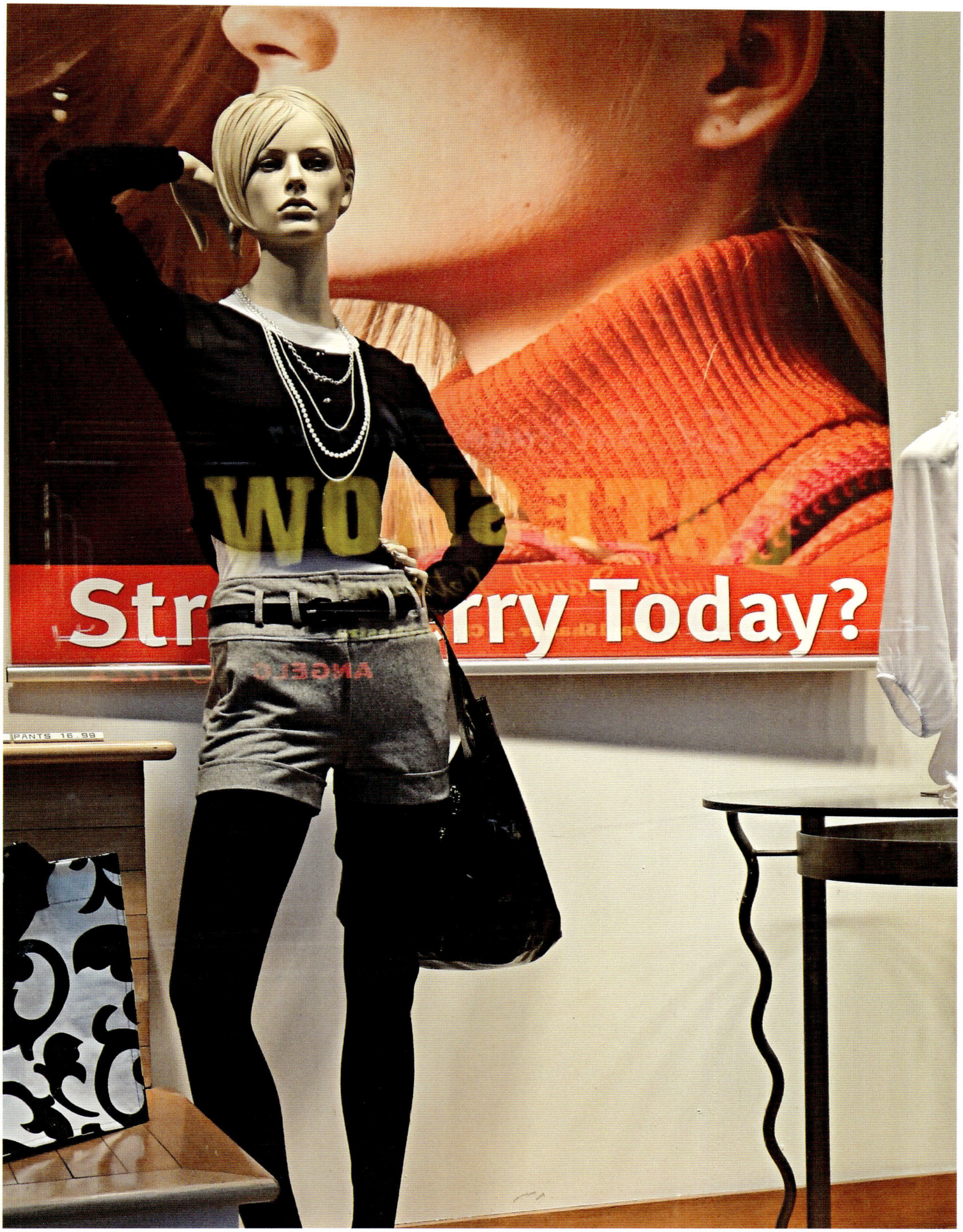
Str
rry Today?

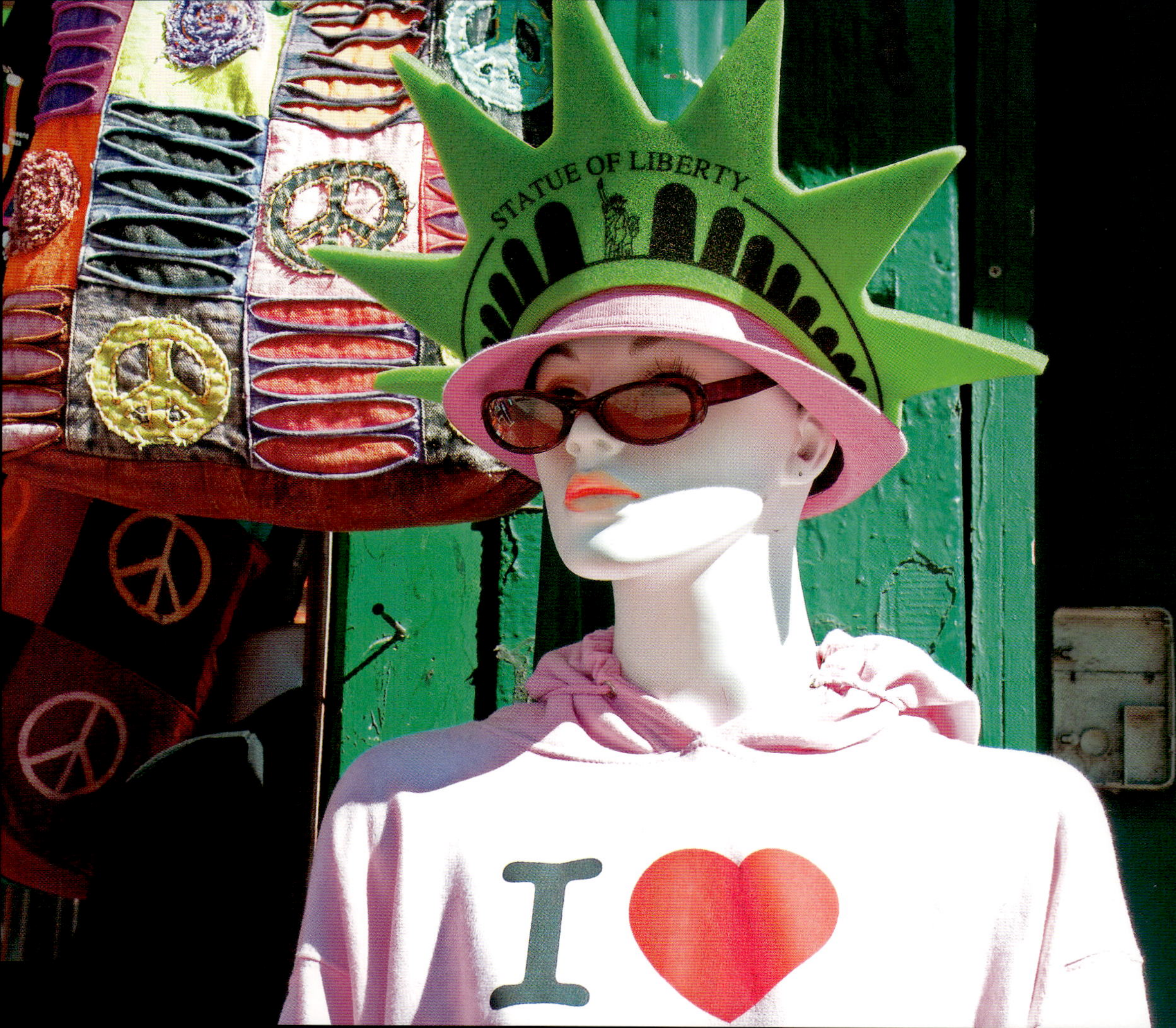
STATUE OF LIBERTY
I ♥

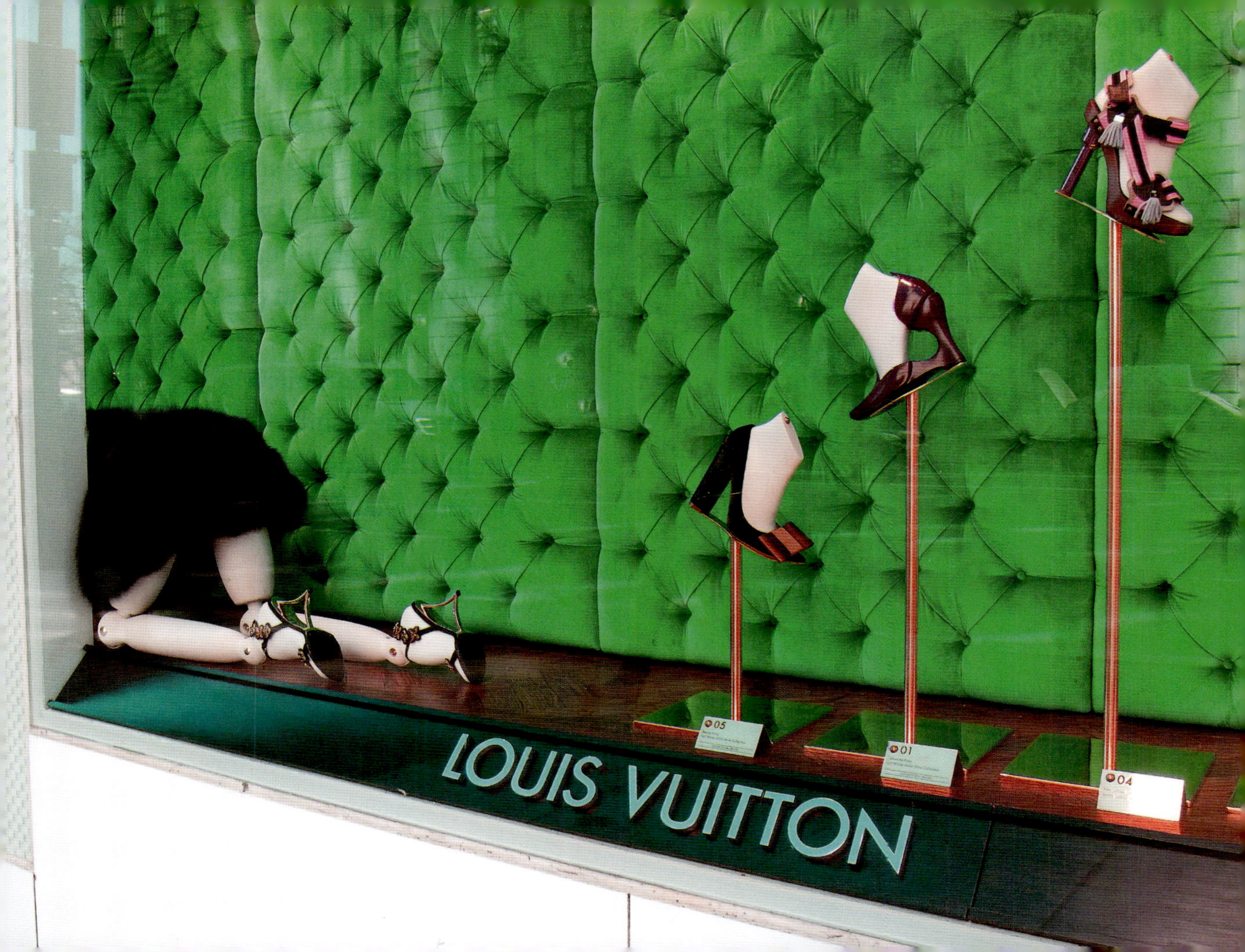
LOUIS VUITTON
05
01
04

11 LANDMARKS

1.

Many a well-known city
takes pride in a local landmark
some eye-seducing structure
or stunning natural wonder
known throughout the land
perhaps throughout the world.

A city and a landmark
can become so intertwined
simply thinking of the city
makes the landmark spring to mind.

Think Paris
  and the chances are
  we see the Eiffel Tower
Think Newport
  we see the stately homes
Think 'Frisco
  and we visualize
  those roller-coaster streets
Think Moscow
  we see its onion domes.

Seattle
  is that needle
  thrusting boldly into space
Miami
  is that gleaming wall
  of oceanfront hotels
Athens
  the Acropolis
Rome
  the Colosseum
and Venice
  those implausible canals.

2.

What is it about a landmark
that makes us take its picture?
You'd think it's an image
we no longer need to see
bombarded as we are
by endless replications
in magazines and journals
photographs and paintings
movies and TV.

It seems a bit bizarre
  that dedicated tourists
hungry for new sights
  will go so great a distance
to stare at something
  they've already seen
and yet
show me some far-famed
  photogenic icon
and I'll show you a tourist
  fiddling with his Nikon
(or Kodak or Lumix or Sony)
  hoping the light is right
gamely trying to Canonize
  this semi-sacred site.

3.

Case in point: New York City
awash in famous landmarks
and celebrated sights
like the belle of Bedloe's Island
  Ms. Liberty
those ever patient carriage horses
  lining 59th
the crossroads of the world
  Times Square
those sumptuous cathedrals
  St. Patrick and St. John
Grand Central's regal Terminal
  the list goes on and on.

No matter that (to some extent)
  they've all seen better days
No matter that they've all become
  pictorial clichés
Still the eager tourists come
  cameras poised for action
shutters clicking tirelessly
  at every tired attraction.

4.

As for those of us who live here
  (yes, I confess)
we've shot our share of landmarks
  in our time.
But we have since discovered
that our city is alive
  with captivating images
(maybe not as grand
  as landmarks
but fresh and arresting
  nonetheless)
waiting to be noticed
  by the open-minded eye.

5.

We've also discovered
those who came before us
such artists of the lens
as Alfred Eisenstaedt, Ruth Orkin,
Helen Levitt, Walker Evans.

These masters of the camera
neither glorified
nor glamorized
New York.
Instead
they surprised and diverted us
delighting us with sights
we hadn't bothered to observe.

6.

Had they wished
they could have offered us
yet one more depiction
of the Hippodrome
or those quintessential nightspots
El Morocco and the Stork
but they didn't.
And what they offered then
my wife offers now:
not your usual images of New York.

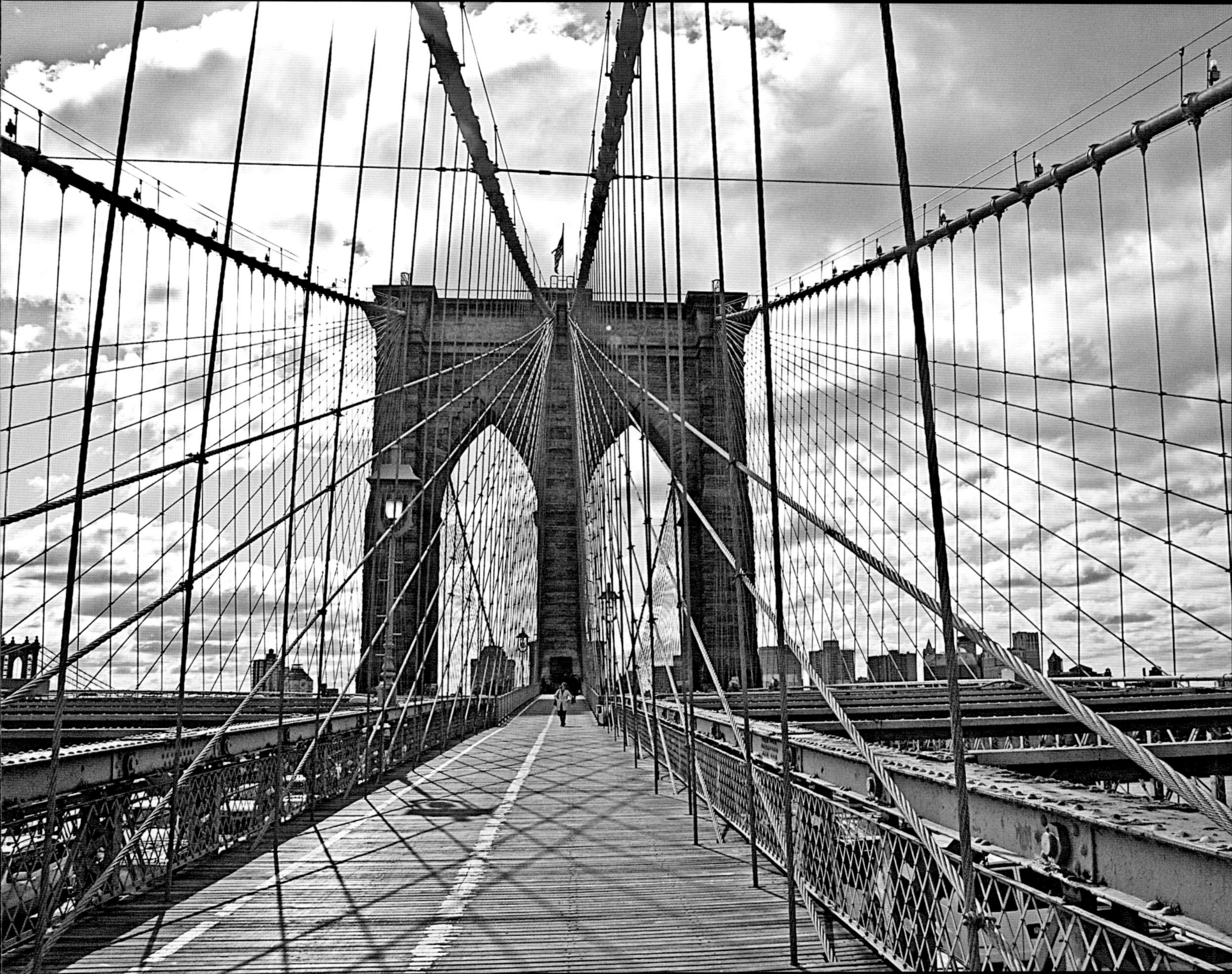

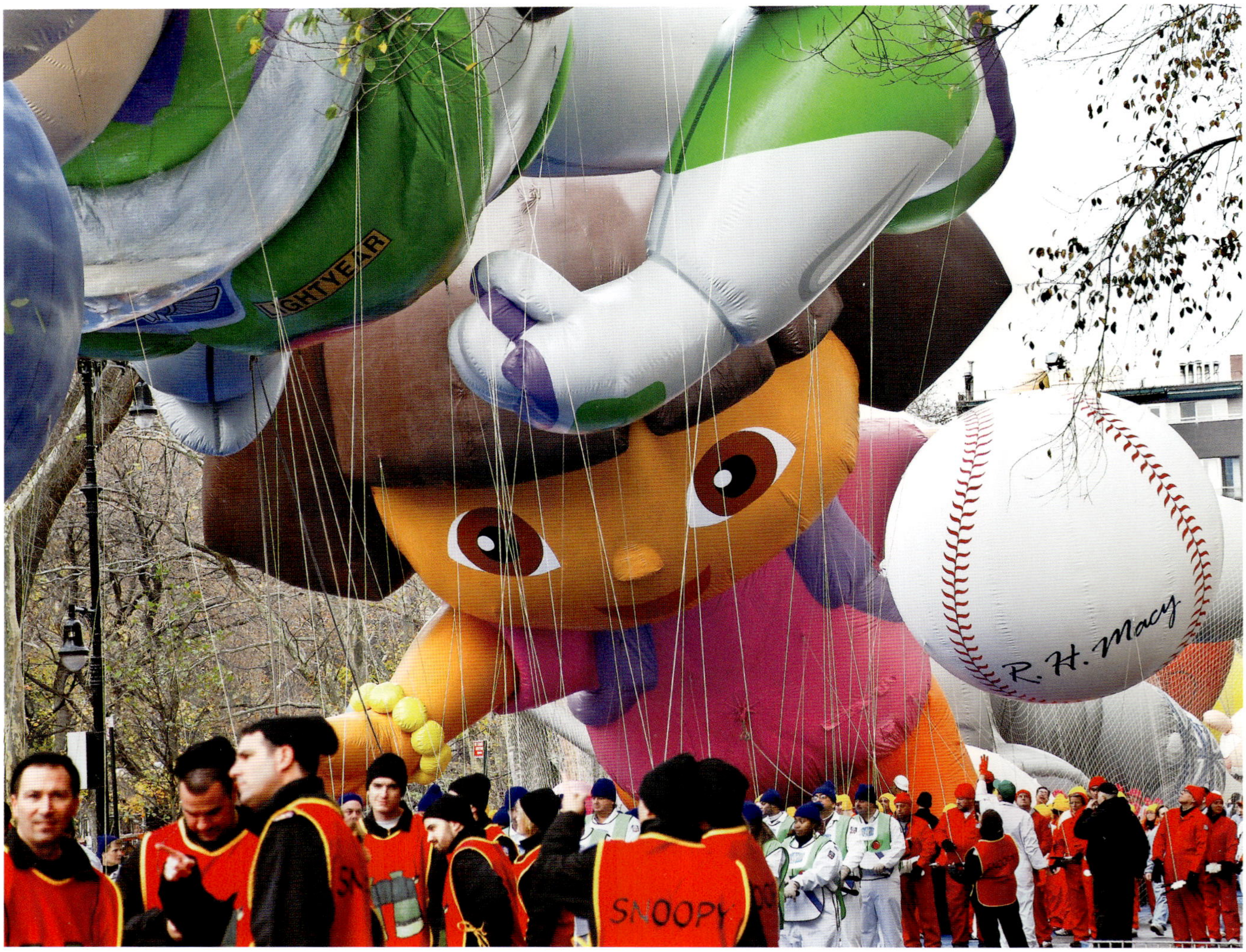
LIGHTYEAR
R. H. Macy
SNOOPY

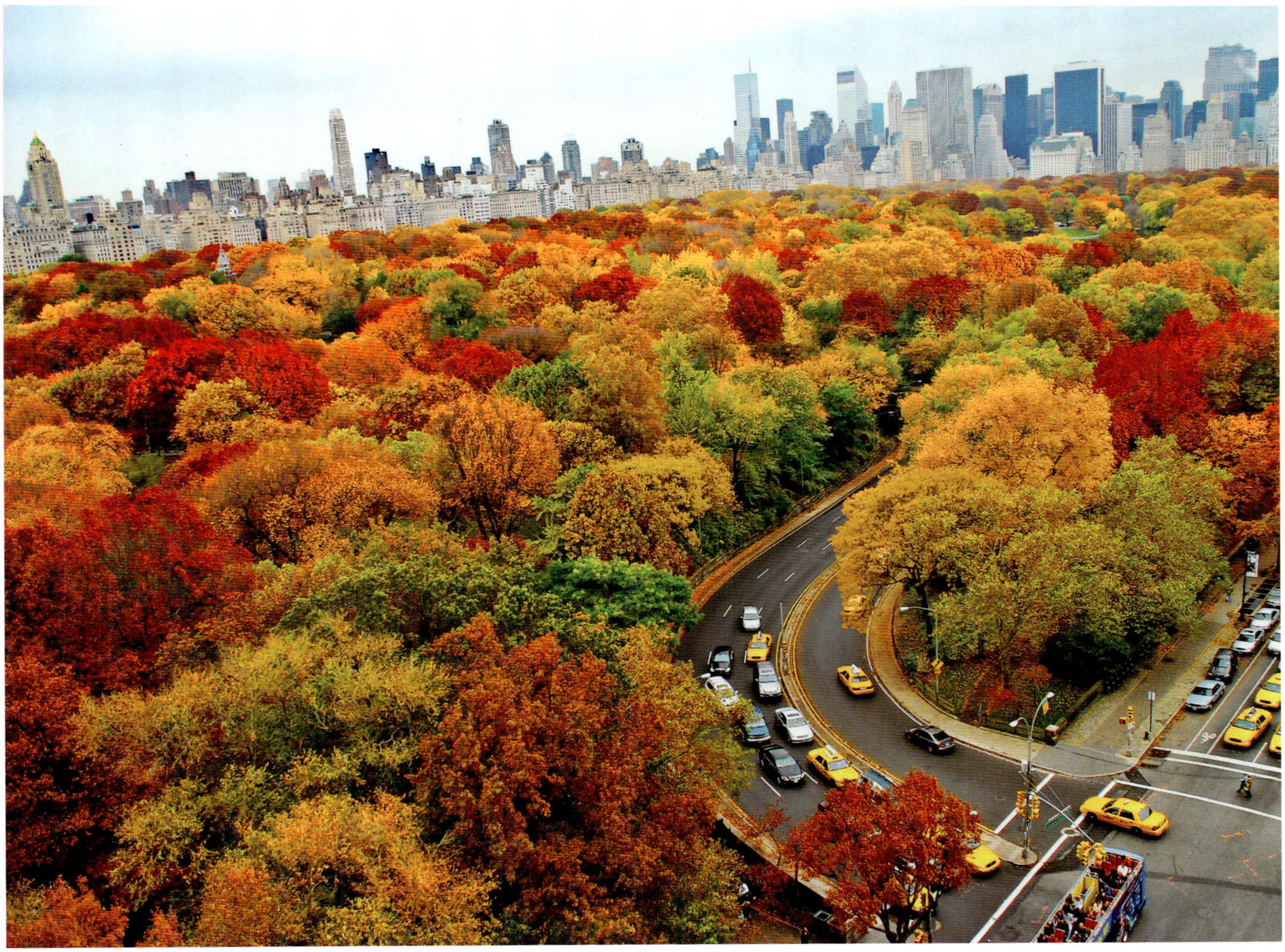

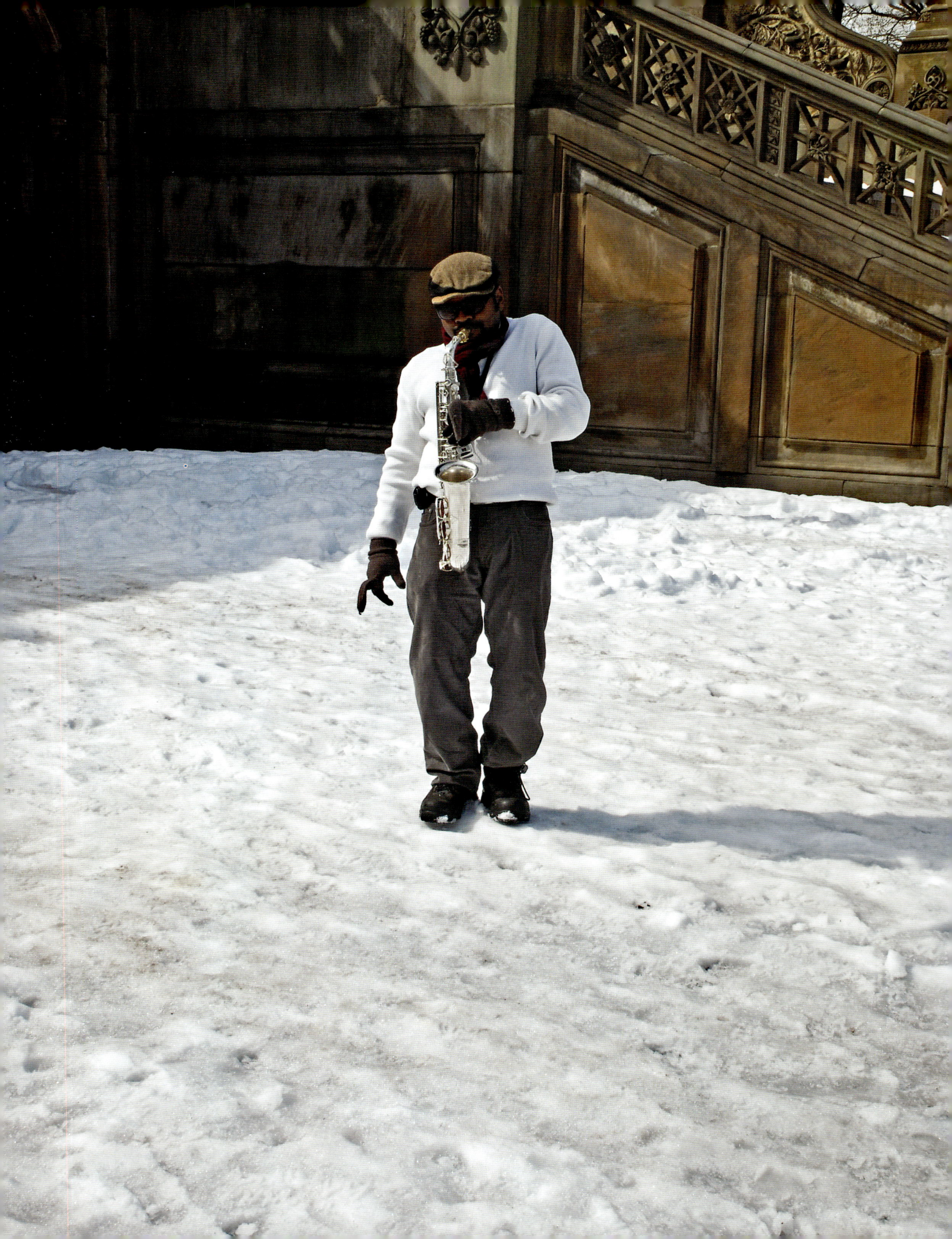

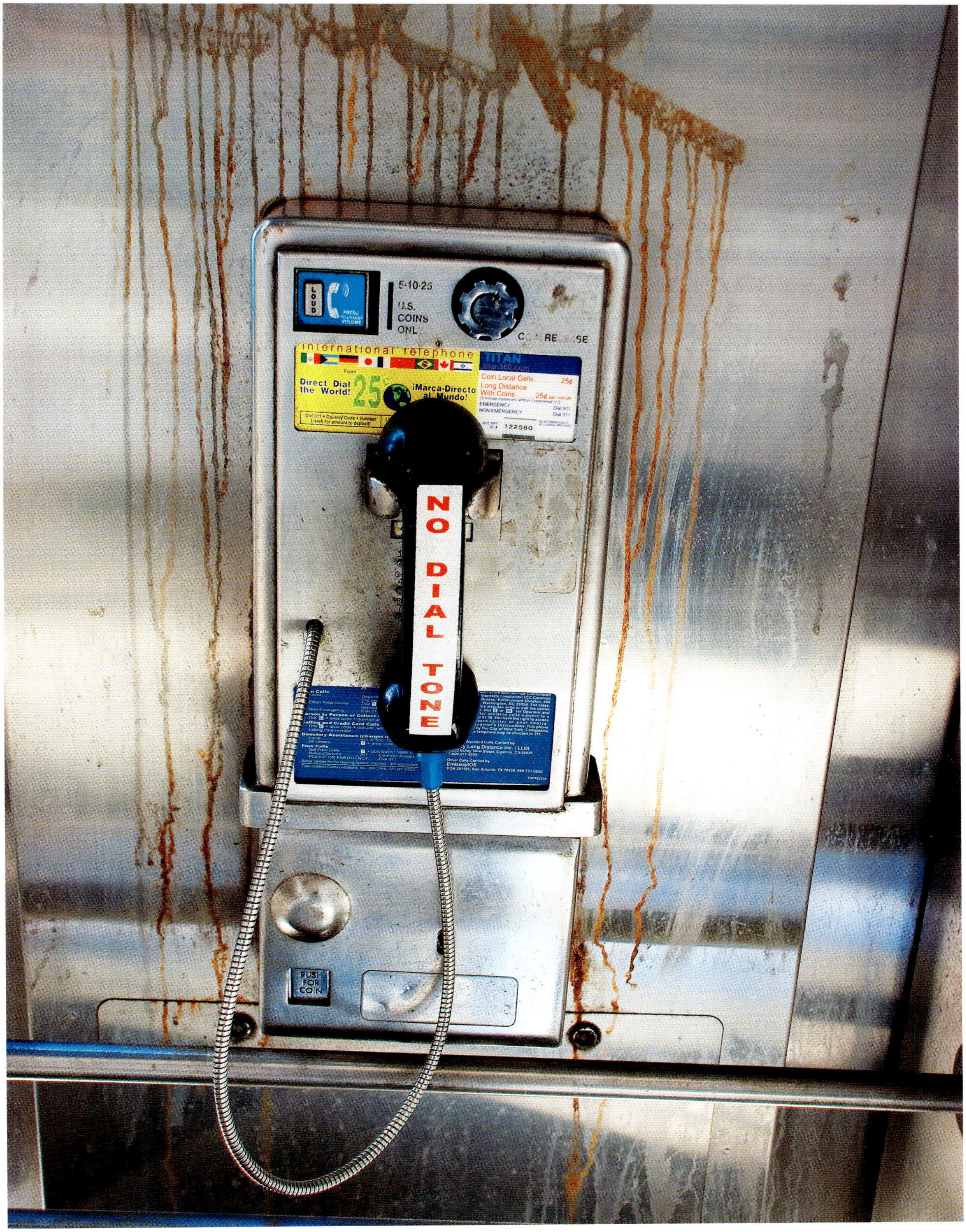
LOUD
5·10·25
U.S.
COINS
ONLY
International Telephone
Direct Dial the World!
25¢
¡Marca-Directo al Mundo!
TITAN
titan360.com
Coin Local Calls 25¢
Long Distance With Coins
EMERGENCY Dial 911
NON-EMERGENCY Dial 311
122580
NO DIAL TONE
PUSH FOR COIN

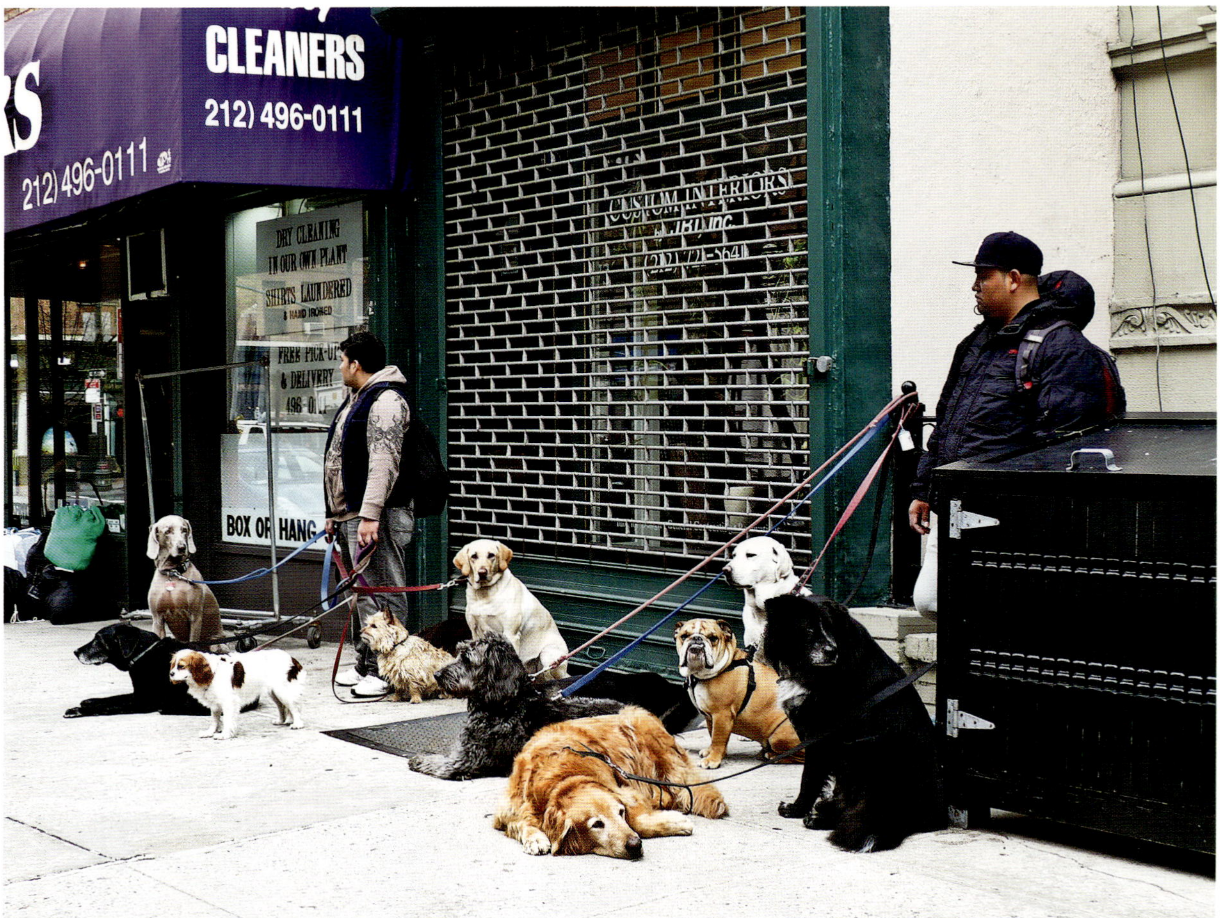
CLEANERS
212) 496-0111
212) 496-0111
DRY CLEANING
IN OUR OWN PLANT
SHIRTS LAUNDERED

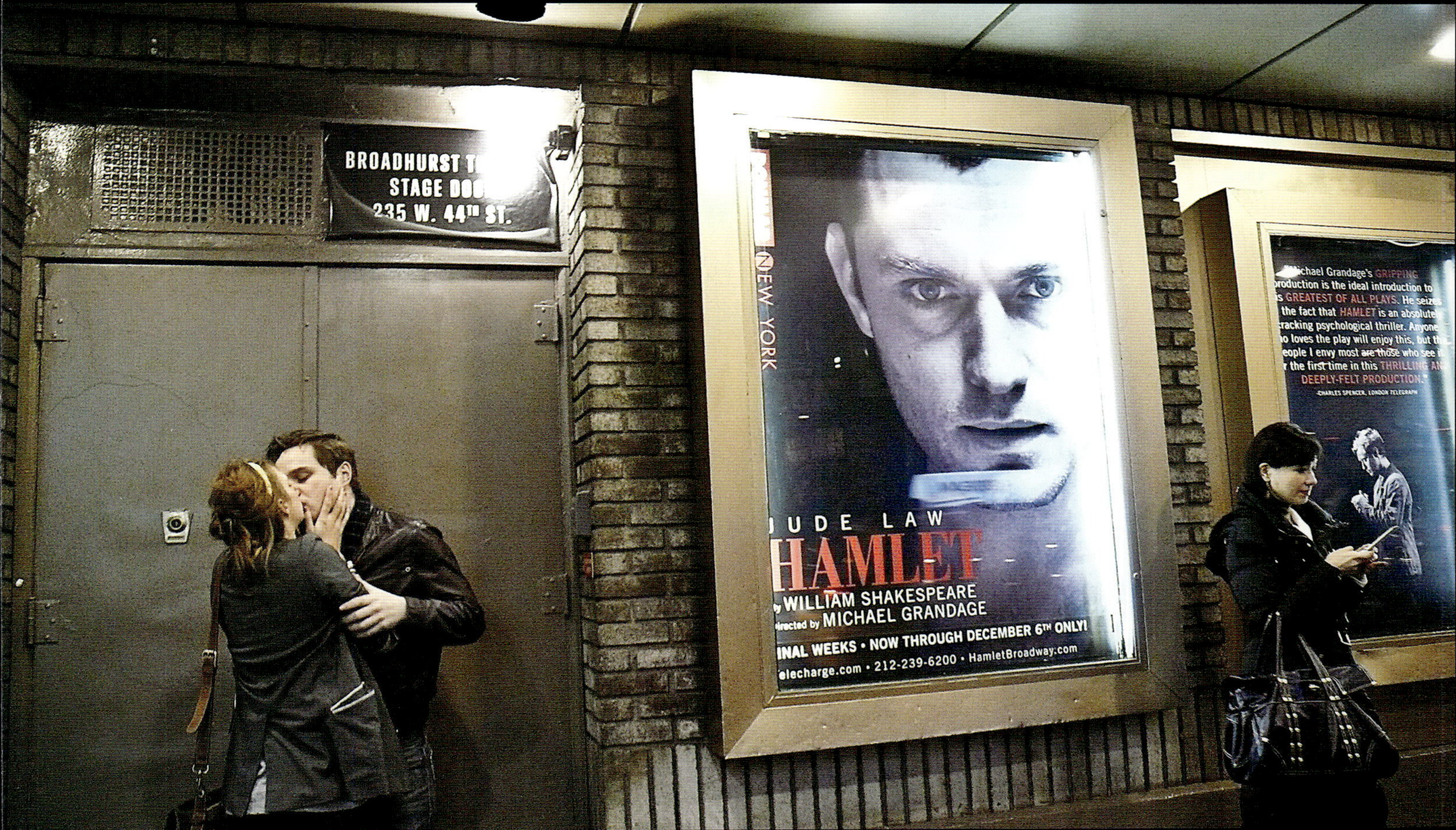
BROADHURST T
STAGE DOO
235 W. 44TH ST.
NEW YORK
UDE LAW
HAMLET
by WILLIAM SHAKESPEARE
directed by MICHAEL GRANDAGE
INAL WEEKS • NOW THROUGH DECEMBER 6TH ONLY!
elecharge.com • 212-239-6200 • HamletBroadway.com
DEEPLY-FELT PRODUCTION."
-CHARLES SPENCER, LONDON TELEGRAPH

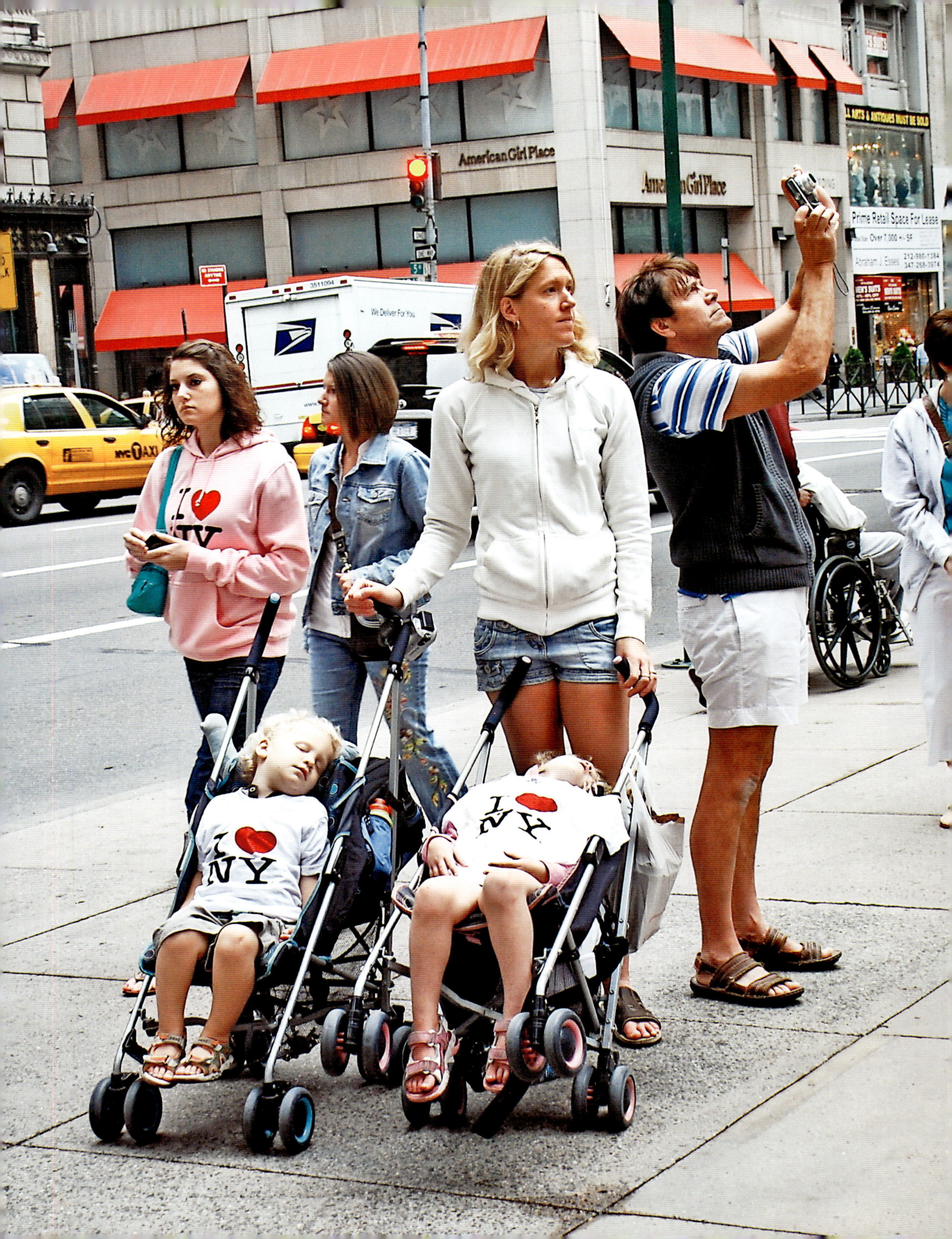
American Girl Place
American Girl Place
Prime Retail Space For Lease
We Deliver For You.
NYC TAXI
I NY
I NY
I NY

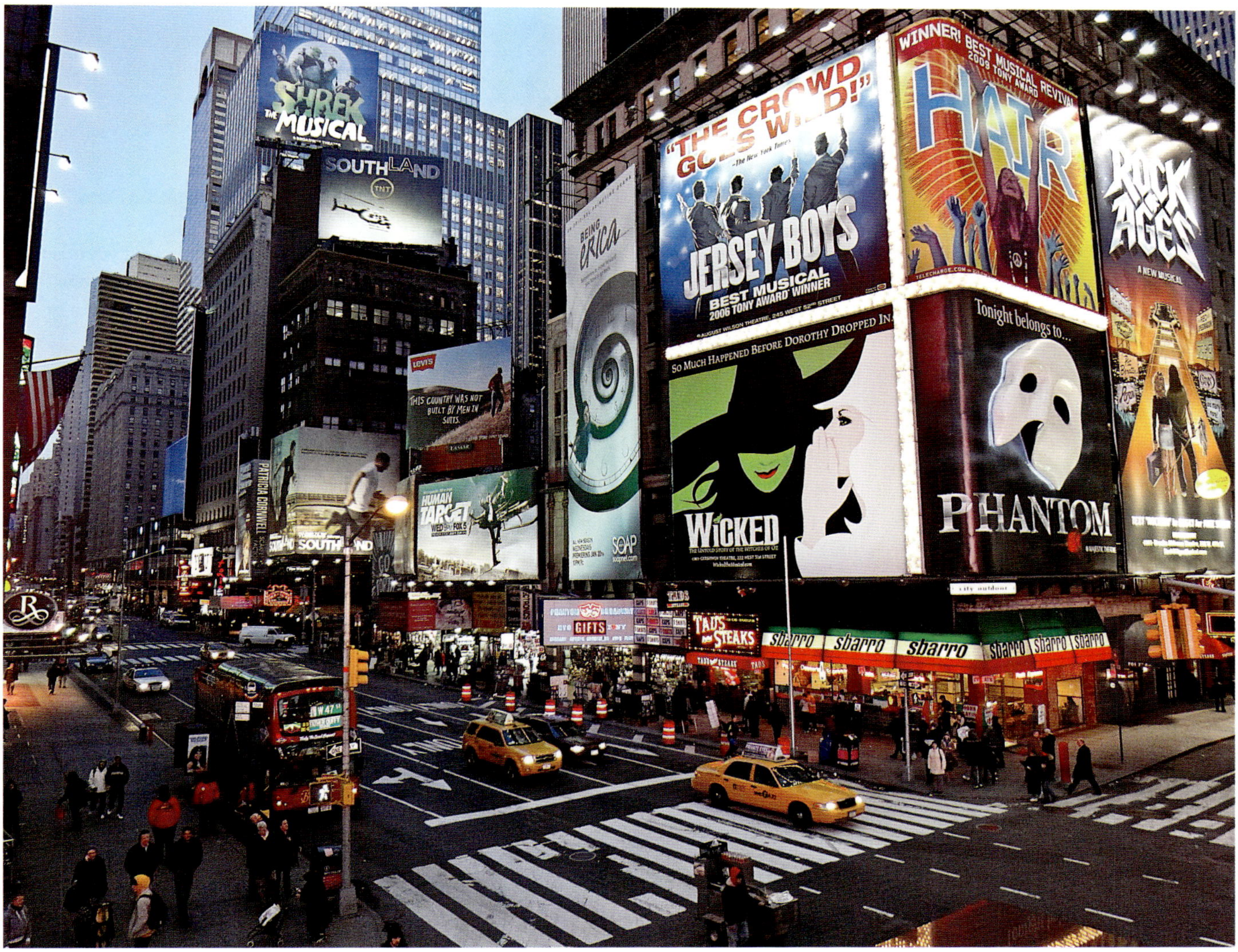
SHREK
THE MUSICAL
SOUTHLAND
TNT
"THE CROWD GOES WILD!"
—The New York Times
JERSEY BOYS
BEST MUSICAL
2006 TONY AWARD WINNER
AUGUST WILSON THEATRE, 245 WEST 52nd STREET
WINNER! BEST MUSICAL REVIVAL
2009 TONY AWARD
HAIR
ROCK
AGES
A NEW MUSICAL
SO MUCH HAPPENED BEFORE DOROTHY DROPPED IN
WICKED
Tonight belongs to...
PHANTOM
BEING erica
SOAP
LEVI'S
THIS COUNTRY WAS NOT BUILT BY MEN IN SUITS.
HUMAN TARGET
PATRICIA CORNWELL
GIFTS
TAD'S STEAKS
sbarro

PHOTO IDENTIFICATIONS

COVER Reflection in puddle, Canal St. & 8th Ave.
pp. 2–3 Building reflected in shiny surface of another building.
p. 4 Head/RCA Building, 5th Ave. & 50th St.
p. 6 Margery reflected in a store display window.

THE OUTDOOR MUSEUM

p. 13 "Devil Clown": deteriorating overlapping posters at a construction site.
p. 14–15 Standpipe/Graffiti doorway, Chinatown.
p. 16–17 Both photos: deteriorating posters at construction sites.
p. 18–19 Glass face: store window display/Botero woman, 59th St. & Columbus Ave.
p. 20–21 The side of a passing truck.
p. 22–23 Botero cat/Flock of sheep by Claude & Francois-Xavier Lalane, 56th St. & Park Ave.
p. 25 Bronze owl by Claude Lalane, Park Ave.

DEBUSSY IN NEW YORK

pp. 28–33 All photos are buildings reflected in shiny surfaces of other buildings.

SUBWAY HAIKU

p. 37 Escalator, 53rd St. & 7th Ave.
p. 39 Bass Fiddle, "Waiting for the A Train"/Gerbil, 77th St. Station (Museum of Natural History).

CONSTRUCTION IN BLUE, BLACK & WHITE

p. 58–59 St. Patrick's Cathedral, 5th Ave. & 50th St./Bethesda Fountain, Central Park.
p. 62 Ice-covered reed, Central Park reservoir.

FIREWORKS

pp. 66–73 Fireworks, Central Park, New Year's Eve.

A CAR LOOKS AT MANHATTAN

p. 76–77 Car headlights at sunset.
p. 78 Truck headlight.
p. 81 Reflection in a car's hood.

SWONNET

pp. 87–95 Central Park, 110th St. reservoir, Boat Lake, Bow Bridge.

LANDMARKS

p. 119 Brooklyn Bridge
p. 120–121 Dora balloon: Macy's Thanksgiving Parade/Central Park, 79th St. transverse.
p. 122–123 Bethesda Fountain/"No Dial Tone": 77th St. & Amsterdam.
p. 127 Theater district, 47th St. & 7th Ave.

FIRST EDITION

Library of Congress Cataloging-in-Publication Data
Gray, Margery.
The outdoor museum : (not your usual images of New York) / photographs by Margery Gray Harnick ; poems by Sheldon Harnick. -- 1st ed.
p. cm.
ISBN 978-0-8253-0675-4 (alk. paper)
1. New York (New York)--Pictorial works. 2. New York (N.Y.)--Poetry.
I. Harnick, Sheldon. II. Title.
F128.55.G73 2012
974.7--dc 232011040975

Book design by Celia Fuller

Technical Coordinator, Matthew Harnick

For inquiries about volume orders, please contact:

Beaufort Books
27 West 20th Street, Suite 1102
New York, NY 10011
sales@beaufortbooks.com

Published in the United States by Beaufort Books
www.beaufortbooks.com

Distributed by
Midpoint Trade Books
www.midpointtrade.com

PRINTED IN CHINA

A LAHR & PARTNERS EDITION
NEW YORK